Improving School Leadership

VOLUME 2:
CASE STUDIES ON SYSTEM LEADERSHIP

Edited by Beatriz Pont, Deborah Nusche, David Hopkins

OECD

ORGANISATION FOR ECONOMIC CO-OPERATION AND DEVELOPMENT

The OECD is a unique forum where the governments of 30 democracies work together to address the economic, social and environmental challenges of globalisation. The OECD is also at the forefront of efforts to understand and to help governments respond to new developments and concerns, such as corporate governance, the information economy and the challenges of an ageing population. The Organisation provides a setting where governments can compare policy experiences, seek answers to common problems, identify good practice and work to co-ordinate domestic and international policies.

The OECD member countries are: Australia, Austria, Belgium, Canada, the Czech Republic, Denmark, Finland, France, Germany, Greece, Hungary, Iceland, Ireland, Italy, Japan, Korea, Luxembourg, Mexico, the Netherlands, New Zealand, Norway, Poland, Portugal, the Slovak Republic, Spain, Sweden, Switzerland, Turkey, the United Kingdom and the United States. The Commission of the European Communities takes part in the work of the OECD.

OECD Publishing disseminates widely the results of the Organisation's statistics gathering and research on economic, social and environmental issues, as well as the conventions, guidelines and standards agreed by its members.

This work is published on the responsibility of the Secretary-General of the OECD. The opinions expressed and arguments employed herein do not necessarily reflect the official views of the Organisation or of the governments of its member countries.

Also available in French under the title:
Améliorer la direction des établissements scolaires:
VOLUME 2 : ÉTUDES DE CAS SUR LA DIRECTION DES SYSTÈMES

Corrigenda to OECD publications may be found on line at: *www.oecd.org/publishing/corrigenda*.

© OECD 2008

OECD freely authorises the use, including the photocopy, of this material for private, non-commercial purposes. Permission to photocopy portions of this material for any public use or commercial purpose may be obtained from the Copyright Clearance Center (CCC) at *info@copyright.com* or the Centre français d'exploitation du droit de copie (CFC) *contact@cfcopies.com*. All copies must retain the copyright and other proprietary notices in their original forms. All requests for other public or commercial uses of this material or for translation rights should be submitted to *rights@oecd.org*.

Foreword

Across the globe, the 21st century is seeing rapid economic and social change. Social and population mobility allied with technological advances and an increased focus on schools to perform mean that students today face very different challenges from their predecessors.

Together, these factors fundamentally alter the role of schools and school leaders and the challenges they face. In many countries school leaders now have more autonomy, but it is coupled with greater accountability. They must not only prepare all their students to participate successfully in the new global economy and society. They must take increasing responsibility for helping to develop other schools, their local communities and other public services. This means that school leaders must become system leaders.

This report highlights examples of innovative practices that focus on system-wide school improvement by encouraging and developing school leaders to work beyond the school borders for the benefit of the school system as a whole. Case studies from Australia, Austria, Belgium, England and Finland are complemented by chapters by leading academics Richard Elmore and David Hopkins. In the final chapter, Beatriz Pont and David Hopkins offer a first international comparison and assessment of the state of the art of system leadership and explore its perceived benefits and potential challenges.

Sustainability is among the most critical of these challenges. The report concludes that system leadership needs to come from principals themselves and from agencies committed to working with them. The Specialist Schools and Academies Trust in England (SSAT) is committed to the principle of "by schools, for schools" and to the sharing of best practice internationally. SSAT worked closely with OECD to develop and disseminate the report.

School leaders are willing and able to take the lead in developing world-class education systems that meet the needs of all students, as this report demonstrates. System leadership can build capacity in education; share expertise, facilities and resources; encourage innovation and creativity; improve leadership and spread it more widely; and provide skills support. The collective sharing of skills, expertise and experience will create much richer and more sustainable opportunities for rigorous transformation than can ever be provided by isolated institutions.

This report is part of a larger OECD study on *Improving School Leadership* to provide analysis to help policy makers develop and implement school leadership policies for improved teaching and learning. Participating countries each provided a country background report following a common framework. The five case studies complemented the knowledge by providing examples of innovative practice. *Improving School Leadership, Volume 1: Policy and Practice* reports on this analysis of school leadership around the world. Offering a valuable cross-country perspective, it identifies four policy levers and a range of policy options to help improve school leadership now and build sustainable leadership for the future.

This book was produced jointly by the Education and Training Policy Division of OECD's Directorate for Education (led by division heads Deborah Roseveare, since June 2007, and her predecessor, Abrar Hasan) and the Specialist Schools and Academies Trust in England (under Sue Williamson, Director, Leadership and Innovation). OECD and SSAT are very grateful to the HSBC Global Education Trust for its generous support. HSBC sponsored the inaugural iNet HSBC Chair of International Leadership, Professor David Hopkins, and hosted the *Improving School Leadership* activity's first international conference and workshop in London in 2006. Thanks are also due to Peter Chambers and Susan Copeland, who edited the report and to Jennifer Gouby who was responsible for preparing the text for publication and administration. Judith Corcoran and Ross Wilkins also provided administrative support.

Table of contents

Boxes

Tables

Figures

Executive summary

The 21st century is still in its first decade, yet many countries have already seen dramatic shifts in the way schools and education systems are managed compared with those of the end of the last century. A prime stimulus for these changes is a combination of shifts in society, including greater migration, changes in social and family structures, and the use (and misuse) of information and communications technologies. Also influential is a greater emphasis on relative performance of different schools and education systems, between schools, school systems and countries.

The strong focus on education by governments and society is entirely appropriate. Only through education can we develop the knowledge and skills that are vital for our countries' economic growth, social development and political vitality. And most importantly, for the success of the children who will be our future generations.

The challenge of system leadership

In this new environment, schools and schooling are being given an ever bigger job to do. Greater decentralisation in many countries is being coupled with more school autonomy, more accountability for school and student results, and a better use of the knowledge base of education and pedagogical processes. It is also being coupled with broader responsibility for contributing to and supporting the schools' local communities, other schools and other public services.

As a result, there is a need to redefine and broaden school leaders' roles and responsibilities. This means changing the way school leadership is developed and supported. It implies improving incentives to make headship in particular more attractive for existing heads and for those who will be taking up school leadership positions in the future. And it implies strengthening training and development approaches to help leaders face these new roles.

One of school leaders' new roles is increasingly to work with other schools and other school leaders, collaborating and developing relationships of interdependence and trust. System leaders, as they are being called, care about and work for the success of other schools as well as their own. Crucially they are willing to shoulder system leadership roles because they believe that in order to change the larger system you have to engage with it in a meaningful way.

This study's approach

This study focuses on a set of innovative practices that provide good examples of systemic approaches to school leadership. These are particular innovative approaches adopted or developed in Austria, England, Finland, Flanders (Belgium) and Victoria

(Australia) which are showing emerging evidence of positive results. Each of these cases is developed in detail in the relevant chapter of this book.

The case studies result from research and visits by OECD staff and education experts to each country. The visits included meetings and discussions with national and local government representatives, and site visits to exemplary schools. The case studies are complemented by articles by two authorities in education leadership: Richard Elmore of the Harvard Graduate School of Education and David Hopkins of the Institute of Education, University of London. The five countries visited were chosen because they met two main criteria: they demonstrated models of school organisation and management that distribute education leadership roles in innovative ways; and showed promising practices for preparing and developing school leaders.

A companion report *Improving School Leadership, Volume 1: Policy and Practice* (Pont, Nusche and Moorman, 2008), looks at 22 countries and regions and provides a set of policy recommendations for improving school outcomes.

The benefits of system leadership

Throughout OECD countries, there is significant co-operation and collaboration on school leadership. While every country participating in the OECD activity has some arrangements for co-operation between schools, one group of jurisdictions has made system leadership the centre of their school improvement strategies. In Flanders (Belgium), England and Finland, they have done so by creating possibilities for co-operation that promote going beyond leaders' own schools to support local improvement. In Victoria (Australia) and Austria, they have launched leadership development programmes for system-wide school improvement.

These innovations focus on system-wide school improvement by encouraging and developing school leaders to work together. Although the approaches were at early stages of development, the researchers found a number of significant benefits emerging. These included development of leadership capacity, rationalising of resources, increased co-operation, leadership being distributed further into schools and across education systems, and improving school outcomes.

The challenges to practice

Nevertheless, the study also found that there are considerable challenges to overcome before the concept of system leadership can be widely implemented. Sustainability is inevitably a critical factor, as is the quality of school leaders – because *system* leaders must first be successful *school* leaders.

The key features identified were: in-school capacity to sustain high levels of student learning; between-school capability (the "glue" that is necessary for schools to work together effectively); mediating organisations to work flexibly with schools to help build in-school capacity along with the skills necessary for effective collaboration; critical mass to make system leadership a movement, not just the practice of a small number of elite leaders; and cultural consensus across the system to give school leaders the space, legitimacy and encouragement to engage in collaborative activities.

The authors note that these conditions for long-term success were not all in place in any of the case studies, but all conditions were seen in some case studies. They add that the cases that demonstrate more of these conditions are more successful in implementing system leadership. Other important factors for system leadership are: recognising and supporting system leaders; identifying and recruiting them; providing professional development; enabling school leaders to cooperate in an environment often still dominated by competition; and scaling up the innovations so that they can influence the whole education system.

Recommendations: Let school leaders lead

The report's authors concluded that systemic leadership needs to come more from principals themselves and from agencies committed to working with them. They suggest that top-down approaches are not likely to work well. Developing ownership by participants, as Victoria (Australia) or the Austrian Leadership Academy are doing, is important.

A more lateral approach may be to create mediating organisations (such as the National College for School Leadership and the Specialist Schools and Academies Trust in England and the Leadership Academy in Austria) to promote system leadership and collaborative activity. Another approach is to foster local education authorities and municipalities in developing and spreading practice, as the Finnish have done. The intention must be not to create a new bureaucracy but to facilitate relationships between schools so that they can collaborate for the good of all students.

There is already significant system leadership activity in the five case study countries, this report finds. System leadership can build capacity in education; share expertise, facilities and resources; encourage innovation and creativity; improve leadership and spread it more widely; and provide skills support.

The collective sharing of skills, expertise and experience will create much richer and more sustainable opportunities for rigorous transformation than can ever be provided by isolated institutions, say the authors. But attaining this future demands that we give school leaders more possibilities in taking the lead.

Chapter 1

Introduction

This chapter describes the focus of this publication, explains the methodology of the case study approach and outlines the criteria used to select case studies. The case studies represent innovative approaches that encourage and develop school leaders to work beyond the school borders for the benefit of the school system as a whole. The case study approach is an innovation in the OECD Education and Training Policy Division's approach to its work. It was chosen because the context and practice of school leadership are undergoing major changes in a short time. To understand the new challenges of leadership and to respond to countries quickly required a different approach than the traditional OECD thematic reviews.

In the 21st century, society and policy makers have focused much attention on schools and schooling. This is because only through education can we develop the knowledge and skills that are vital for our countries' economic growth, social development, and political vitality - and for the success of our future generations.

In this new environment, schools and schooling have received broader mandates. Greater decentralisation is coupled with more school autonomy, more accountability for school and student results and a better use of the knowledge base of education and pedagogical processes. At the same time, schools are facing challenges such as increased migration, changes in social and family structures and the use of information and communications technologies. All of these are affecting the roles and functions of schools and their leaders.

School leaders' tasks have broadened and intensified, and require a new framework for practice. All in all, there is a need to redefine and broaden school leaders' roles and responsibilities. This means changing the way school leadership is developed and supported. It implies improving incentives to make headship in particular more attractive for existing heads and for those who will be taking up school leadership positions in the future. It also implies strengthening training and development approaches to help leaders face these new roles.

One of school leaders' new roles is increasingly to work with other schools and other school leaders, collaborating and developing relationships of interdependence and trust. System leaders, as they are being called, care about and work for the success of other schools as well as their own. Crucially they are willing to shoulder system leadership roles because they believe that in order to change the larger system you have to engage with it in a meaningful way.

1.1 The OECD *Improving School Leadership* activity

The OECD conducted a study of school leadership to give policy makers information and analysis that will help them formulate and implement school leadership policies leading to better education. The activity aimed to: *i)* synthesise research on issues related to improving leadership in schools; *ii)* identify innovative and successful policy initiatives and practices; *iii)* facilitate exchanges of lessons and policy options among countries; and *iv)* identify policy options for governments to consider.

More specifically the activity has aimed to provide in-depth analyses of some questions that are vital to school leadership:

- What are the roles and responsibilities of school leaders under different governance structures?

- What seem to be promising policies and conditions for making school leaders most effective in improving school outcomes?

- How can effective school leadership be best developed and supported?

- What policies and practices would be most conducive to these ends?

To reply to these questions more effectively, the OECD conducted two complementary approaches. It collected information necessary to compare country developments, while at the same time adopting a more innovative and forward looking approach to policy making.

All 22 participating countries and regions were involved in an *analytical strand*, in which they provided a country background report exploring school leadership policies and practices and the key challenges countries face. These are rich documents which provide research evidence as well as policy descriptions.

Participating countries

Australia, Austria, Belgium (Flemish Community), Belgium (French Community), Chile, Denmark, Finland, France, Hungary, Ireland, Israel, Korea, The Netherlands, New Zealand, Norway, Portugal, Slovenia, Spain, Sweden, United Kingdom (England), United Kingdom (Northern Ireland), United Kingdom (Scotland).

In addition, a small number of *case studies of innovative practices in school leadership* complement the work by exploring in detail some of the more innovative practices, their challenges and successes.

These two strands of work have resulted in the publication of two books:

- Improving *School Leadership, Volume 1: Policy and Practice* (Pont, Nusche and Moorman, 2008) reports on the overall findings of the OECD study of school leadership.

- This book, *Improving School Leadership, Volume 2: Case Studies on System Leadership*, provides the basis to explore the emerging systemic role of school leaders and provides some policy pointers for policy makers and practitioners. It does so principally by analysing a set of country case studies looking at models of school organisation and management and approaches to leadership development that are aiming for system improvement.

1.2 The innovative case study approach

The purpose of the case studies is to explore innovative practices in school leadership and their policy implications. Five carefully selected studies each explore the two key factors framing the overall activity. The first is new models of school organisation and management that distribute leadership roles in innovative ways. The second is promising programmes and practices to prepare and develop school leaders. For both factors, the case studies are intended to give policy makers descriptions and analysis of innovations and their implementation. In addition they aim to identify both the policy conditions in which the innovations are being conducted and any further implications for policy suggested by the cases.

Two additional articles, "Leadership as the practice of improvement", by Richard Elmore, of the Harvard Graduate School of Education and "Realising the potential of system leadership", by David Hopkins, of the Institute of Education, University of London, examine the background to effective school leadership practices.

These five case studies and two articles bring together the latest in-depth thinking and practice on school leadership from many international experts. A final chapter surveys the relevant literature, presents a cross-case analysis, assesses benefits and challenges and draws conclusions for policy and practice.

In addition, the case studies were complemented with two international conferences. The first was hosted in London in July 2006 by the HSBC Global Education Trust. This presented and discussed the two papers by Elmore and Hopkins and the conceptual framework of this strand of the work. The second conference was held in Dublin in November 2007, hosted by the Irish and Northern Irish Departments of Education. During this conference the case study reports were presented and discussed, leading to conclusions about cross-case comparisons. This book, and this stream of work, also benefit from having the comparative report, *Improving School Leadership, Volume 1: Policy and Practice*, as its companion volume and from the discussions that informed that aspect of the project.

Overall this book summarises the major findings from different national practices, identifies implications for state and national policy, and makes recommendations for further research and development. It aims to advance knowledge about school leadership practice, development, and policy by examining innovative approaches to system leadership and the transformation of educational systems more generally.

This book aims to advance knowledge about school leadership practice, development and policy by examining innovative approaches to system leadership and the transformation of educational systems.

Why was this approach taken?

The case study approach is an innovation in the OECD Education and Training Policy Division's approach to its work. It was felt necessary because the context and practice of school leadership is undergoing major changes in a short space of time. To understand the new challenges of leadership and to respond to countries quickly required a different approach than the traditional OECD thematic reviews.

The case studies provide in-depth information on innovations that can inform debate, guide practice, provide reference and help frame school leadership policies in OECD countries. The case studies were selected according to criteria resulting from the recommendations of participating countries, research literature, and expert consultants (Box 1.1) and focused on two key areas.

A: Models of school organisation and management that distribute leadership roles in innovative ways

School leaders, who have provided guidance throughout this activity, have agreed from the start that effective school leadership is not exclusive to formal offices or positions; instead it should be distributed across a number of individuals in a school. Principals, managers, academic leaders, department chairs, and teachers can contribute as leaders to the goal of learning-centred schooling. The precise distribution of these leadership contributions can vary. Such aspects as governance and management structure, amount of autonomy afforded at the school level, accountability prescriptions, school size and complexity, and levels of student performance can shape the kinds and patterns of school leadership. Thus principals must be not only managers but also leaders of the school as a learning organisation. They interact with teachers to create a productive, cohesive learning community.

This perspective suggests several specific areas to focus on:

- "System improvement," where the school leaders take responsibility for contributing to the success of other schools as well as to their own school; or where regional or local level teams engage leaders in re-culturing and working collaboratively to support one another in achieving common goals of student learning.

- Partnerships or collaborations of schools with other organisations in which the organisation and management arrangements distribute leadership across a combination of individuals, organisations and groups.

- School-level learning communities in which a combination of managerial and teacher leadership build "professional communities" and "collective efficacy". They do this through shared commitment to challenging learning goals; collective responsibility for student performance; continuous improvement; decisions based on high quality and timely data; and staff, student, and community engagement.

B: Promising practices for the preparation and development of school leaders

Analysing different approaches to training and development of effective school leaders can help policy makers better formulate and implement school leadership policies. School leaders today need a daunting array of knowledge and skills. At a minimum, they need to know something about curricula, pedagogy and student and adult learning. They need skills in change management, group dynamics, interpersonal relations and communications. Depending on their governance context, they may well need skills in planning, budgeting, human resource management, marketing and fund raising.

Training and professional development for school leaders across OECD countries is of variable quality and availability. While there is evidence that many countries now provide school principals and senior staff with significantly more training, support and guidance than in the past (*e.g* England's Headteacher Induction Programme [Headship Early Provision from September 2006], the Australian National Professional Qualification for Headship, the Swedish four-step approach to principal training), opportunities for school leaders in this area leave room for improvement.

The case studies will identify innovative practices to develop and support high quality school leaders. They include:

- national or regional academies for preparation and continuing professional development promoting effective leadership aligned with the desired vision of schooling and student outcomes;

- alternative mechanisms to recruit and prepare school leaders, conducted through non-traditional organisations rather than universities and schools;

- collaborations authorised by regional authorities in which individual partners (*e.g* university-school district partnerships, intermediate unit collaborations) jointly define their needs, design an academic programme aligned with those needs, and offer certified programmes to selected candidates;

- school or local level professional development specifically designed to promote the competencies required for academic leadership.

Selection of innovative case studies and methodology

The OECD Secretariat identified potential candidate sites for case study by consulting with countries and using a variety of sources: information provided by countries; research; input from experts and stakeholders in the field; and knowledge developed in the international workshops organised on relevant issues.

The selection of case studies was made according to a set of specific criteria (Box 1.1). The criteria were developed to reflect the variables of chief interest in this activity.

Box 1.1 Criteria for the selection of innovative case studies

The core criteria for both aspects include:

- the final set reflects the diversity of education governance systems, financing arrangements, and political cultures of the countries represented in the activity;

- the full range of relevant stakeholders is involved;

- the practice has been in operation for long enough to establish its operational viability;

- the practice focuses on educational results and reflects a clear theory of action grounded in the current literature with promise of achieving those results;

- the practice can demonstrate initial results suggesting that it is on track to achieve its intended outcomes;

- full access to the site and to relevant data is afforded.

More particularly, for each of the two main aspects of the studies, the cases chosen should meet the criteria below.

A: Models of school organisation and management that distribute leadership roles in innovative ways. The activities identified for case studies should:

- demonstrate models of school organisation and management where leadership roles and responsibilities are distributed in new ways;

- take a systemic orientation: the leaders' behaviours should influence student outcomes in the whole of the school or larger system, or explore the interactions of the school with larger elements of the education or community systems.

B: Promising programmes and practices for the preparation and development of school leaders. The activities selected for case studies should:

- prepare and develop school leaders using innovative approaches reflecting the broader roles and responsibilities of leaders, the purposes of schooling, and the operation of core school technologies to achieve intended outcomes;

- be designed to produce leaders who work to build student-centred schools with capacity for high performance and continuous learning and improvement towards that end;

- take a system-wide perspective: the innovative programmes should align with the larger goals and processes of the system concerning school improvement, student performance, and enhanced efficiency and effectiveness.

After selecting the case studies, OECD expert teams visited each country for four to five days. The visits were organised by the countries in collaboration with OECD so that the teams were able to get an overview of general school leadership policy and the particular practices the OECD had selected. This involved meetings with key stakeholders in all countries, including national, regional and local policy makers as well as leadership teams, unions, parents and school boards, and school visits, as well as specific training institutions or programmes. These visits enabled the OECD teams to prepare the detailed case study reports that are presented in this volume.

Chapter 2

Realising the potential of system leadership
by
David Hopkins

This chapter sets out an approach to "system leadership" leading to sustainable educational transformation. The author proposes a definition of system leaders as those who are willing to shoulder system leadership roles and work for the success of other schools as well as their own. He elaborates the concept and argues that the movement towards system leadership can be increasingly defined in terms of concepts, capacities, roles and strategy. The chapter concludes by proposing a model for system leaders: they focus on three domains of the school – managing the teaching and learning process, developing people and developing the organisation – but they also strive for equity and inclusion through acting on school context and culture. System leadership is the key driver in ensuring that every student reaches their potential and that every school becomes great.

Traditional leadership and management approaches are well able to resolve technical problems. In the future however leaders will face problems for which there is no immediate solution, and will have to build the capacity to deal with them. This requires a different kind of leadership.

The literature on leadership has mushroomed in recent years, as have leadership courses and qualifications. Many represent different views of leadership and claims on truth, which I for one find a little confusing. In this paper I will set out an approach to "system leadership" which leads to sustainable educational transformation. So, the purpose of this paper is to:

- propose a definition and elaborate the concept of system leadership;

- explore how system leaders can use the diversity within the system to create a new educational landscape through a process of "segmentation";

- conclude by proposing a model for system leadership that incorporates a theory of action.

2.1 Defining and conceptualising system leadership

"System leaders" are those head teachers who are willing to shoulder system leadership roles, who care about and work for the success of other schools as well as their own.

"System leaders" are those head teachers who care about and work for the success of other schools as well as their own.

In England there appears to be an emerging cadre of these head teachers; a contrast to the competitive ethic of headship so prevalent in the nineties. By their efforts and commitment these leaders are beginning to transform the nature of leadership and educational improvement in this country. Interestingly there is also evidence of this role emerging in other leading educational systems in Europe, North America and Australia as seen in the case studies in this book.

In terms of the argument here, this leads me to a simple proposition:

If our goal is "every school a great school", policy and practice must focus on system improvement. This means that school heads must be almost as concerned about the success of other schools as about their own schools. Sustained improvement of schools is not possible unless the whole system is moving forward.

Our recent research on system leadership began to map the system leadership landscape (Hopkins and Higham, 2007). It identified far more system leadership activity in England than previously expected. In charting the system leadership movement, we are working inductively from the behaviours of the outstanding leaders we collaborate with. Some of the key aspects of the role are:

- the moral purpose of system leadership;

- system leadership roles;

- system leadership as adaptive work;

- the domains of system leadership.

Moral purpose

The first thing to say is that system leadership, as Michael Fullan (2003; 2005) has argued, is imbued with moral purpose. Without that, there would not be the passion to proceed or the encouragement for others to follow. In England, for example, that moral purpose is addressing issues such as gaining a better understanding of the factors behind improvement in teaching and learning, and changing the situation where deprivation is still too good a predictor of educational success.

I would argue therefore that system leaders express their moral purpose through:

- Measuring their success in terms of improving student learning and increasing achievement, and striving both to raise the bar and narrow the gap(s).

- Being fundamentally committed to the improvement of teaching and learning. They engage deeply with the organisation of teaching, learning, curriculum and assessment in order to ensure that learning is personalised for all their students.

- Developing their schools as personal and professional learning communities, with relationships built across and beyond each school to provide a range of learning experiences and professional development opportunities.

- Striving for equity and inclusion through acting on context and culture. This is not just about eradicating poverty, as important as that is. It is also about giving communities a sense of worth and empowerment.

- Appreciating that the classroom, school and system levels all influence each other. Crucially system leaders understand that in order to change the larger system you have to engage with it in a meaningful way.

Although this degree of clarity is not necessarily obvious in the behaviour and practice of every head teacher, these aspirations are increasingly becoming part of the conventional wisdom of the best of our global educational leaders.

System leadership roles

A variety of system leader roles consistent with such a moral purpose are emerging. At present, in England, these are (Hopkins and Higham, 2007):

- Developing and leading a successful educational improvement partnership between several schools. Such partnerships are often focused on achieving more than any one single institution could do. They include partnerships on: curriculum design and specialisms, including sharing curricular innovation to respond to key challenges; 14-to-19 consortia; behaviour and hard to place students. While many such partnerships are "soft" organisational collaboratives, others have moved to "harder", more fomalised arrangements such as federations (to develop stronger mechanisms for joint governance and accountability) or education improvement partnerships (to formalise the devolution of responsibilities and resources from their local authority).

- Choosing to lead and improve a school in extremely challenging circumstances, building a culture of success to sustain high value added.

- Partnering another school facing difficulties and improve it, either as an executive head of a federation or as the leader of a more informal improvement arrangement. Leaders here work from a lead school into a low achieving or underperforming school (or schools) that require intervention. "There is a growing body of well-documented evidence from around the country that, where a school is in serious trouble, the use of an executive head teacher / partner head teacher and a paired arrangement with that head's successful school can be a particularly effective solution, and is being increasingly widely applied" (NCSL, 2005, p. 3).

- Acting as a community leader to broker and shape partnerships and/or networks of wider relationships across local communities to support children's welfare and potential, often through multi agency work. Such system leadership reflects the English national agenda on Every Child Matters and responds to, as Osbourne (2000, p. 1) puts it, "the acceptance [that] some … issues are so complex and interconnected that they require the energy of a number of organisations to resolve and hence can only be tackled through organisations working together (p. 1). … The concept of [a] full-service school where a range of public and private sector services is located at or near the school is one manifestation (p. 188)".

- Working as a change agent or expert leader within the system, identifying best classroom practice and transferring it to support improvement in other schools. This is the widest category and includes:

  - heads working as mentor leaders within networks of schools, combining an aspiration and motivation for other schools to improve with the practical knowledge and guidance for them to do so;

  - heads who are active and effective leaders within more centrally organised system leadership programmes, for instance within the consultant leader programme, school improvement partners (SIP) and national leaders of education (NLE);

  - heads who with their staff develop exemplary curricula and teaching programmes that are transferable to other schools and settings.

These roles could be divided into formal roles that are developed through national programmes and have clear protocols, such as consultant leaders; school improvement partners (SIPs) and national leaders of education (NLPs); and informal roles which are locally developed and are far more fluid and organic. Such flexibility is often an important element of these system leadership roles.

The formal and informal roles hold a very significant potential to effect systemic educational improvement. If a sufficient cadre of system leaders were developed and deployed, there would be:

- a wider resource for school improvement, making the most of our leaders to transfer best practice and reduce the risks involved in innovation and change;

- an authentic response to failing schools (often those least able to attract suitable leaders);

- a means to resolve the emerging challenges of, on the one hand, falling student rolls and hence increasingly non-viable schools and, on the other, pressures to sustain educational provision in all localities;

- a sustainable strategy for retaining and developing head teachers as a response to the current shortages (a survey by Hutchings *et al.* in 2006 warned that 40% of head teacher posts would be filled with difficulty in the coming years).

System leadership as adaptive work

No doubt these roles will expand and mature over time. What is significant about them is that they have evolved in response to the adaptive challenge of system change. This is the third of the aspects we need to discuss. It was Ron Heifetz (1994) who focussed attention on the concept of an adaptive challenge: a problem situation for which solutions lie outside current ways of operating. This is in stark contrast to a technical problem for which the know-how already exists. This distinction has resonance for educational reform. Put simply, resolving a technical problem is a management issue; tackling adaptive challenges requires leadership. Often we try to solve technical problems with adaptive processes, or more commonly force technical solutions onto adaptive problems. Figure 2.1 illustrates how this issue underpins the transition from prescription to professionalism, and emphasises the importance of capacity building.

Figure 2.1 System leadership as adaptive work

Technical solutions

Adaptive work

System leadership

Technical problems can be solved through applying existing
know how – adaptive chalenges create a gap between a
desired state and reality that cannot be closed using existing
approaches alone.

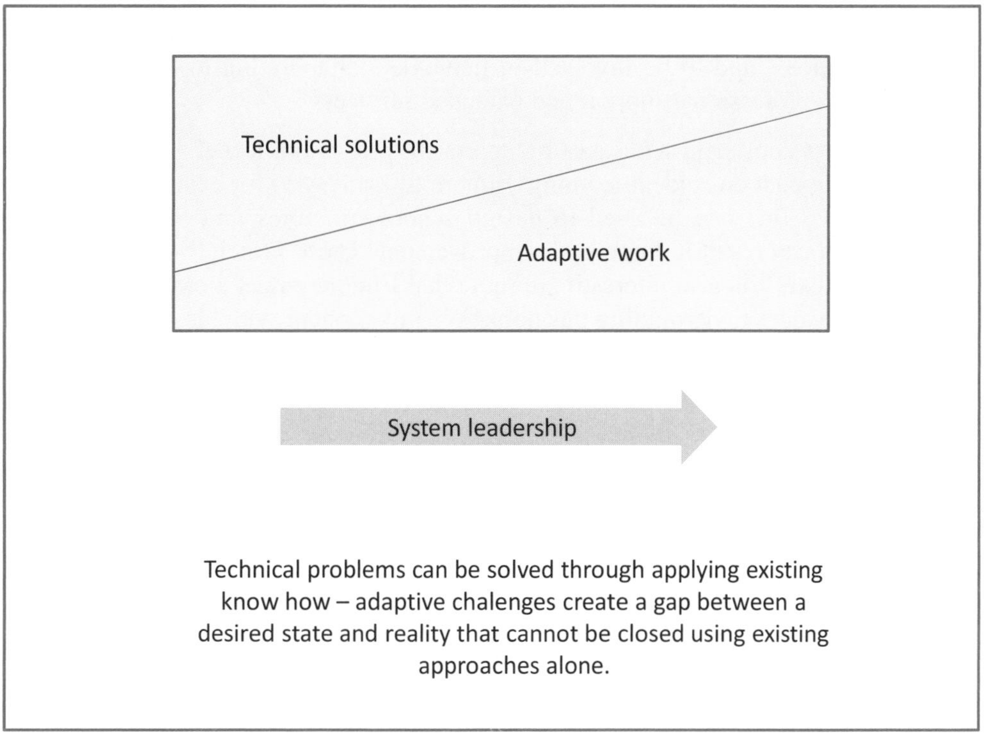

Almost by definition, adaptive challenges demand learning, as they require new ways of thinking and operating. In these instances it is people who are the problem, because an effective response to an adaptive challenge is almost always beyond the current competence of those involved. Inevitably this is threatening, and often the prospect of adaptive work generates heat and resistance.

Mobilising people to meet adaptive challenges is at the heart of leadership practice. In the short term leadership helps people to meet an immediate challenge. In the medium to long term leadership generates capacity to enable people to meet a continuing stream of adaptive challenges. Ultimately, adaptive work requires us to reflect on the moral purpose by which we seek to thrive, and demands diagnostic enquiry into the obstacles to those purposes.

The domains of system leadership

The fourth issue is what are the domains of system leadership: what does the task involve? One of the clearest definitions is the four core functions proposed by Ken Leithwood and his colleagues (2006):

- setting direction: to enable all learners to reach their potential, and to translate a vision into a whole school curriculum with consistency and high expectations;

- managing teaching and learning: to ensure that there is a high degree of consistency and innovation in teaching practices to enable personalised learning for all students;

- developing people: to enable students to become active learners and to create schools as professional learning communities for teachers;

- developing the organisation: to create evidence based schools and effective organisations, and to be involved in networks collaborating to build curriculum diversity, professional support and extended services.

This outline is consistent with existing approaches to school leadership that have had a demonstrable impact on student learning. Elmore (2004:80-81) for example distils some guiding principles that can be used to design school structures and stimulate training programmes that can result in large scale improvement. These principles are summarised in Box 2.1 overleaf. It is also interesting to note that Elmore enters a caveat that is much in tune with the values underpinning this book. We fully concur with his suggestions that:

"… the exact form or wording of the principles is less important than the fact that they are an attempt to derive general guidance from practice and research in a form can be tried in multiple settings and revised and elaborated with experience."

Box 2.1 Elmore's principles for large scale improvement

Maintain a tight instructional focus sustained over time

- Apply the instructional focus to everyone in the organisation.

- Apply it to both practice and performance.

- Apply it to a limited number of instructional areas and practices, becoming progressively more ambitious over time.

Routinise accountability for practice and performance in face-to-face relationships

- Create a strong normative environment in which adults take responsibility for the academic performance of children.

- Rely more heavily on face-to-face relationships than on bureaucratic routines.

- Evaluate performance on the basis of all students, not select groups of students and – above all – not school- or grade-level averages.

- Design everyone's work primarily in terms of improving the capacity and performance of someone else –system administrators of principals and teachers, principals of teachers, teachers of students. In a well-developed system, the order should be reversed as well.

Reduce isolation and open practice up to direct observation, analysis, and criticism

- Make direct observation of practice, analysis, and feedback a routine feature of work.

- Move people across settings, including outsiders into schools.

- Centre group discussions on the instructional work of the organisation.

- Model desired classroom practice in administrative actions.

- Model desired classroom practice in collegial interactions.

Exercise differential treatment based on performance and capacity, not on volunteerism

- Acknowledge differences among communities, schools, and classrooms within a common framework of improvement.

- Allocate supervisory time and professional development based on explicit judgements about where schools are in developmental process of practice and performance.

Devolve increased discretion based on practice and performance

- Do not rely on generalised rules about centralisation and decentralisation.

- Loosen and tighten administrative control based on hard evidence of quality of practice and performance of diverse groups of students; greater discretion follows higher quality of practice and higher levels of performance.

My own work with schools in England represents a similar logic to school improvement (Hopkins, 2001). This as Elmore has proposed is the crucial domain of system leadership. Figure 2.2 contains an illustration of the activities that contribute to a capacity for learning within a school and that are facilitated, established and energised by system leaders. It represents an attempt to capture how schools establish a learning focus and how elements of school improvement come together in practice. It begins from two assumptions. The first is that *all students* have a *potential for learning* that is not fully exploited (Line 1). The second is that the students' learning capability refers to their ability to access that potential through *increasing their range of learning skills* (Line 2). This potential is best realised and learning capability enhanced, through the range of *teaching and learning models* that the teacher uses with her/his students (Line 3). The deliberate use of a range of teaching and learning strategies with high meta-cognitive content is one of the richest features of personalised learning.

However, as has already been stressed the teaching and learning strategies are not "free-floating", but *embedded in the schemes of work and curriculum content* that teachers use to structure the learning in their lessons (Line 4). This leads to the whole school dimension through the staff development infrastructure the school has established, the *emphasis on high expectations*, the careful attention to consistency of teaching and the discussion of pedagogy that pervades the culture of the school (Line 5). It is these forms of internal collaboration on personalised learning and "professional" teaching that enable schools to *network* in order to raise standards across local areas, nationally and even globally (Line 6).

Figure 2.2 The logic of school improvement

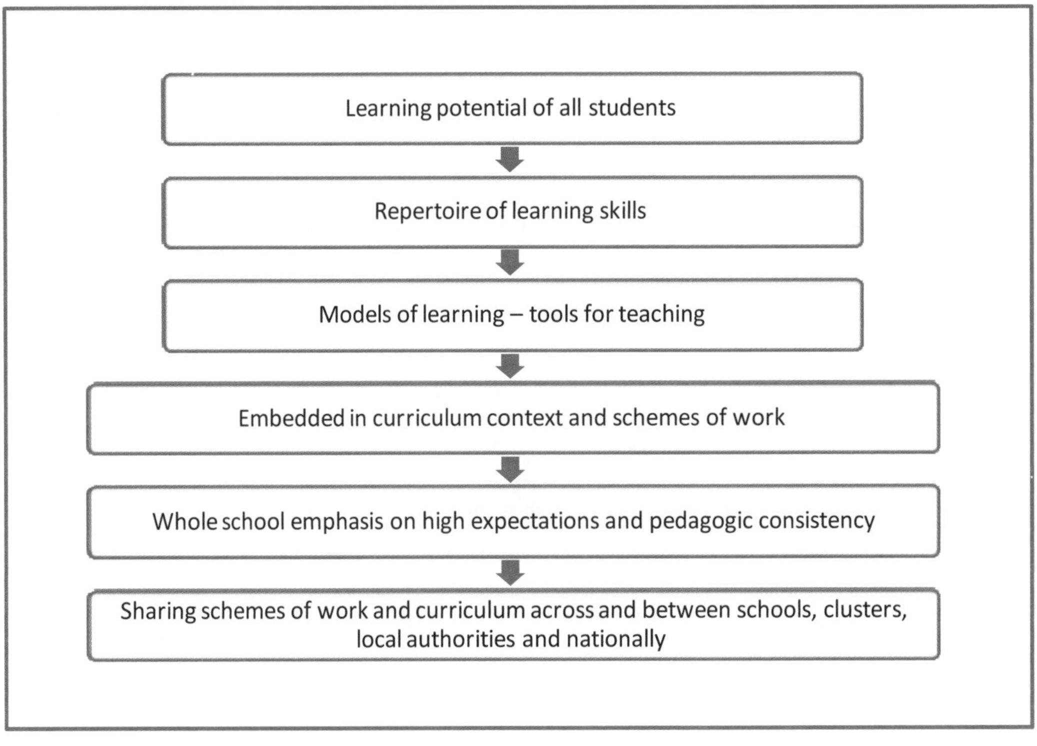

Finally, while it is true that system leadership is a relatively new concept, it is not an academic or theoretical idea, but has developed out of the challenges that system reform is presenting us with and the thoughtful, pragmatic and morally purposeful responses being given by our leading principals and heads. Ultimately, the test of system leadership is twofold: is it having an impact where it matters? And, can our school leaders answer the hard questions? Let us briefly answer each question in turn.

There is now growing evidence in the English secondary school system that this approach to system leadership is having a positive impact. Three examples make the point:

- Waverley School, under leadership of Sir Dexter Hutt from Ninestiles, improved from 16% 5 A-Cs at GCSE in 2001 to 62% in 2004.

- Sir Michael Wilshaw has instilled excellent behaviour, a focus on teaching and learning, and high expectations at Mossbourne Academy which is also having wider impact in the community.

- Valley Park School, in a partnership led by Sue Glanville, improved from 31% 5A*-C in 2004 to 43% in 2005. The lead school, Invicta Grammar, also benefited by developing its leadership team and curriculum offer.

Although these results are very encouraging, they do not claim to be comprehensive. Our research programme is beginning to build the evidence base more systematically (see for example Higham and Hopkins, 2007).

As regards to the hard questions, Michael Barber (2005) phrases them like this:

- Who are your key stakeholders in the local community? Do they understand your vision? Are they committed to it? How do you know?

- Have you established a core belief that every pupil (yes, every pupil) can achieve high standards? And then have you reorganised all the other variables (time, curriculum, teaching staff, and other resources) around the achievement of that goal? If not, why not?

- Is each pupil in your school working towards explicit short and medium term targets in each subject?

- Does each teacher know how his/her impact in terms of results compares to every other teacher? Have you thought about whether governors or parents should have access to this data? And what do you do to make sure that teachers who perform below the top quartile are improving?

- How do you ensure that every young person has a good, trusting relationship with at least one significant adult in your school?

- What do you and your school do to contribute to the improvement of the system as a whole?

These are the types of questions that the best system leaders test themselves against and are now comfortable with. When all our school leaders can do so, then surely we will be well on the way to every school being a great school.

2.2 Segmentation and system leadership

Reform efforts often fail to achieve a system-wide impact because of the high degree of segmentation in the school system. It is here where system leadership can have its most powerful effect. In all countries there are large groups of schools at varying stages of the performance cycle, between low and high performing. For every school to be great we need to use this diversity to drive higher levels of performance throughout the system. System transformation depends on excellent practice being developed, shared, demonstrated and adopted across and between schools.

It is important to realise however that this aspiration of system transformation being facilitated by the degree of segmentation existing in the system only holds when certain conditions are in place, crucially:

- There is increased clarity about the nature of intervention and support for schools at each phase of the performance cycle.

- Schools at each phase are clear about the most productive ways to collaborate so as to capitalise on the system's diversity.

The following discussion reflects experience in the English secondary school system, but the analysis is designed to be generally applicable.

There are probably six clearly identifiable levels of performance in the current structure of English secondary schools that are recognised by both statisticians and those tasked with improving schools. They, together with their key strategies for improvement, are:

- *Leading schools* (possibly 10% of secondary schools): These are the highest performing schools, which have the capacity to lead others. Their route to further improvement and contribution to the system comes in at least two forms: first, becoming leading practitioners through disseminating best practice and networking; and second, working formally and systematically with lower performing schools through some federation arrangement to improve the partner school's performance.

- *Succeeding, self-improving schools* (possibly 20% of secondary schools): Schools that have consistently above average levels of value added and exhibit aspects of best practice that can benefit the system. Their route to further improvement and contribution to the system comes in networking their best practice, using their leading teachers to mentor in other schools and to take students from local schools into their areas of specialism.

- *Succeeding schools with significant areas of underperformance* (possibly 20% of secondary schools): These schools although successful on published criteria have unacceptable numbers of underperforming teachers or departments who are masked by the averaging out of published results. Their route to further improvement and contribution to the system comes on the one hand contributing as above to other schools from their areas of strength and being the recipients of such support in their weaker areas.

- *Underperforming schools* (possibly 25% of secondary schools): Defined as those secondary schools in the lowest quartile of value added, who may have adequate or good headline results, but are consistently failing to add value to the progress of their students. Their route to further improvement is to use the data discussed with the school improvement partner (SIP) as a basis of raising standards across the school. They will need sustained consultancy in the early stages of an improvement process from a school with a similar intake, but far higher value added using a modified version of the federations intervention described below.

- *Low attaining schools* (possibly 20% of secondary schools): Defined as those secondary schools below the 30% A*-C GCSE floor target but with a capacity to improve. Their route to further improvement requires sustained support through some federation arrangement or involvement, consultancy support through the national strategies and possibly an improvement grant.

- *Failing schools* (possibly 5% of secondary schools): Defined as being well below the floor target and with little capacity to improve. At a minimum these schools will require intervention in the form of a hard federation or membership of the intensive support programme. If these strategies are not successful in the short term, then closure or Academy status may be the only answer.

A summary of this approach is set out in Table 2.1. In the right hand column is a basic taxonomy of schools based on an analysis of secondary schools in England. The number of categories and the terminology will vary from setting to setting, the crucial point being that not all schools are the same and each requires different forms of support. The second column shows strategies for supporting schools at different phases of their development. Again these descriptions are grounded in the English context, but they do have a universal applicability. There are two key points here:

- One size does not fit all.

- These different forms of intervention and support are increasingly being provided by schools themselves, rather than being imposed and delivered by some external agency. This approach to system transformation relies fundamentally on school to school support as the basis of the improvement strategy.

**Table 2.1 The six school types of English secondary schools and
their key strategies for improvement**

Type of school	Key strategies – responsive to context and need
Leading schools	Become leading practitioners Formal federation with lower-performing schools
Succeeding, self-improving schools	Regular local networking for school leaders Between-school curriculum development
Succeeding schools with internal variations	Consistency interventions such as assessment for learning Subject specialist support to particular departments
Underperforming schools	Linked school support for underperforming departments Underperforming pupil programmes; catch-up
Low attaining schools	Formal support in federation structure Consultancy in core subjects and best practice
Failing schools	Intensive support programme New provider such as an Academy

The segmentation approach requires boldness in setting system level expectations and conditions. There are four implications in particular that have to be grappled with:

- All failing and underperforming (and potentially low achieving) schools should have a leading school that works with them in either a formal grouping federation (where the leading school principal or head assumes overall control and accountability) or in more informal partnership. Evidence from existing federations in England suggests that a national system of federations could deliver sustainable improvement in a short time. For example a number of federated schools, as has been seen, have improved their 5 A*-Cs at GCSE from under 20% to over 50% in two years.

- Schools should take greater responsibility for neighbouring schools to encourage the move towards networking and collaborative arrangements outside of local authority control. This would be on the condition that these schools provided extended services for all students within a geographic area, but equally on the acceptance that there would be incentives for doing so. Encouraging local schools to work together will build capacity for continuous improvement at local level

- The incentives for greater system responsibility should include significantly enhanced funding for students most at risk. The potential effects for large scale long term reform include:

  - a more even distribution of at risk students and associated increases in standards, due to more schools seeking to admit a larger proportion of at risk students so as to increase their overall income;

  - a significant reduction in sink schools even where at risk students are concentrated, as there would be much greater potential to respond to the social-economic challenges (for example by paying more to attract the best teachers; or by developing excellent parental involvement and outreach services).

- A rationalisation of national and local agency functions and roles to allow the higher degree of national and regional co-ordination for this increasingly devolved system.

These proposals have a combination of school and policy level implications. This is consistent with the current phase of adaptive change in the overall system. If we are to move towards a system based on informed professional judgement, capacity has to be built both at the school and system level as both schools and government learn new ways of working, establish new norms of engagement and build more flexible and problem oriented work cultures.

2.3 Towards a model of system leadership

The new educational landscape is becoming better defined through a more systematic approach to segmentation and the power of system leadership. System leadership will develop from the actions of our best educational leaders. In *Every School a Great School* (Hopkins, 2007), I make an initial attempt to capture the main elements of this emerging practice (Figure 2.3). The individual elements in the model build to present a theory of action for leadership in the new educational context.

Figure 2.3 Emerging model of system leadership

The model's logic flows from the inside out. Leaders seek to empower teachers and others to make schools a critical force for improving communities. It is based on this paper's argument that sustainable educational development requires educational leaders who are willing to shoulder broader leadership roles: who care about and work for the success of other schools as well as their own.

Let me briefly unpack the elements in the model. It begins in the centre with the acknowledgement that such forms of leadership are imbued with moral purpose, as defined earlier. This is a necessary but not sufficient condition. Although I am not a great believer in heroic theories of leadership, it is clear that our best system leaders share a characteristic set of behaviours and skills. As illustrated in the next ring of the diagram, these are of two types. First, system leaders engage in "personal development", usually informally through benchmarking themselves against their peers and developing their skills in response to the context they find themselves working in. Secondly, all the system leaders we have studied have a strategic capability: they can translate their vision or moral purpose into operational principles with tangible outcomes.

The third ring of the model shows that the moral purpose, personal qualities and strategic capacity of the system leader are focused on three domains of the school: managing the teaching and learning process, developing people and developing the organisation. System leaders engage deeply with the organisation of teaching, learning, curriculum and assessment in order to personalise learning for all their students, reduce within school variation and support curriculum choice. In order to do this they develop their schools as personal and professional learning communities, with relationships built across and beyond each school to provide a range of learning experiences and professional development opportunities. They also realise that all this requires a robust and reliable school organisation, and they work towards achieving this.

System leaders strive for equity and inclusion through giving their communities a sense of worth and empowerment.

Although a growing number of outstanding leaders exemplify these qualities and determinations, they are not necessarily "system leaders". A system leader not only has these aspirations and capabilities but also, as seen in the outer ring of the model, strives for equity and inclusion through acting on context and culture and through giving their communities a sense of worth and empowerment. They do this by assuming one of the system leadership roles described earlier.

So, in concluding, the movement towards system leadership movement can be increasingly clearly defined in terms of concepts, capacities, roles and strategy. It has the exciting potential that the practices of system leadership will grow out of the future demands of system leaders. System leadership is the key driver in ensuring that every student reaches their potential and that every school becomes great. That is what school transformation is all about.

References

Barber, M. (2005), "A 21st Century Self Evaluation Framework", Annex 3 in *Journeys of Discovery: The Search for Success by Design,* keynote speech at the Annual Conference of National Center on Education and the Economy, Florida.

Elmore, R. F. (2004), *School Reform from the Inside Out*, Harvard Education Press, Cambridge, MA.

Fullan, M. (2003), *The Moral Imperative of School Leadership*, Corwin Press, London.

Fullan, M. (2005), *Leadership and Sustainability*, Corwin Press, London.

Heifetz, R.A. (1994), *Leadership Without Easy Answers*, Harvard University Press, Cambridge, MA.

Higham, R, and D. Hopkins (2007), "System Leadership for Educational Renewal in England: the Case of Federations and Executive Heads", *Australian Journal of Education,* Vol. 51, No 3, pp. 299-314.

Hopkins, D. (2001), *School Improvement for Real*, Routledge/Falmer, London.

Hopkins, D. (2007), *Every School a Great School*, McGraw Hill/Open University Press, London.

Hopkins, D. and R. Higham (2007), "System Leadership: Mapping the Landscape", *School Leadership & Management*, 27(2), pp. 147-166.

Hutchings, M., *et al.* (2006), *Survey on Teachers*, General Teaching Council (GTC), *www.gtce.org.uk* Accessed 26 August 2006.

Leithwood, K., C. Day, P. Sammons, A. Harris and D. Hopkins (2006), *Seven Strong Claims about Successful School Leadership*, National College for School Leadership / Department for Education and Skills, Nottingham.

NCSL (National College for School Leadership) (2005), *Advice to the Secretary of State on Complex Schools,* NCSL, Nottingham.

Osborne, S.P. (ed.) (2000), *Public-Private Partnerships*, Routledge, London.

Chapter 3

Leadership as the practice of improvement
by
Richard F. Elmore

This chapter explores the relationship between accountability and school leadership. The argument is as follows: accountability systems work to the degree that they engage the knowledge, skill, and commitment of people who work in schools. The success of accountability policy depends on the development of what the author calls the practice of improvement – explicit strategies for developing and deploying knowledge and skill in schools. Accountability tends to lead to an underinvestment in knowledge and skill, and an overinvestment in testing and regulatory control. Correcting this distortion requires changing the relationship between policy and practice, particularly around the definition and development of leadership. The author develops a model of school leadership practice consistent with his proposed theory of accountability. He reviews ways in which policies might be used to increase leadership capacity for school improvement. Accountability policy will not increase school performance unless there is substantial investment in developing human capital focused on school improvement.

It is an ordinary day at Hamilton Elementary School, in an urban setting in the north-eastern United States. Students and teachers are working with a satisfying and orderly hum. The hallways are neat and clean and are hung with student work. Classrooms are busy. Students move through the hallways in a (mostly) quiet way. The school's mission statement – Learning for All – is posted prominently in the front hallway. The principal moves from classroom to classroom, greeted by children and teachers. Hamilton is classified under the US *No Child Left Behind Act* as a school in need of improvement. Its mathematics scores on the state test are significantly below the level required to meet the annual yearly progress standard; its reading and writing scores have moved in and out of that zone over the past four years. It is a high poverty school in a largely immigrant neighbourhood. There are four primary languages in the school, Haitian Creole, Spanish, Chinese, and English; about one-third of the students either are, or have been in the last two years, in English immersion classes.

The problem the school is focusing on at the moment is the implementation of a new maths curriculum. The system in which Hamilton resides adopted a very challenging, high level curriculum two years ago, to accompany its high level literacy curriculum. The teachers at Hamilton are having difficulty with the curriculum. It requires teachers to teach in a very different way than they are accustomed to. A typical lesson starts with a brief set-up of a problem, then students are asked to work individually and in groups to propose solutions to the problem, during which the teacher is supposed to coach students without providing direct instruction. The individual and group work is followed by some students presenting their work and others critiquing it.

The principal has found that in most classrooms teachers are unable to move away from direct instruction as the main pedagogical technique; they focus on factual and procedural details at the expense of the maths concepts; they frequently misunderstand the maths concepts they are expected to teach; and they do not expect students to be able to work at the level the curriculum requires. "There is a mismatch between the ability level of our students and the level of the curriculum," one teacher says. Just down the hall from this teacher, however, is a classroom in which the curriculum is being implemented with a great deal of skill with children similar to those in other classrooms. This teacher has become a model for the district; district curriculum staff regularly bring visitors to observe. Other teachers at Hamilton, however, have not observed this teacher.

The principal at Hamilton is stymied. "I've done just about everything I know how to do to engage teachers in this work, and we're just not making progress beyond the initial burst of enthusiasm that teachers felt when we first start working with higher level content. I think we're all pretty demoralised. The testing system is relentless, whether you know what you're doing or not. If we miss annual yearly progress again, we'll be in corrective action, which carries even stricter sanctions. I don't see how that is going to help us. We're still the same school with the same teachers and the same kids. How does it help to beat us up more than before?"

Hamilton's story is acted out in various versions across a wide variety of schools and school systems in the US School administrators accept the terms of accountability for performance, even though they may argue with the specific way in which the accountability system treats them. Teachers are working more or less at the limit of their knowledge and pedagogical skill. School systems are making changes that they think will move them to higher levels of performance, often, as is the case with Hamilton's district, taking serious risks by adopting very high level curricula that require teachers and students to work in very different ways. But in many instances – probably most – they find themselves stuck at some point, not having a clear idea of what to do next.

This paper is about the role of leadership in the improvement of schools like Hamilton. Hamilton is a composite of dozens of schools I have been in over the past four or five years, schools that are struggling to do what they are expected to do under the terms of an accountability system they understand in only the most basic way. People in these schools show up for work committed to doing a good job. They are attached to the children they teach. They are, for the most part, very aware that they are not doing a good job, according to the terms of the accountability system, but they don't have a clear idea of what to do differently. Often they are challenged to teach at higher levels – as with introduction of the new literacy and maths curricula in Hamilton's district. They feel challenged by these curricula, but they often – indeed usually – do not feel supported in their attempts to learn how to teach in different ways. They are, for the most part, not persuaded by the teacher down the hallway who seems to be doing better. They live in their own world with their own students. Leaders with good intentions are trying to change these schools, often themselves with only the simplest ideas of how this work is done.

This paper explores the relationship between accountability and leadership. The argument is as follows: accountability systems work to the degree that they engage the knowledge, skill, and commitment of people who work in schools. Indeed, the success of accountability policy depends on the development of what I will call practices of improvement – explicit strategies for developing and deploying knowledge and skill in classrooms and schools. The politics of accountability tend to lead to an underinvestment in knowledge and skill, and an overinvestment in testing and regulatory control. Correcting this distortion requires changing the relationship between policy and practice, particularly around the definition and development of leadership. This paper develops a theory of accountability that is different from the prevailing view expressed in policy. It develops a model of school leadership practice consistent with the new theory of accountability. And it provides an initial working model of how school improvement works as a developmental process and how policies might be used to increase leadership capacity for school improvement. Accountability policy will not increase school performance without a substantial investment in human capital aimed at developing the practice of school improvement in a diverse population of school leaders.

Accountability policy will not increase school performance without a substantial investment in human capital aimed at developing the practice of school improvement in a diverse population of school leaders.

3.1 (If) accountability is the policy, (then) improvement is the practice

The idea of accountability for performance has a firm grip on education policy in virtually every industrialised democracy. The social, economic, and political roots of these policies is worthy of its own extensive analysis (Manna, 2006; Debray, 2006). Suffice to say for our purposes that these roots run deep, and the general direction of these policies is relatively immune to change.

Policy speaks of "holding schools accountable for results". Schools, and the people in them, are expected to come to understand what policy makers (and presumably the broader society) expects of them through the application of some combination of performance standards, assessments, classification schemes, oversight and sanctions.

Over time, they are expected to change their behaviour, individually and collectively, to meet these expectations. In this way, then, policy produces performance. What is interesting about this formulation of accountability policy is that, while it dominates policy discourse, there is little in the history of social interventions, or in the practice of schooling, to support it.

The first problem lies in the attribution of the effect (performance) to the cause (accountability policy). One can, of course, measure the aggregate "effects" of accountability policy on school performance – and policy researchers do this whenever and wherever they can find the data (proof of Abraham Kaplan's first law of instruments – "give a child a hammer and suddenly everything in the world needs pounding".) These studies are good for provoking debate and for generating and allocating political credit and blame, essential parts of the institutional behaviour of democracies. But they have little or nothing to do with the actual cause and effect relationships that determine school effectiveness or performance.

We have known explicitly for at least 30 years, and probably implicitly for a good deal longer, that it is not the policy, or the programme, that directly produces the effect. We have known that if policies produce any effects at all, they do so by altering the distribution of effects around some mean, typically in marginal ways. Hence, the main effect of any policy is practically meaningless as scientific construct. The distribution of effects is far more meaningful – an idea that is hard to express in political terms. We continue, for example, to talk about the main effects of vouchers and charter schools despite the fact that these effects are typically small and variable from one study to the next, and despite the fact that most of the information about the effects of these interventions lies in their distribution, not in the main effect. We have also known that the main effect of any intervention is typically quite small, relative to the ambient noise in the larger context. It is now virtually a given that variability in effects among sites within a given intervention exceeds variability between the interventions themselves, or between the intervention and the control condition. In plain language, this means that context dominates treatment in any large scale social intervention. In the language of old fashioned analysis of variance, interaction effects dominate main effects. The effects most worth knowing about in policy analysis, and the least analysed, are interaction effects (Elmore, 2004; Coburn, 2003; Datnow *et al.*, 2000).

Despite these robust and repetitive patterns in policy research, policy discourse continues to focus on main effects, as if the world were organised neatly around clearly delineated policies, and as if everything important that happens in the world were directly traceable to some policy decision made by someone whose electoral fortunes depend on its success. This misconception is driven not by an understanding of the actual world in which policies operate, but rather by the incentive structure within which policymakers operate. You don't get political credit for interaction effects.

In the context of accountability and school leadership, the "main effects" view of policy has produced a number of very costly misconceptions. Not the least of these is that school performance will increase to the degree that schools and school systems "implement" accountability policy. In this view, the federal government holds states accountable, governors and legislatures hold their state agencies accountable, state agencies hold school systems accountable, school systems hold the schools accountable, and school leaders hold students and teachers accountable. We have known for a very long time, of course, that this "fidelity" or "compliance" model of policy implementation does not work, and never has. Policies "work" not to the degree that they force everyone

– in this case schools – to do what the policy requires, but rather to the degree that they move different parts of the distribution of schools in a similar direction using different types of policy instruments. Again, this view seems too complex and too nuanced for a world in which political credit is generated by doing something visible and claiming credit for it.

An even more costly misconception of the main effects view is that schools will do better if they are given clear information about their performance. In this view, delivering clear information to schools and their communities about their performance will have a galvanising effect on the people who work in them, and will cause them to do something they would not otherwise have done to improve teaching and student performance. When I talk to my students and to groups of practitioners about this view of accountability, I ask them to imagine schools, on a grand scale, in which teachers have systematically squirreled away in their classroom closets all their best and most powerful instructional ideas and practices, saving them for the day when the accountability system smacks them on the head. Then, magically, the good ideas come out of the closet and school performance, just as magically, increases. In fact, people in schools are working pretty reliably at the limit of their existing knowledge and skill. Giving them information about the effects of their practice, other things being equal, does not improve their practice. Giving them information in the presence of new knowledge and skill, under the right conditions, *might* result in the improvement of their practice, which *might*, in turn, result in increased student performance. In the 1970s, Thomas Schelling, the Nobel laureate economist, called this distinction, "doing the right thing versus knowing the right thing to do". Accountability policy, as it's presently constituted, makes no such distinction.

As I work with schools and school systems around issues of accountability and school improvement, I am constantly amazed at how little they seem to know about things that I consider to be central to the process of school improvement. I want to stress that these are schools that have been operating in a performance-based accountability system for at least a decade. They were subject to strong state accountability systems before the advent of *No Child Left Behind*. For the most part, they have got the message that accountability for student performance is their present and future. They can tell you in rough terms where they lie in some distribution of schools and districts, and they can tell you whether they are facing sanctions, and what kind, under accountability policies. In this sense, they have internalised the main message of accountability policy. But they have almost no knowledge of how to respond to accountability policy effectively – at either the school or the system level.

The distribution of schools I work with is extremely bi-modal. The majority have only the smallest, most rudimentary understanding of what to do in response to accountability policy. A significant minority have relatively well-worked-out strategies, and a smaller minority within this group have strategies that appear to be working. A small fraction are somewhere between the vast majority who don't know what they are doing, and the significant minority who seem to. If accountability policy were "working", in the implementation view, this distribution would look very different. If policymakers were interested in the effects of accountability policy, they would know something about this distribution, and they would be trying to do something about it. In point of fact, accountability policy does not work when it doesn't take account of the knowledge and skill requirements for its success. These requirements vary considerably from one setting to another.

What the present conception of accountability lacks is a **practice** of school improvement to go with the **policy** of accountability. Accountability policy is, for the most part, resting on a weak, unreliable and mushy base of knowledge, skill, and practice. The state of knowledge is evident in the distribution of effects, but this distribution is not part of routine discussions of the policy. In Schelling's language, it matters a great deal less in these conditions whether people want to do the right thing – for the most part, they do – but in vast numbers they don't know what is the right thing to do, or how to do it. Furthermore, and more distressingly, accountability policy itself is based on the premise that they don't need to know, because doing the right thing is all that is necessary.

In an institutional structure in which the governance of schools is increasingly defined by accountability for performance, leadership *is* the practice of improvement – like it or not (Fullan, 2005). We can talk about broader, more philosophically-grounded definitions of school leadership, but the necessary condition for school leaders' success in the future will be their capacity to improve the quality of instructional practice. In the near term, this work will have to be done in an environment which does not acknowledge the value or necessity of practice.

Leadership is the practice of improvement.

In sum, then, accountability policy won't work without a corresponding practice of school improvement. Furthermore, the practice has to work at a scale and to be distributed in a way that markedly alters the distribution of quality and performance among classrooms and schools. To my knowledge, no one has taken on this problem in the education system of any industrialised country. Is it worth doing, or at least trying to do? What would such a practice look like? What are the knowledge and skill requirements of such a practice? And what kind of institutional infrastructure would be required to develop and support it?

3.2 An alternative view of accountability and leadership

In order to get at the knowledge and skill requirements of leadership for improvement, we have to have an alternative working theory of accountability. In our work on accountability, we have found that it is useful to think about accountability as a problem of **institutional response**, rather than implementation, compliance or fidelity. Schools don't suddenly "get" accountability as a consequence of a policy being formed at some remote place and implemented at another; schools already **have** accountability. All schools, regardless of their type, status or institutional basis, have a solution to the accountability problem embedded in their existing organisational context and culture. They have answers to the questions of **to whom** they are accountable, **for what**, and **how**. These answers may not be consistent with what policymakers think they should be, but schools nonetheless have them. Some schools solve the problem by focusing on a particular group of parents, some by trying to please the local superintendent, some by focusing on internal constituencies like a particular group of favoured teachers. Accountability policy, in other words, doesn't "introduce" the idea of accountability to schools. It rather operates by reshaping existing modes of accountability around an alternative idea of accountability for performance to a specific, often remote, governmental authority (Abelmann *et al.*, 1999).

So the effect of an external accountability policy depends not on whether, or how well, schools or school systems "implement" that policy, but on how they **respond** to the incentives the policy puts in place in their external environment. Accountability policies are only one among many possible signals that schools and school systems have to respond to in their environment. Furthermore, most schools operate in multiple accountability systems simultaneously and have to choose which ones to favour in any given instance. The most obvious case of this phenomenon is high schools, which have to operate in a performance-based accountability system judging their performance based on test scores. At the same time they operate in an attainment based system, which judges them on the basis of their success in placing students in post-secondary institutions. These two systems are not aligned, and, in fact, are in certain critical ways in conflict with each other. Instead of asking whether schools and systems "implement" accountability policies, we should ask what their responses are to the panoply of incentives they face, what the determinants of these responses are, and how they adjust to alterations of these incentives over time.

The first, most obvious, finding from our research is that schools and school systems respond differently, depending on their *capacity* and their *internal accountability*. In simple terms, which I will elaborate later, capacity is the fund of skill and knowledge that the organisation can bring to bear in responding to external pressure, and internal accountability is the degree of coherence in the organisation around norms, values, expectations, and processes for getting the work done. We speak of "high capacity" organisations as those that have, or have access to, knowledge and skill that can be put to use in responding to external pressures, and "low capacity" organisations as those that do not (Cohen and Lowenburg Ball, 1999; Cohen *et al.*, 2006). We speak of organisations with high internal accountability as those with high agreement around values and an organisational scheme that makes that agreement evident in practice. We speak of organisations with low internal accountability as those with weak agreement and atomised, highly variable practice. Not surprisingly, in our studies, most schools lie at the low capacity, low internal accountability end of the distribution. Perhaps a little more surprisingly, we do not find major systematic differences among different types of schools (public, private, religious, charter, etc.) on these dimensions. In our work, it matters far more what your level of capacity and internal accountability is than what type of school you are.

A school's response to an accountability policy depends heavily on the conditions in its environment. Schools are more likely to develop capacity for high level instruction and internal accountability if they are in an institutional environment that provides support for these factors. It is not, however, a foregone conclusion that a school that exists in a supportive environment responds to that environment in ways that improve its capacity and internal accountability. Many schools get stuck at a given level in ways that are difficult to understand, and they seem unable to make productive use of the resources in their environment.

Think now about leadership in this view of accountability. The first thing that comes to mind is that leadership provides a focusing function, sorting out signals in the ambient environment, valuing some over others, and modelling the organisation's solution to the accountability problem around those signals. The second is that leadership is both a marker for capacity and a factor in determining the organisation's ability to mobilise and use capacity in its environment. A knowledgeable leader counts as a measure of capacity, but she also heavily influences how well the organisation uses its internal capacity and develops its capacity with external resources. Likewise, leadership is both a marker for determining how internally coherent the organisation is and for developing internal accountability. Knowledgeable and skilful leaders are generally (but not always) a proxy for high internal accountability, and leadership is instrumental in developing internal accountability.

In our work on accountability and school improvement, accountable leaders are not passive or reactive leaders. That is, they don't do what they are told to do. They don't even spend much time trying to figure out and "game" the accountability systems they operate in. They operate in a more strategic frame. They use the accountability system to position themselves and their organisations in a favourable place to gain resources and capacity, and they tend to use capacity as an instrument for developing organisational coherence. Accountable leaders know that success in a performance-based incentive system does not stem from compliance, but rather from the strategic use of resources to improve performance, which in turn allows them to build capacity.

Notice that I have said nothing about whether performance, as defined by the accountability system, is worth achieving in some objective sense, or against some normative principle. We have found, against conventional wisdom, that schools with high capacity and high internal accountability seem to do well on whatever the tests are, regardless of whether their instructional philosophy is aligned with the tests. It is also possible that doing well in a performance-based accountability system does not correspond to doing good. Saying that we know some of the practices of highly effective leaders under conditions of performance-based accountability systems is definitely not the same thing as saying that what they are doing is good, either for their students or for society as a whole. Nor is it clear that policymakers have any particular advantage, other than their formal institutional position, for saying what is good. For the most part, they do not have the expertise to make judgment about what is good practice educationally. Accountability policy sets a framework of incentives within which skilful leaders learn to operate; whether what they are doing is worth doing is a separate question that is argued out in the political arena and is not self-evident at any particular time.

We have found that schools with high capacity and high internal accountability seem to do well on whatever the tests are, regardless of whether their instructional philosophy is aligned with the tests.

3.3 Understanding improvement practices

Leadership *practice* is what connects policy to performance in schools. It is important to understand what this proposition means in order to grasp what effective practice looks like. First, practice is not a personal attribute or characteristic of leaders; it is a collection of patterned actions, based on a body of knowledge, skill, and habits of mind that can be objectively defined, taught, and learned. Americans, in particular, tend to have essentialist or attribute theories of leadership: skilled leadership, in this view, is a personal attribute, unique to the individual, like a particular posture, facial expression, or conversational style. (Americans also have essentialist views of teaching – a topic we will address later – and essentialist views of intelligence in general.) The problem with essentialist views of leadership is that they can never be generalised to scale. By definition, only a fraction of the population of potential or actual leaders have the attributes identified with effective leadership, and that fraction never equals anything like the number required for system-wide improvement. To be sure, most effective practices of leadership are initially the product of gifted individuals operating in creative ways. But these practices have to be separated from the individuals who created them in order to be useful at scale. As a gifted practitioner once said to me, "It's only genius the first time you do it. After that, it belongs to everyone." In order to become a practice, patterns of behaviour must be objectified and separated from the individuals who use them.

Second, practice must be based on a ***theory of action***, a causal model that can be falsified with evidence of its consequences. A theory of action is a set of logically connected statements that, in our case, connect the actions of leaders with their consequences for quality and performance in the organisation[7]. The statements might have to do with resource allocation, with the design and structure of professional development, with the creation of collegial networks, etc. Theories of action are essential to the separation of the practice from the person. They have to be stated in order to be shared, and they have to be evaluated against evidence of their success in order to be judged. All theories of action are, of course, contingent – their actual effectiveness varies according to the settings in which they are enacted. Contingency does not, however, mean that all practices are situational, nor does it mean that theories can't be adjusted to meet predictable contingencies. For example, in order for an organisation to work effectively in a performance-based accountability system, leadership has to exercise control over resource allocation, targeting time and money on developing knowledge and skill. It's unlikely that this type of theory will vary a great deal across settings, but it is likely that the conditions under which one gains control of resource allocation and the options available for the use of resources would vary considerably.

Third, practice is embedded in the particular incentive structures and particular institutional settings in which it is used. Another way of saying this is that practices cannot be generalised, except in superficial ways, beyond the institutional settings in which they are developed. Powerful knowledge of practice does not transfer, for example, from the private sector to the management of schools without considerable work in specifying, developing, and adapting it. Again, using the resource allocation example, there may be powerful resource allocation models from outside the education sector that have value in helping school leaders think about how to manage money and time. These models do not become "practice," though, until they are adapted to school settings, and to the particularities of incentives in those settings, and then worked into the repertoire of school leaders. Most great ideas about organisation and management don't make this transition because their advocates don't have the patience or the insight to understand how practice develops.

Finally, we are interested not in practice in general but in practices that lead to school improvement. For this purpose, I will use a simple definition of improvement: ***improvement is increases in quality and performance over time.***

Graphically, this would be displayed as performance and quality on a vertical axis, time on a horizontal axis, and improvement would be a more or less steady movement in a north-easterly direction. This definition, of course, begs the question of what we define as quality and performance – a question I will return to later. And it raises the question of why put both performance and quality on the vertical axis since, in the cosmology of performance-based accountability, performance is a proxy for quality. Again, I will address this issue later. For the time being, then, improvement is moving the herd roughly north-east. This definition might apply to teachers and classrooms within schools, to schools within systems, or to schools and systems within state or national jurisdictions.

What do I mean, then, by "***practices of improvement***"? I mean theories of action that lead to systematic increases in quality and performance over time. What I would like to do, in a preliminary way, is to sketch out what a theory of action might look like in order to illustrate the broader argument I will make later about how we might think systemically about the development of leadership in the education sector. But here it is necessary to issue a stern consumer protection warning. These insights about practices of improvement are based on my own work with schools and school systems around problems of accountability and school improvement, not a systematic body of research, which, incidentally does not exist. So what follows should be seen as the provisional beginning of a conversation about leadership practice and school improvement.

Improvement occurs in predictable stages and practices of improvement vary by stage

A school in which decisions around content and pedagogy are delegated to the classroom level, in which teachers have no relationships with each other around instructional practice, in which there are no discussions among teachers or administrators about evidence of student learning, is a school with extremely low internal accountability. Such schools are relatively immune to external influences of any kind because they have no receptors for new knowledge and skill and no way of using it when it is present. Moving a school like this through an improvement process requires a focus on creating occasions for discussion and analysis of instructional practice, creating a demand for new knowledge and skill, managing time and money in a way that promotes occasions for learning, and opening up classroom practice to outside influences on curriculum and pedagogy.

A school with a well-developed approach to curriculum and pedagogy, routine grade-level and content-focused discussions of instructional practice, and structured occasions to discuss student performance is a school with relatively high internal accountability. Moving a school like this requires skill in using the existing internal infrastructure to develop and sustain focus and motivate teachers to tackle progressively more difficult problems of practice. The problem with such schools is that they often lose focus, or become complacent, not they lack the wherewithal for improvement.

Notice that these two schools represent different points on a continuum of internal accountability – the first, an essentially atomised organisation ill-equipped to mount any sort of response to pressure for performance, or to use any external knowledge; the second, a school in the process of developing a stronger internal accountability system whose problem is how to use this system to focus on increasingly challenging problems of practice.

We could imagine a number of different points on the continuum, but these two are enough to illustrate the main issue: school improvement is a developmental process[1]. High performance and quality are *not* a state but a point along a developmental continuum. Like most developmental processes, this one involves more or less predictable stages. Moving a school through these stages requires, first, an understanding that there is a developmental process going on; and second, an understanding of what distinguishes schools at one stage of development from another. In addition, there is a

---

1. Here, I take gentle exception to my colleague and friend, Michael Fullan and his colleagues, who have recently published a book describing improvement using the term "breakthrough", by which I think they mean discontinuous shifts in quality and performance that change the fundamental nature of the organisation. This has not been my experience working with schools, nor do I think the data on school improvement support this conclusion, even though I think the practices they describe in their book are consistent in many ways with what I am describing here. See Fullan *et al.*, (2006).

value in thinking of these schools on a continuum to demonstrate that, while the practices of improvement may vary by stage, the practice of improvement in general requires mastery of practices across stages. You cannot understand how to manage a school with a well-developed internal accountability system unless you have knowledge of how such systems develop. Likewise, you cannot create an internal accountability system unless you understand what one looks like in a more or less fully developed state.

The idea that different types of leaders are appropriate to schools at different stages of development – the contingency theory of leadership – strikes me as particularly pernicious in this context. In Massachusetts currently, for example, certain groups are advocating the training of "turn around" specialists for failing schools. These turn around specialists have been likened to the people who deal with oil well fires – cap the well, put out the fire, return the oil field to normal. There is a presupposition that this work requires a specific set of skills that are different from those of running schools. Understanding improvement as a developmental process is the antithesis of this model of leadership. If your sole purpose is to turn around a failing school – and then move on to the next one – you could well make decisions that undermine its longer term development. Indeed, most short term turn around strategies necessarily involve heavy use of managerial control, rather than developing the internal connective tissue of the organisation necessary to respond effectively over longer term. These strategies also have a certain heroic quality that appeals to Americans' views of leadership – "Who was that masked man?" The hero rides out of town in a cloud of dust.

More importantly, it is difficult to shape a developmental practice of improvement if practitioners specialise in schools at a single stage of development. If the process is continuous, the practice should be more or less continuous too. Practitioners who have taken schools through a range of stages of development, and thus have developed a broad range of knowledge and skill, are a precious commodity because their practice can be captured and taught to others. These people are relatively rare, and they tend to practice in isolation. Most systems have no capacity to learn from these practitioners. Systems usually lack the kind of detailed knowledge of practice at the school level that is required to support improvement. In all but a few of the systems I am currently working with in the United States, the most knowledgeable and skilled leaders are treated simultaneously as messiahs and pariahs by their superiors and peers.

Briefly put, the default culture in most schools is one in which practice is atomised, school organisation reinforces this atomisation by minimising occasions for collective work on common problems, so the school lacks the basic organisational capacity to use any kind of external knowledge or skill to improve practice. These schools exist in a myriad of contexts with a myriad of specific conditions – language groups, income groups, community cohesion and mobility, etc. As schools begin to develop toward a higher degree of internal accountability, their success depends increasingly on their capacity to identify and respond to specific problems in their context. Usually this occurs through deliberate work on the development of internal processes and structures that can, in turn, be used to develop common norms and expectations for instructional practice and student learning. Schools don't improve by following a set of rules; they improve by engaging in practices that lead them to be successful with specific students in a specific context. Hence, sustained improvement depends on the development of diagnostic capacity and on the development of norms of flexibility in practice. Leaders in these settings succeed to the degree that they engage in more or less continuous learning, and model that learning for others in the organisation.

Improvement is seldom, if ever, a smooth or continuous process

Typically, schools, or school systems, for that matter, do not advance through the improvement process at a more or less steady rate once they have begun. Most schools describe periodic states in which they "get stuck" or "hit the wall". Typically, these states occur after a new practice has been adopted but before it has become deeply seated in the organisation, or after a deeply seated practice has been in place for a while and a new problem surfaces in the organisation which the practice can't address. The early stage version is often called "the implementation dip." Let's say a school adopts a new literacy curriculum, or an extension of an existing one that is designed to deal with students who have serious language deficits. Incorporating a new practice into an existing one, or displacing an old one with a new one, involves a stage of learning, challenging new practices and changing a mindset about what it is possible to do. It is not unusual for performance data to go into a stall – sometimes for a year or two – and in some cases even to decrease as the new practice finds its place in the repertoire of teachers and administrators.

Sometimes when a practice has become well seated in the organisation and has been associated with positive increases in quality and performance, it loses its capacity to produce those increases and performance goes flat. Most of the schools I work with, having gone through what they consider to be very difficult processes of increasing internal accountability and the adoption of new instructional practices, hit a plateau within a year or two. For the people who work in these schools this is often a psychologically devastating experience. It is not unusual to hear people say things like, "I thought we had it together and it seemed like we were doing so well, and then things went flat. We don't know what to do next."

When you look at the evidence of student performance and classroom practice in these schools a number of possibilities emerge. First, it is often the case that some groups of students are simply not responding to the new practice. Teachers' sense of success is fuelled by the students who are responding, but at some point the lack of response from certain students becomes a drag on the school's overall performance. Second, it is often the case that teachers and principals overestimate, by a significant amount, how much their practice has actually changed. When we do more systematic classroom observations, we often discover that some of the more challenging parts of the new instructional practice are simply not present, or not present in a powerful enough form to affect student performance. Finally, it is often the case that the original intervention wasn't challenging enough, and the school simply needs to ratchet up its expectations for practice and performance, which involves another difficult adjustment of practice and expectations.

In general, developmental processes – biological, geological, economic, political, organisational, or human – do not follow simple straight line trajectories. A more common pattern that generalises across a number of developmental processes is called "punctuated equilibrium"[2]. People or systems might move relatively rapidly, sometimes

---

2.   The term "punctuated equilibrium" originates in evolutionary biology, specifically a famous paper authored by Eldridge and Gould (1972). Eldridge and Gould argue that major changes in speciation occur in small populations at the periphery of large, stable central populations. These "small peripheral isolates" become a "laboratory for evolutionary change", and result in discontinuous shifts in the major population. Eldridge and Gould portray the process of evolution as a form of continuous gradualism, punctuated by discontinuous changes. For a review of the controversy surrounding the idea of punctuated equilibrium (Prothero, 1992). The application of the idea to development of individuals and social organisations has been more implicit than

in a discontinuous way, through a particular stage of development identified as "progress". This stage is often followed by a period of equilibrium, in which the factors that produced the previous stage of development stabilise, and the factors that produce the next stage of development are latent and unobservable, or at least can't be measured through the same measures one would use to gauge "progress". Equilibrium is followed, again, by a stage of disequilibrium in which a constellation of accumulated forces produces a discontinuous development.

Learning, whether it occurs in students or adults and whether individual or collective, is a developmental process. We should not expect it to occur in a uniform, linear fashion. The practice of improvement is the management of learning for collective purposes; hence, knowledge of development is central to the practice of leadership.

Improvement occurs across at least three domains: the technical, the social-emotional, and the organisational

At least three processes are occurring simultaneously as schools get better at what they are doing (Kegan and Lahey, 2002; Heifetz, 1994). Changes in instructional practice occur with some consistency across classrooms that represent more powerful forms of learning for students and adults. Changes occurring in students', teachers' and administrators' sense of efficacy result from changes in practice and changes in student learning. And changes occur in the structure, processes, and norms around which the work of adults and students is organised. If you imagine development as a more or less wavy line, moving from south-west to north-east, on a graph with performance and quality on the vertical and time on the horizontal, the organisation is simultaneously *i)* getting better at its core functions; *ii)* changing the way adults and students think about their role in the process of learning; and *iii)* increasing internal accountability by managing the organisation in progressively more coherent ways.

The practice of improvement, then, occurs across these three domains; the practice of leaders requires knowledge, skill, and fluency of practice in each, and across all three. Leaders cannot choose to be "good" at some domains and "not-so-good" at others; to be effective they have to be competent across all domains. What does this look like in practice? It means monitoring instructional practice more or less continuously. It means seeding the creation of organisational structures, processes, and norms that make instruction transparent, so that it can be analysed and changed in response to feedback about its effects. It means modelling inquiry and learning as the central dimensions of practice, creating expectations that the improvement of practice is a continuous process. It means developing practices of challenge and support that help people deal with the social and emotional difficulties entailed in improvement. And it means using the basic features of the organisation – structures, processes, norms, resources – as instruments for increasing the knowledge and skill of people in the organisation.

---

explicit, but the idea corresponds closely to much of the current literature on adult development, organisational and economic development such as Hirschman, A. (1970).

The practice of improvement consists of making the familiar strange: objectifying practice, treating organisations as instruments

One of the most difficult aspects of mastering this practice is learning to treat existing instruction and organisation in an agnostic and instrumental way. Just as our theories of leadership are essentialist, so too are our theories of teaching. We identify the person with the practice. Teachers are thought to be either "good" or "bad" depending on deeply seated personal attributes. Teachers think of themselves as more or less coterminous with their practice; they *are* what they teach. To challenge the practice is to challenge the person. This view of teaching is, among other things, profoundly unprofessional, no, *anti*-professional – imagine a physician arguing that her surgical practice is a consequence of purely personal tastes, or an airline pilot announcing that he is making his landing approach based on his personal aesthetic considerations. It is also deeply anti-intellectual – good practice, in the essentialist view, depends on who you are, not what you know or what you can do. But the main problem with the essentialist view is that it effectively precludes any possibility of improvement of instruction at scale. There are never enough people with the "right" attributes to go around. It makes what is essentially a learning process into a selection process, and in doing so makes it impossible to treat human skill and knowledge as the main instrument of improvement.

The same might be said about the standard stance of school leaders toward their organisations. Structure, process, norms, and resources are what they are, in the essentialist view; the job of the leader is to manage within them, not to treat them as instruments for making things happen. To disturb the form of the organisation is to surface for critical scrutiny all the treaties, implicit and explicit, and all the accommodations that have been made to individuals, their interests and their (in)competencies. To assert that structure is instrumental to learning is to assert that the collective interests of the organisation supersede the individual interests of its members. Typically, low-performing, atomised schools are organisations in name only; they are the congealed residue of private interests.

Typically, low-performing, atomised schools are organisations in name only; they are the congealed residue of private interests.

We have learned to use two specific practices, adapted from other professions, to develop the capacity of leaders to objectify their own practice and to help practitioners learn to treat the organisation in which they work agnostically and instrumentally. One practice involves the use of protocols to observe, analyse, and develop practice. We observe instructional practice using protocols that focus as much as possible on the visible evidence in the classroom, *not* on the personal attributes of the teacher and not on the observer's normative stance toward what is being observed. We also use protocols for discussion of these observations that focus mainly on developing a body of evidence from which we can draw inferences about learning and student performance. We try to the extent possible to focus on the evidentiary claims that people in leadership positions make to justify their practices, or their theories of action, rather than on the personal attributes of the leaders. The use of protocols depersonalises practice; it separates the practice from the person; it objectifies the practice, and in doing so it makes the practice something that can be changed through learning and further practice.

The use of protocols separates the practice from the person; in doing so it makes the practice something that can be changed through learning and further practice.

Another technique we use is to work with practitioners on their theories of action – asking them to state in as simple terms as possible what the main causal connections are between what they influence or control and what they are trying to achieve by way of quality and performance. Again, the value of this work is that it helps practitioners to objectify their practice, to put it in terms that someone else can understand and that, if necessary, can be used to communicate with others and to teach them what the underlying line of thought and action is. It also depersonalises the practice, so that people can feel free to treat their own most deeply held values and beliefs as empirical propositions that can be subject to verification through evidence on the effects of what they do.

A large part of the practice of improvement for leaders is making the invisible visible. Most people in school leadership positions are more or less socialised to a relatively dysfunctional culture. Part of that socialisation process is learning to take most aspects of the organisation and its culture for granted and to focus on a narrow range of things that the default culture tells you that you *can* do. Part of the process of teaching leaders to actively manage the process of improvement is to make all the implicit rules, norms, and agreements that set constraints on action explicit, and subject to analysis and change.

We work with leaders on the central cultural artefacts of their organisations: the schedule, the assignment of teachers to grade levels and classes, the use of preparation time, the use of meetings, the management of time and money, the consultation and planning processes, etc. With each of these artefacts we try to get leaders to explain how they might be used to focus instructional practice, to create challenge and support for teachers and students, to create opportunities for enhancement of knowledge and skill. Rather than treating the "givens" of the organisation as constraints on action, we try to create a bias toward treating them as instruments for making things happen.

As improvement progresses, leadership refracts

Up to this point, I have, for the sake of simplicity, committed the common fallacy of confounding leadership with role. I have spoken of "leaders" and "teachers" as if they were mutually exclusive categories, and left the impression that leadership inheres in positional authority – in the principalship, in the superintendency, etc. Now it's time to rectify this fallacy.

As the literature on communities of practice suggests, collective learning requires distributed cognition. As networks or organisations get better at what they do, specialised expertise tends to develop in multiple sites; networks of influence develop around those sites; and leadership tends to become defined less by position and more by expertise. The literature on communities of practice tends to romanticise this process, suggesting that formal organisation plays little or no role in the development and distribution of knowledge and practice. In fact, there are situations in which the development of practice relies more on social networks, and less on formal organisation – punk bands, modern dance and meditation, for example. But the problem of improving practice and performance around learning is not one of these situations. Improvement of educational practice at scale requires some kind of formal infrastructure, and, as improvement progresses, leadership tends to follow the demands of learning, individual and collective, rather than the demands of formal organisations.

The metaphor of refraction is useful, if not exact. The basic idea is that the qualities and direction of light change as it passes through different media – air, water, lenses, etc. The notion is that leadership takes substantially different forms in organisations in the early stages of improvement than it does in organisations that are more advanced, and the ***practices*** of leadership become substantially more complex and powerful as they engage the energy and commitment of people in the organisation. Organisations in the early stages of improvement rely heavily on role-based definitions of leadership, and, as they cope with the early stages of improvement they tend to import practices of improvement into traditional roles. Principals take on increasing responsibility for the instructional side of the organisation, and often try to convert other administrative roles in the organisation into instructional support roles – assistant principals, for example. As improvement advances, it becomes clearer that role-based definitions of leadership are inadequate, both because teachers who take improvement of their own practice seriously become more expert on instructional issues than their supervisors and because the flow of work through the organisation becomes too demanding and too complex to manage exclusively from the top. So the work of leadership tends to flow out into the organisation.

The practices of leadership become substantially more complex and powerful as they engage the energy and commitment of people in the organisation.

Notice that two things are happening simultaneously as leadership refracts – people are learning how to use their own individual expertise for collective purposes, and they are also learning a new set of knowledge and skills associated with managing work across organisational boundaries. As this process advances, people in positions of formal leadership increasingly manage less in the direct mode, and more in the indirect mode. Their work is less in direct management of the conditions that influence instruction and performance and more in managing the learning and development of people whose responsibility directly affects instruction.

There are all sorts of ways in which this process can go awry. The most common is that positional leaders underestimate the level of complexity and the demands of the work as the organisation begins to improve, and they don't adapt the structure of the organisation to the tasks it has to perform. As teachers start to differentiate from one another in terms of their expertise, leaders fail to acknowledge what is going on and continue to manage as if everyone in the organisation were equal. It is not unusual, for example, for teachers who are highly enthusiastic and committed to professional development in the early stages of improvement to become increasingly frustrated as the process advances because the level of the professional development and the work doesn't increase as their expertise increases. Professional development becomes a compliance task rather than a learning opportunity. The organisation is not flexible enough to adapt to changes in their expertise, or to use that expertise as a resource in the organisation. Often people with positional authority are threatened by the idea that others might know more than they do about key functions of the organisation.

Another common way the process of differentiation goes awry is that leaders change the form of the organisation without changing the nature of the work. Principals often can't give up direct management of instruction once they have had the experience of being successful at it. They deliberately design the organisation so that people who have expertise are treated as specialists and not as leaders – they narrow responsibilities and treat people as subordinates rather than as active agents of improvement. Hence, they lose most of the advantages of expertise, and they narrow the range of learning available to others in the organisation.

The more advanced the improvement process, the more complex the work, the more complex the processes of leading the work, and the more distributed the work becomes. The idea of distributed leadership has gained a good deal of visibility, for good reason. At its core, distributed leadership describes the way expertise and influence is distributed in schools and school systems. In general, consistent with our work on internal accountability, the more dense the networks in a given school, the more likely that school is to function effectively in the face of external demands. What the distributed leadership literature does not deal with directly, although it does implicitly, is the practice of leadership in a distributed system and how it develops over time. My sense is, from observing improving schools, that they don't just *distribute* leadership – that is, put more influence in the hands of people with expertise – they also *develop* leadership. That is, they actively create a common body of knowledge and skill associated with leadership practice and put people in the way of opportunities to learn it.

One common question we ask during school visits is "who's chairing the meeting?" We're frequently asked to observe planning meetings of various kinds in schools. One good unobtrusive measure of how leadership is defined, distributed, and developed is how the organisation decides who is going to chair the meeting. Often, in advanced organisations, the principal is a participant but not the chair. When the explanations about who chairs have to do with positional authority, it is clear that there is a largely role-based definition of leadership. When the explanations have to do with who has the expertise and whose turn it is to try out a new set of skills, then it is clear that the organisation has a more developmental view.

Performance and quality are imperfect proxies for each other – improvement requires attention to both

Throughout this discussion I have used performance and quality more or less synonymously as indices of improvement. It is now time to unpack these concepts. Quality is a matter of professional judgment. Performance is a matter of external measurement. Both are central to large-scale improvement. An illustration and some analogies will help to illustrate.

There is a body of knowledge now about the acquisition of reading skills in the early grades. It consists of a set of more or less well defined practices, accompanied by evidence on the effects of those practices. When knowledge in a field reaches this stage of development, it becomes professionally irresponsible not to use it. The practices constitute indices of quality – that is, we can say that we expect to see certain practices in schools and classrooms as an index of quality in those settings. Evidence on the effects of the practice constitutes performance, and the external measurement of performance constitutes the core of accountability. In the healthcare sector, there are standards of practice embedded in the practice of physicians, and in the organisation of practice – these standards of care define quality. We also measure the effects of practice and monitor the performance of healthcare organisations as a way of making decisions about performance and cost effectiveness.

The problem comes when, as inevitably happens, there are disconnects between quality and performance. As noted earlier, practices associated with successful reading instruction often don't work in certain contexts for certain children, and it becomes the responsibility of practitioners to figure why they are not working and to do something about it. In this case, the school may have met the quality standard for reading instruction, but is not meeting a performance standard because the quality standard doesn't cover the particular situation it finds itself in.

Likewise, many schools look much better on performance measures than they do upon inspection of their practice. Schools in general, and high-performing schools in particular, produce a large part of their performance with social capital, not with instruction. Families and communities bear a large part of the role of educating young people – often directly, such as in the purchase of tutoring services to compensate for the shortcomings of instructional practice in schools; often indirectly, such as creating pressure for attainment and performance in the lives of children independently of what the school does. For this reason, it is wise to treat the population of high performing schools with some scepticism as a source for "successful" practices, or "high quality" instruction. My experience – however limited – working with high performing schools is that it is an extremely bi-modal population. Some high-performing schools actually do contribute significantly to students' learning and performance through instructional practice. Many high-performing schools are stunningly mediocre in their practice, and produce most of what they do with social capital.

Many high-performing schools are stunningly mediocre in their practice, and produce most of what they do with social capital.

In the work of improvement, performance measures are hardly ever completely adequate for judging how well a school is doing, or for making decisions about how to focus resources for the improvement of instruction. Most performance measures are late in coming, and apply to cohorts of students who are no longer present in the grade where they were tested – fourth graders are tested in the spring, the results come in the fall (if we're lucky); the fourth graders are now fifth graders, and we are put in the situation of inferring what would work for this year's fourth graders from data on last year's fourth graders. In college courses on inference, we would not stand for this kind of sloppy reasoning; in accountability systems we regard it as good practice.

In addition, the grain size of external measurements is much too large to use as a basis for detailed instructional decisions. Item level scores on tests are notoriously unreliable as a basis for making predictions about future performance. Item level scores associated with individual students are even worse. The utility of external measurements to school-level practitioners lies in their description of aggregate level effects, not in the fine grained data necessary for instructional decisions.

External measures of school performance are mainly useful to higher level authorities in making aggregate judgments about the performance of schools and school systems. Policymakers argue that the test data should be useful to schools in making detailed decisions about instruction (a) because they lack the knowledge of basic educational measurement to know the difference; and (b) because they need to justify the cost and frequency of testing by saying tests are broadly useful for decisions of all kinds.

In this situation, the rational thing for school practitioners to do is to focus on formative assessment data that is very close to the instructional process – teacher-made assessments – and to monitor the quality of instruction against some external standard of practice very carefully. This is, in fact, what most "real" professions do. They develop relatively clear standards of practice to guide their detailed daily decisions and monitor the consistency of their practice with those standards relatively carefully. Over time, they and others engage in empirical research designed to push out the boundaries of knowledge and practice, using aggregate evidence of effectiveness to reinforce or critique existing practice.

Leadership in this situation consists of creating and sustaining the structures and processes necessary to monitor and evaluate practice within the organisation against quality standards that are, to the extent possible, based on defensible criteria outside the organisation. Being sceptical about the utility of external performance measures is an important part of this process. Teaching people in the organisation how to manage against performance measures while at the same time sustaining a commitment to quality is an essential part of the practice.

In our non-degree professional development programmes at Harvard University, I have taken to routinely asking the assembled administrators and teachers how many of them have taken a basic course on educational measurement. In an audience of 50 to 100 participants, the usual count is two or three. These people are usually ringers – they are typically assistant superintendents for measurement and evaluation whose job is to run the testing operation in their school systems. Now, imagine what the state of healthcare would be if practising physicians didn't know how to read ECGs, EEGs or chest x-rays, didn't know how to interpret a basic blood analyses, or didn't know anything about the test-retest reliability of these simple diagnostic measures. Imagine what it would be like if your basic family practitioner in a health maintenance organisation didn't know how to interpret a piece of current medical research questioning the validity of the standard test for colorectal cancer. Imagine what it would be like to be a practitioner in a healthcare organisation in which every piece of evidence required for patient care came from a standard test of morbidity and mortality administered once a year in the organisation. The organisation you are imagining is a school system.

We have created an accountability regime at the system level, without the professional infrastructure necessary to make it work at the delivery level. This regime invites practitioners to engage in unprofessional and incompetent behaviour – usually without knowing it – in the interest of doing what policymakers – who are equally uninformed – want them to do, thereby producing electoral credit. It is difficult, but not impossible, to lead in such a regime. At the very least, the regime is not designed to promote the kind of leadership required to make it work.

Improvements in performance usually lag behind improvements in quality

Developmental processes, of which school improvement is only one, are characteristically see-saw relationships among key variables. One variable has to advance before another one can; the latter variable advances, while the former stays constant or declines, and finally acts as a constraint on the latter. In biophysical systems increasing the food supply increases the population of a food-consuming animal, and this population out-consumes the food supply, putting a constraint on the population, which in turn increases the food supply, etc.

Such is the likely relationship between quality and performance in schools. Our judgments of quality are relative to a particular time and a particular state of knowledge and skill. A good part of what we know about quality depends on what we learn from measures of performance. I have noticed in many schools that substantial improvements in the quality of instructional practice are preceded by a considerable amount of time improvements in measured performance. I have also noticed that practitioners' sense of what it is possible to do is highly sensitive to what they take to be the effects of their practice. So, for example, with the introduction of a substantially new mathematics curriculum that requires much more complex pedagogy on the part of teachers and a much more active role on the part of students, we often see in our observations that there are significant changes in instructional practice, but the formative and external measures of performance stay the same, or, in some cases decline. The problem is not that the teachers and students have got it wrong; they're actually working very hard to get it right. The problem seems to be that the effects of instruction on teachers' practice and student performance are more complex than a simple input-output model. The model is something more like a critical mass function – that is, the practice has to reach a certain level to displace the earlier, less effective practice, and student learning has to reach a certain level in order to displace the students' prior constructions of mathematical knowledge. Once this happens – notably after what seems like a good deal of teaching at a relatively high level – performance seems to respond. This relationship might not exist in laboratory conditions, where the situation is more tightly constructed. Schools are social organisations and the individual performance of members is, in part, contingent on the performance of others.

At any rate, the implications of this relationship between quality and performance are significant for leadership practice. First, leaders have to know enough about the practice itself to know what the cognitive and emotional obstacles are to acquiring it and doing it fluently. Second, leaders have to have some systematic understanding of the various ways developmental processes work in order to be supportive and helpful to people who are struggling. Third, leaders have to be patient and to expect a possible seesaw relationship between quality and performance, watching for evidence of changes in student learning before they become evident in external measures of performance.

It is also important to observe that the design of most accountability systems is no friend of the developmental view of leadership practice. The incentive structure of most accountability systems puts a premium on direct and immediate effects on performance. This view is based on exactly no knowledge of how the improvement process actually works. There is no empirical basis for the performance targets in accountability policies because there is no research relating performance to the presence of other factors in the environment of schools. The gap between what good leadership practice might look like and what the accountability environment signals it should look like is, at the moment, quite wide.

3.4 Principles of leadership development

Accountability works to the extent that it is supported by practices of improvement. Performance is a collective good. Its value exceeds that which can be produced by any single individual, organisation or system acting in its own narrowly construed self-interest. For reasons too complex to develop here (but developed at length in other places), the politics of accountability leads predictably to an underinvestment in the capacities required to produce the collective good called performance. There are deep systemic reasons why we have tended to under invest in the very capacities required to make accountability systems work. Correcting this situation requires changing the relationship between policy and practice, particularly around the definition and development of leadership. The following four principles are designed to provide some initial guidance in how leadership might be defined more clearly as a collective good and made more productive in a regime of performance based accountability.

(1) Honour the principle of reciprocity

Fundamental to the political economy of accountability is the principle of reciprocity. Accountability is essentially a contractual relationship in which a principal contracts with an agent to act in a particular way – in this case, to produce a certain level of performance. In order to work, this relationship has to be beneficial to both parties. The principal receives the benefit of the agent's performance (in the case of policymakers this benefit accrues largely in the form of electoral credit) and the agent receives both the authority that inheres in acting for the principal and whatever the material benefits are in the transaction. As we have noted above, accountability is a special case of the principal-agent relationship, since, unlike many such relationships, the principal cannot depend on the agent to know what to do. If practitioners knew how to solve the performance problems they faced in schools, accountability systems would be unnecessary, or at least would look very different from what they do. So the principal-agent relationship is complicated in the case of accountability systems by the fact that in order to get what the principal demands, the principal and the agent have to act co-operatively to build the knowledge and skill of the agent to do the work. This is where the principle of reciprocity comes in.

The principle of reciprocity, in its simplest form, says that *for every unit of performance I require of you, I owe you a unit of capacity to produce that result.* In practice, this means that accountability for performance requires investments in capacity that are equal to the expectations they carry. Now, there are lots of complexities we can introduce to the principle in its simplest form. We can assume, for example, that there is lots of unused capacity in the system that can be mobilised to produce results, and the accountability system has to first exhaust that unused capacity before the simple form of the principle applies. We can assume that teachers really do know how to teach at higher levels, but for some reason they simply aren't doing it. We can assume that principals really do know how to manage resources in the service of improvement, but for some reason they're not doing it.

Another complication around the principle of reciprocity is who gets to decide what kind of capacity is needed to produce a given level of performance. If we leave the decision to policymakers, it is clear that they have very strong incentives to under invest in capacity and to treat accountability systems simply as instruments to mobilise unused capacity. If we leave the decision to practitioners – especially to practitioners who, themselves, don't know what they need to know in order to improve performance – it is likely that we will either overinvest or invest in the wrong things.

The solution to the problem of reciprocity in the real world of school improvement has to be incremental. First, policy itself has to acknowledge the principle of reciprocity – something accountability policies presently do only marginally, if at all. Second, practitioners and policymakers have to build a strong institutional relationship around the link between capacity and performance. In auto emissions control policy, for example, there are elaborate institutional settings and processes for arguing out what it is feasible to produce, given the existing evidence on the characteristics of the internal combustion engine and the government's goals for pollution control. No such settings exist in education. In their absence, policymakers are more or less free to set performance standards anywhere they want, and practitioners are forced to live with the consequences. If the policy succeeds, the policymakers claim credit. If it fails, they blame the practitioners. Either way, they get electoral credit. We tend to underinvest in capacity because there is little or no discipline in the system to enforce the principle of reciprocity.

The infrastructure that would be required to enforce the principle of reciprocity would be one that combines the expertise of researchers to track the effects of various practices of improvement combined with the engagement of networks of practitioners to develop, test, and evaluate their own use of these practices. Without a body of evidence at a level of specificity that would inform practice, it would be very difficult to say what the capacity requirements of strong leadership are and whether the government is meeting its responsibilities under the principle of reciprocity.

(2) Treat leadership as a human investment enterprise

The model of leadership that emerges from the practice of improvement has three important characteristics: (1) It focuses on the practice of improving the quality of instruction and the performance of students; (2) It treats leadership as a distributed function rather than as a role-based activity; and (3) It requires more or less continuous investment in knowledge and skill, both because the knowledge base around instructional practice is constantly changing and because the population of actual and potential leaders is constantly depleting and replenishing itself.

In this view, leadership is a knowledge-based discipline. The practices associated with leadership exist independently of the people who use them, and they are subject to constant testing against the rigours of practical work and evidence of effectiveness. Leadership does not inhere in the personal characteristics of the individual; it inheres in the knowledge, skill, and behaviour of the individual.

Accountability as it is conceived thus far requires more or less continuous improvement of performance. If accountability systems were fairer than they are now, the requirement of continuous improvement would apply equally to nominally high performing schools as to nominally low-performing schools. The model of leadership that applies to continuous improvement is one in which the system is constantly investing in the capacity of people at all levels to master and lead the improvement of instructional practice.

One thing I have noticed about education as a system, relative to knowledge-based enterprises in other parts of society (healthcare operations, consulting firms, law firms, research and development organisations, information technology organisations) is that education systems typically have almost no human resource management function. Human resource management in the typical school system consists of hiring new teachers and administrators. Professional development, if it exists as an administrative function, is typically located in another part of the organisation. Supervision and evaluation are shoved down in the organisation to the school level, where they become routinised and disconnected from anything having to do with instructional practice. So whereas most knowledge-based enterprises have a unified structure for recruiting, hiring, inducting, mentoring, training, supervising, and promoting individuals, all organised around the goals of the system, educational systems have a host of separate functions that typically work at cross purposes to each other. Policy aggravates this problem by treating accreditation as a regulatory issue and professional development as a grant-in-aid activity. The current requirement in *No Child Left Behind* that there be a "qualified teacher" in every classroom is a travesty in a system that has no capacity to manage human resources systemically.

In a knowledge-based human resource management system, recruitment into leadership positions begins the minute a novice teacher contacts the organisation for employment. Every individual would be evaluated not just on their qualifications for employment, but also on their potential to assume leadership in the organisation.

- **Every novice teacher** would be supervised by an experienced teacher who modelled not just excellent instructional practice but also practices of observation, analysis, problem-solving and work with peers that characterise successful approaches to improvement.

- **Every intermediate teacher** would be given some leadership responsibility in some part of the instructional improvement enterprise, under the mentoring and supervision of a more expert practitioner. Teachers would be given more or less continuous feedback on their practice, not only in the instructional domain, but also in the practices of improvement – working with peers on instructional issues, taking leadership responsibilities in groups, creating and demonstrating instructional solutions to pressing problems of performance, etc.

- **Teams of teachers and novice administrators** would be given responsibility for working through organisation and management functions around problems of instructional practice – designing schedules that provide time for teachers to pursue common work, designing group work around instructional practice, designing induction activities for novice teachers, etc.

- **The potential cohort of principals** would be created from the group of more experienced teacher leaders, and these individuals would operate in a setting outside their present school under the supervision of another principal with increasing responsibility for school-level management functions.

- **System-level administrators** would be recruited from the ranks of teacher leaders and school-level administrators with strong instructional knowledge and managerial skills.

The incentive structure in this system is the same as in any knowledge-based enterprise – positional authority follows the contours of expertise. It is the responsibility of experts to induct, socialise, and manage novices; evaluation and supervision centres on mastery of practice; and lateral accountability is as important as vertical accountability because much of the work is accomplished in groups.

In the context of current practice in public education, this kind of human resource management system sounds extreme. In the context of most knowledge-based enterprises, it is routine. Students who take my courses, and who are changing careers from law and healthcare, are dumbfounded at how weak the human resource management systems are in schools and school systems.

I have heard every possible explanation for why it is impossible to create such a system – it costs too much, it combines too many functions with too much specialised knowledge in a single place, it requires skills and knowledge that people in the organisation don't have, and (my favourite) it undermines the positional authority of too many people. In fact, the small population of schools that have advanced to the outer edges of the practice of improvement have had, of necessity, to create human resource systems that look very much at the school level like a good human resource management system would look at the system level.

The problem is not that people can't invent these systems. The problem is that the broader managerial and policy environment is unresponsive to them when they are invented. This is yet another example of how accountability systems don't work in the absence of knowledge and skill, and how accountability systems don't fill the knowledge and skill gap in the absence of explicit attention to the principle of reciprocity.

(3) Invest in social capital [3] around practices of improvement

Knowledge and skill in accountability structures are collective goods, not private goods. That is, the knowledge and skill necessary to improve the performance of schools doesn't belong to those schools, or to people who work in them, it belongs to the system as a whole – if, that is, accountability is about systemic improvement. Accountability systems, to be sure, send mixed signals – on the on hand, they seem to want to induce competition among schools as a way of spurring performance, on the other they seem to regard performance as something that should be common to all schools. If knowledge and skill become a private good, then accountability works not to promote systemic improvement but simply to shift schools around in the distribution of performance, or to advantage one set of actors over another. Policy should be concerned, as I argued above, as much or more with shape of the distribution of performance as it is with the aggregate effect of policy on performance. If this is true, then policymakers have no choice but to treat knowledge as a public good.

The problem of how to create and deploy knowledge in the leadership of improvement is a classic problem of social capital. The knowledge itself doesn't reside in the individuals; it resides in the relationships among individuals engaged in the practice. What a teacher or principal "knows" has no value, except insofar as it can be used to create or enhance knowledge and skill in others. One teacher's success working through a particular problem of practice has immediate value for her and her students, but it does not produce value for the school in which she teaches without intentional action on the part of her colleagues. One school's success has immediate value for the students, practitioners and parents in that school, but its public value is limited by its position as one unit in a system, and therefore its public value is limited to its direct beneficiaries. In order for an accountability system to produce performance as a public good, it has to be accompanied by a system of social relationships that take knowledge out of the private domain and make it public – within classrooms in schools, among schools, and among systems of schools within a larger polity.

The analysis of practices of improvement above suggests that the kind of skill and knowledge required to create improvement is very specific – specific to the instructional issues practitioners are trying to solve, specific to the stage of improvement in which a school finds itself, specific to the particular mix of students in the school, etc. Decisions about the adaptation and use of knowledge have to be made very close to the ground. This aspect of improvement practice suggests that investments in social capital should be densest at the level of the classroom and school, and should become less dense at higher levels of the system. Networks of teachers working with researchers and curriculum developers on the solution of particular problems of practice, networks of principals operating across schools around common problems of practice, vertical teams of administrators and teachers trying to solve problems of systemic improvement – all of these kinds of social networks exemplify what social capital formation would look like in an accountability system focused on improvement. Such networks exist. I myself have been involved in the formation of two such networks – one for school superintendents

---

3.   The most direct application of the idea of social capital to school improvement and accountability is Bryk and Schneider (2002) and Dasgupta and Serageldin (eds.) (2000).

focused on system-wide instructional improvement, one for principals in a single school system focused on systemic improvement in that system. Insofar as these networks exist, however, they tend to exist on a purely voluntary basis, with no supporting infrastructure from public authorities who are responsible for accountability. Voluntarism is good, but it also feeds variability, and variability feeds inequality of access to knowledge. Voluntarism cannot be the basis for systemic improvement.

Voluntarism cannot be the basis for systemic improvement.

Accountability systems tend, by the natural application of political incentives, to drift in the direction of regulation and hierarchical command and control. This drift moves policy away from investments in the social capital necessary to create, nurture and expand practices of improvement. It also tends to push leadership in the direction of positional authority and hierarchical control. Governments do what they know how to do unless otherwise disturbed. One thing governments know how to do is to promulgate regulations, run enforcement processes, and administer sanctions. This view of governmental action could not be further from the role required of government in the creation of social capital.

(4) Build the strategic function[4]

One thing that is striking about schools and educational systems, at least in the United States, is the absence of anything that might be called a strategic function. I work with a number of large US school systems – systems with anywhere from 50 000 to one million students. These are organisations that spend in the hundreds of millions to billions of dollars. They employ thousands to tens of thousands of people. They make decisions affecting the lives of millions of people. In no system I currently work with is there anything I would call a well developed strategic function. By this I mean a part of the organisation that is dedicated solely to making the various pieces of the organisation fit together coherently around a single strategic vision of what kind of performance, at what level, is required for the organisation to sustain itself. This would include the specific organisational structures, resource allocations, and investments in human skill and knowledge required to make those commitments work. I know of several superintendents and principals who are brilliant strategists. They personally have a vision for how the pieces of the organisation fit together, and they act on those visions. If they were mowed down by a bus tomorrow their schools and systems would revert immediately to the default model that existed before they came. Furthermore, their brand of leadership typically consists of having people in the organisation try to guess their intentions, and read their actions, in order to figure out what the big picture is. As a consequence no one really knows exactly what the big picture is. These leaders often create documents they call strategic plans. The rhetoric in these plans is usually inscrutable to all but the small circle of people who drafted them. The point is that, while they might be brilliant strategists, they are not brilliant leaders because they have not institutionalised the strategic function in their organisations.

---

4.   Childress, S. *et al.*, 2005. This paper grows out of four years of work with senior administrators in nine large U.S. school systems. It develops a framework for the strategic function in education systems, and it provides a structure for a larger set of working papers and case studies that we have used in the project.

I must say this absence of a strategic function is practically unique to educational organisations. Public utilities, healthcare organisations, research and development organisations, and, for heaven's sake, even universities now have strategies that have actual consequences for issues like who they hire, how they spend money, and how they organise themselves to do the work. I find it very peculiar that educational systems, supposedly working in a tight and unforgiving accountability environment, still have not developed anything resembling a strategic function.

Strategy is a key responsibility of leadership, broadly defined. When we work with superintendents and principals on these issues, we start by having them state a theory of action by which what they do, on a daily basis, influences instructional practice. Then we work with them on how they treat the basic functions and structures of the organisations. For principals, these would be schedules, supervision, collective work, allocation of discretionary resources, relations with community and parents. For superintendents, they would be curriculum and professional development, supervision, administrative structures, accountability processes, and discretionary budget decisions. We then try to develop practices that convert these givens in an organisation into strategic resources that can be used to accomplish purposes. We try to help them use the resources of their employees to come up with ideas about how to manage against specific performance objectives. The mindset required to do this work is counter cultural to school people. That is, strategy requires you to see everything in the organisation as instrumental to the achievement of some collective goal. Educators, for the most part, are used to thinking of everything as "given" and then trying to find some modest source of leverage from outside to move the organisation. This work is, they report to us, the most difficult work that practitioners have done.

Strategy requires you to see everything in the organisation as instrumental to the achievement of some collective goal.

As leaders become socialised to the work of improvement, it is important to have some place they can learn how to create and manage a strategic function at the school and system level. This does not mean creating a specialised part of the organisation with "strategy" over the door. Nor does it mean that they should get better at producing school improvement plans, which are almost universally useless as strategic documents. It means that members of the organisation participate in the development of a strategy that embodies real decisions about real resources, structures, and processes that have real consequences for the way the work is done. It means that people are taught to think about the time of people in the organisation as money that has already been spent, and as the most important resource the organisation has to improve its work. It means that people are taught to treat existing structures and process as malleable and as instruments for getting things, not as expressions of the property rights of individuals in the organisation to particular benefits and privileges. It means that everyone – including students and parents – should be able to say what the basic commitments of the organisation are, how they will be accomplished, and what their role is in achieving them.

As with other practices of improvement, this one is best learned on the spot, confronting real problems, facing real people, under real conditions – not in university classrooms, and probably not even, except in an introductory way, in workshop settings. The most powerful way to learn strategy is through social networks in which the work is targeted on things that have to be done and in which there is lateral accountability and support among colleagues to do the work. Which brings me to my final recommendation.

(5) Locate the learning as close as possible to the work

Elmore's second law is, "the effect of professional development on practice and performance is inverse to the square of its distance from the classroom." (Elmore's first law, for those who are interested is, "children generally do better on tests they can read than those they can't".) As a general design principle for the development of leadership, the influence of learning on practice is greater the more direct and immediate the application to practice. In my own work, I insist, if I am to engage in longer-term professional development activities with administrators, that they commit to a regular regime of classroom observations, systematic analyses of instructional practice, and collective problem-solving around the practice of instructional improvement. In graduate coursework on instructional improvement, we spend the first five weeks of a 13-week course watching, analysing, and drawing inferences from video tapes of teachers teaching. After this, students are required to do their observational study outside of class, and their final research project has to be a plan for improvement that includes direct work with teachers and administrators in schools. I do these things because I want to drive home the view that professionals are experts who have a practice. Anyone who pretends to lead an organisation whose core functions involve decisions about practice should herself have a practice that directly connects to that core function.

The effect of professional development on practice and performance is inverse to the square of its distance to the classroom.

For the most part, we have no working theory about how to organise learning for professionals in this field. The institutional structure of learning is largely driven either by entrenched institutional interests (cash-for-credit certification programmes at colleges and universities) or by entrepreneurship that is disconnected from any strategic vision of how to generalise learning in the field (leadership academies). There is no clinical practice in the field on which to base judgments about more and less effective ways to learn it, so the ideas of anybody with a little money is as good as anyone else's. This way of organising knowledge is typical of pre-professional occupations. They refuse to specify norms of practice and, for the most part, they refuse to exercise real control over entry to the occupation, and therefore they exercise only modest influence over the quality of practice generally.

My bias is to make investments in learning as bottom-heavy as possible – putting most of the resources not in formal institutions but in professional networks, anchoring the work in instructional practice rather than in managerialism, and making the criteria of success the improvement of instructional quality and student performance. Insofar as established institutions have a role to play in the development of practices of improvement, they should have to compete for the business by demonstrating that they have the expertise and the capacity to manage network-based learning systems. The first priority should be on improving the practice of people in the field, and using the knowledge gained from this effort to train others in the field for leadership positions.

One thing that policymakers would discover if they were to underwrite such a learning system is that the costs of accountability are considerably higher and of a different order than what they presently assume. Accountability systems currently function in an almost purely regulatory mode. The human investment side of the work is either ignored altogether or funded as a purely symbolic gesture. Putting money behind the development of more powerful instructional practices and more powerful practices of improvement requires a different view of what accountability is about and what constitutes success. It is essentially a major human investment strategy; and major improvements in the level and distribution of performance require major work on the practices that produce performance.

3.5 Leadership, policy and practice

Accountability policy "works" by affecting the way schools, as organisations, respond to external signals about their performance. The key determinants of that response are the capacity of schools to produce high levels of instructional practice reliably, which is a function of the knowledge and skill of teachers and administrators, and the internal accountability, or coherence, of the organisation around norms, expectations, and routines for getting the work done. Improvement – defined here as increases in performance and quality over time – is the process by which schools move from relatively atomised and ineffective organisations to relatively coherent and effective organisations. The process of improvement, like all developmental processes, is neither continuous nor linear; it looks more like a process of punctuated equilibrium: periods of significant increases in performance, followed by periods of consolidation. Leadership, in this context, is primarily about (a) managing the conditions under which people learn new practices; (b) creating organisations that are supportive, coherent environments for successful practice; and (c) developing the leadership skills and practices of others. Leadership of improvement, if it is to result in the improvement of quality and performance at scale, must be conceived as a practice – a collection of patterned actions, based on a body of knowledge, skill, and habits of mind that can be objectively defined, taught, and learned – rather than a set of personal attributes. As improvement advances, leadership refracts; it ceases to follow the lines of positional authority and begins to follow the distribution of knowledge and skill in the organisation.

The single greatest weakness of accountability policy as it is presently constructed is its failure to invest adequately in the human knowledge and skill required to form strong practices of improvement. From a policy perspective, the agenda for developing leadership is primarily an agenda of creating the institutional structures that support the development of the knowledge and skill to lead improvement, and the social capital that connects the individuals' knowledge and skill in ways that contribute to the development of practices of improvement. The most effective investments will be close to the ground, and will create human resource systems that develop the knowledge and skill of educators. Being close to the ground means having networks and institutional arrangements that connect people in classrooms and schools with the knowledge required for their work, and with other practitioners faced with similar problems of practice. Effective human resource systems develop the knowledge and skill of educators from the earliest stages of entry to the profession to the latest, rather than focusing on a single role or a single career stage.

The role of public policy in this domain has to focus on improving practice by focusing on the dimensions of the problem that cannot be addressed by individuals and schools working alone in their own spheres. More specifically, public policy has to do three things. It has to create the legal and institutional framework that requires the education profession to say what its practice is. It has to create the infrastructure by which knowledge about content and pedagogy will be made available to practitioners. And it has to create the career structure required to develop human talent for leadership roles. Public policy has to show its commitment to the principle of reciprocity by providing financial support, and constructing the infrastructure, for the improvement of practice equal to the demands for performance that accountability policy makes on individuals and institutions. And public policy has to begin to discipline its expectations to fit with empirical evidence on what schools can achieve by way of performance, given the resource investments and the state of practice on the ground.

References

Abelmann, C. and R. Elmore with J. Even, S. Kenyon and J. Marshall (1999), "When Accountability Knocks, Will Anyone Answer?", in Elmore, R. (2004) *School Reform from the Inside Out: Policy, Practice, and Performance*, 133-199.

Bryk A. and B. Schneider (2002), *Trust in Schools: A Core Resource for Improvement*, Russell Sage Foundation, New York.

Childress, S., R. Elmore, A. Grossman (2005), "Promoting a Management Revolution in Education", Working Paper, Public Education Leadership Project, Harvard Business School and Harvard Graduate School of Education, Cambridge, MA.

Coburn, C. (2003), "Rethinking Scale: Moving Beyond Numbers to Deep and Lasting Change", *Educational Researcher*, 32(6), 3-12.

Cohen D. and D. Lowenburg Ball (1999), "Instruction, Capacity, and Improvement", Report, Consortium for Policy Research in Education (CPRE), Philadelphia, PA.

Cohen, D., S. Moffitt and S. Goldin (2006), *Policy and Practice*, Consortium for Policy Research in Education, Philadelphia, PA.

Datnow, A., G. Borman and S. Stringfield (2000), "School Reform Through a Highly-Specified Curriculum: Implementation and Effects of the Core Knowledge Sequence", *Elementary School Journal*, 101 (2) 36, 167-191.

Debray, E. (2006), *Politics, Ideology, and Education: Federal Education Policy during the Clinton and Bush Administrations*, Teachers College Press, New York.

Dasgupta, P. and I. Serageldin (eds.) (2000), *Social Capital: A Multifaceted Perspective*, World Bank, Washington, D.C.

Eldridge, N. and S.J. Gould (1972), "Punctuated Equilibria: An Alternative to Phyletic Gradualism", in Schopf, T.J.M. *et al. Models in Paleobiology*, Cooper and Co., San Francisco, CA, 82-115.

Elmore, R. (2004), *School Reform from the Inside Out: Policy, Practice and Performance*, Harvard Education Press, Cambridge, MA.

Fullan, M. (2005), "The New Work of Leaders", in *Leadership and Sustainability*, Corwin, Thousand Oaks, CA, 45-52.

Fullan, M., P. Hill and D. Crevola, D. (2006), *Breakthrough*, Corwin, Thousand Oaks, CA.

Heifetz, R. (1994), *Leadership Without Easy Answers*, Harvard University Press, Cambridge, MA.

Hirschman, A. (1970), *Exit, Voice, and Loyalty: Responses to Decline in Firms, Organisations, and States*, Harvard University Press, Cambridge, MA.

Kegan R. and L. Lahey (2002), *How the Way We Talk Can Change the Way We Work: Seven Languages for Transformation*, Jossey-Bass, San Francisco, CA.

Manna, P. (2006), *School's In: Federalism and the National Education Agenda*, Georgetown University Press, Washington, D.C.

Prothero, D. (1992), "Punctuated Equilibrium at Twenty: A Paleontological Perspective", *Sceptic*, 1 (3), 38-47.

Chapter 4

The Finnish approach to system leadership
by
Andrew Hargreaves, Gábor Halász and Beatriz Pont

This chapter analyses the particular Finnish approach to school leadership that contributes to the country's educational success. In a decentralised environment and in response to pressures brought about by declining school enrolments and resources, Finnish municipalities are developing different approaches to school leadership distribution and co-operation. Their reforms are geared to improve schooling for local children in a new environment by ensuring that principals are responsible not only for their own schools but also for their districts. There is shared management and supervision as well as evaluation and development of education planning. This chapter also explores key features at the heart of what is widely seen as Finland's education miracle. Finland was selected by the OECD Improving School Leadership activity because of its innovative approach to distributing school leadership in a systemic way.

This chapter is based on a study visit to Finland, organised by the Finnish Ministry of Education at OECD's request. The chapter provides some theoretical background for understanding system leadership and its impact, and analyses the key Finnish context and features that make for successful schooling outcomes. It continues with a review of their system leadership approaches and provides a discussion of lessons learned and some recommendations on how these approaches can be made sustainable in Finland.

4.1 The OECD case study visit to Finland

Finland was selected by the OECD as an example of a systemic approach to school leadership, because of its particular approach to distributing leadership systematically. From reading the literature and in discussions with Finnish representatives, it seemed that their approach fit the criteria defined for the selection of the OECD case studies (Chapter 1) and would represent a model of system leadership co-operation for the benefit of student and school outcomes.

The visit provided the team with a national perspective on leadership policy and with some examples of leadership practices in municipalities and schools in different areas in Finland (Tampere and Jarvenpää). In Helsinki, the team met with representatives from the Ministry of Education, from the National Board of Education, from the Association of Municipalities, from the Teachers and School Principals Union, from the Helsinki Municipality Education Services and from two school leadership development providers. We then visited two municipalities which provided useful examples of how leadership in education is practiced at the municipality and school level. We met the education representatives in both municipalities, a group of school principals and visited one school in each municipality, where we met with the principal and leadership teams, teachers and also some very inspiring students (Annex 4.A1).

The study team was composed of the rapporteur, Prof. Andrew Hargreaves, Thomas More Brennan Chair in Education in the Lynch School of Education in Boston College, Massachusetts; Dr. Gábor Halász, former Director-General of the National Institute for Public Education in Budapest and now scientific advisor in this institution and Professor of Education at ELTE University (Budapest); and Beatriz Pont from the OECD Secretariat. The rapporteur took the lead in writing the case study report, with the support of the other team members. We take the opportunity to thank the Finns for their openness and discussions.

The purpose of this chapter is to provide information and analysis for policymakers and researchers on models of school organisation as well as management and leadership approaches that are aiming for systemic improvement. It aims to describe the way Finland has adopted innovative and successful initiatives and practices in order to distribute leadership in innovative ways. The chapter provides some theoretical background for understanding system leadership and its impact. It reviews the emerging literature on the development of Finland as an advanced and high performing knowledge economy, and on the reasons for its increasingly high standards of educational performance over the past decade. It follows by reviewing the country's system leadership approaches and provides a discussion of lessons learned and some recommendations on how these approaches can be made sustainable in Finland.

4.2 Theoretical grounding on system leadership

This chapter examines the relationship between school leadership and system-wide improvement in one particular national setting, Finland. But before analysing this particular Finnish approach, we need a common understanding of what we mean by system leadership and why we think that there is an important relationship between shared and distributed leadership on the one hand and successful outcomes on the other. In research and in practice, articulating the relationship between school leadership and improvement on a system-wide basis is a relatively new venture. Leadership has been found to have a modest though significant effect on school achievement (Mortimore *et al.*, 1988; Silins and Mulford, 2002) though it is still the second most influential variable affecting achievement after teaching (Leithwood *et al.*, 2006). Leadership effects are largely exerted within the school and mainly indirectly through influencing the adults who affect the children (Leithwood *et al.*, 1999). Providing intellectual stimulation, supplying professional development and other support, developing a vision of and focus on learning with others, creating a strong professional learning community through team commitment to learning and achievement – these are the key ways that leaders have exerted their effects on learning, achievement and performance among students.

Despite this demonstrated potential of school leadership to exert positive effects on student performance, the degree of its impact has been and still is limited by a number of factors.

- In many countries, school leaders have served more as elected managers of their schools or been slowly promoted from within them. While this has served schools well in maintaining efficient co-ordination of operations during times of relative stability, it has hindered them in contexts of rapid change which call for administrators to behave more as leaders who are responsible for changing the practices, relationships and cultures of those who they represent (Bolivar and Moreno, 2006).

- The movement towards large-scale reform in the latter part of the twentieth century, with its accompanying emphases on more detailed government intervention and high stakes testing, turned leadership which inspired communities to achieve and improve upon their purposes, into management that emphasised delivering the short-term policies and purposes of others (Fink and Brayman, 2006; Hargreaves and Goodson, 2006).

- In a number of countries, more prescriptive strategies focused on raising achievement in measured results through management of performance, have yielded some successes and tangible performance gains in the short-term, but in most places these have now reached a plateau (Fullan, 2006; Hopkins, 2007). Moreover, the gains that have been registered have largely been in easily tested basic skills more than in the high level competencies that are essential for developing knowledge economies (OECD, 2001; Hargreaves, 2003; New Commission on the Skills of the American Workforce, 2007).

- The most substantial and significant effects on student outcomes continue to reside beyond the immediate school setting in which school leaders currently exert their influence, and these effects remain stubbornly persistent over time (Berliner, 2006).

- In many countries, almost half of the current generation of school leaders is due to retire within the next five years, creating significant challenges to leadership recruitment, stability and effective continuity and succession, especially where leadership effects overly rely on the impact of single individuals (Leithwood *et al.,* 1999; Hargreaves and Fink, 2003; The Wallace Foundation, 2007; PricewaterhouseCoopers, 2007).

- The replacement cadre of school leaders is bringing into the job different generational expectations, dispositions and skill sets than their older predecessors

– especially in relation to exercising more collaborative forms of leadership, and managing work-life balance (Harris and Townsend, 2007).

The effect of these interlinked changes, pressures and expectations is to push school leadership in new directions so it can become both more successful and also sustainable. The limitations of top-down large scale reform in education, are now calling for school administrators to act as leaders who can develop and inspire their teachers' commitment to and capacity for producing higher-level learning – for all students. The use of collaborative styles and strategies is not only more suited to building higher order competencies and capacities among teachers and students alike, but it also enhances work-life balance by ensuring the burdens of leadership do not rest on one set of shoulders and it helps secure more stability and effective succession by creating larger pools of leadership and thereby making succession events less contingent on grooming or selecting particular individuals. Finally, the existing skewed distribution of school versus out-of-school influences on student outcomes can be shifted if the responsibilities of leadership extend to acting on and influencing the external variables that affect student performance – if leaders help their schools to affect the things that currently affect them.

The key challenge of school improvement today, then, is for school administrators to become leaders who develop and raise high level achievement by working with, learning from and influencing the behaviours of others within and beyond their schools. Instead of being managers who implement policy, school administrators will increasingly need to become leaders of their schools who can also exercise leadership in the environment beyond their schools, and articulate the connection between the two. The educational leader of the future, therefore, will increasingly be a system leader as well as a school leader.

Instead of being managers who implement policy, school administrators will increasingly need to become leaders of their schools who can also exercise leadership in the environment beyond their schools.

What do we mean by system leadership? Various contributions help us understand the nature and significance of this concept and strategy:

Leading learning organisations

Effective organisations are able to learn continuously, not just as an aggregation of individuals, but also collectively as a group. Leaders of and in such learning organisations grasp that their organisations are rapidly changing, complex and interconnected systems. They are able to have and articulate clear mental maps of where they are going, to see the "big picture" of their organisation, to understand how different parts of it are connected to each other and the whole, to connect their personal learning to the organisation's learning, and to employ processes that provide swift feedback and learning of how the organisation or initiatives in it are proceeding, so future action can be taken that is effective and appropriate (Senge, 1990; Senge *et al.*, 2000). When schools behave and are led as problem-solving learning organisations, then they enhance their effectiveness and improve their outcomes with students (Leithwood and Louis, 1998; Mulford, 1998).

Leading learning communities

When the intellectual processes and feedback mechanisms of learning organisations become embedded in the attitudes, behaviour and overall culture of people within it, these organisations become learning communities. These communities of practice (Wenger, 1998), professional communities (Louis and Kruse, 1995; McLaughlin and Talbert, 2001) or professional learning communities (Newmann and Wehlage, 1995; Hord, 2004), engage and inspire professionals to collaborate together to improve learning and other outcomes, by sharing and analysing practice and by using data to inquire into and evaluate progress and problems over time (Newmann, King and Youngs, 2000). Successful learning communities are places where people care for each other as individuals, and commit to the moral purpose the organisation is pursuing, as well as pursuing technical tasks of analysis and improvement together (Hargreaves, 2003; Giles and Hargreaves, 2006). Schools that operate as strong learning communities have more successful outcomes in performance results (Rosenholtz, 1989; Newmann and Wehlage, 1995), and they deal with change more effectively (Fullan, 2003; Hargreaves, 2007a). Paradoxically, while learning communities depend on and develop leadership throughout the school, in Anglo-Saxon countries at least, this seems in turn to be a result of effective leadership by the school principal in building such communities (Stoll and Louis, 2007).

Distributed leadership

Within the overall sphere of school leadership, teacher leadership has more significant effects on student achievement than principal leadership (Leithwood and Jantzi, 2000). This has led to considerable advocacy for the development of greater teacher leadership in schools (Harris, 2001; MacBeath and Mortimore, 2001; Crowther *et al.*, 2002; Hopkins and Jackson, 2003; Lieberman and Miller, 2004). Spreading leadership out in this way is referred to by some as distributed or distributive leadership (Harris, 2001), though in its more robust forms, this distribution extends beyond teachers to students (Levin, 2000), parents and support staff. Indeed, Bolam, Stoll, and Greenwood (2007) show that schools which include support staff within their learning communities are more effective than those which employ a narrower range of distribution.

Spillane (2006) uses distributed leadership less as a way to promote a particular kind of leadership practice, than to analyse how, and how far leadership is already distributed within schools. Others also recognise that distributed leadership assumes many forms with varying degrees of effectiveness, in different conditions – formal or informal, downward delegation or upward assertion, etc. (Hay Group Education, 2004; Hargreaves and Fink 2006; PricewaterhouseCoopers, 2007). In this respect, it is not just the extent of distributed leadership, but its nature and consequences that are important for school improvement.

Leadership succession

The contemporary challenge of leadership, in systemic terms, is not only to distribute and develop leadership across space, but also to develop and articulate it over time. Individual leaders must address the needs of and relationships between short-term and long-term improvement within their own tenure (Kotter, 1996; Hopkins, 2001; Schmoker, 2006; Dodd & Favaro, 2007), but must also consider how leadership effects will last beyond them, after they themselves are gone, so their benefits are spread from one leader to the next.

Highly effective schools are often characterised by high leadership stability (James *et al.*, 2006). This can be achieved by individual leaders or leadership teams remaining in their schools for long periods, or by developing clear plans and effective processes for leadership succession. Especially at a time of high demographic turnover in leadership, thinking about and caring for the future is an essential aspect of system leadership. Lasting improvement depends on planned succession, leaving a legacy, mentoring new leaders and creating great leadership density and capacity from which future high level leaders will come (MacMillan, 2000; Gronn, 2003; Hargreaves and Fink, 2004; Fink and Brayman, 2006) within a common vision of institutional and societal progress.

Lateral leadership

If the magnitude of school leadership effects is to be increased, leaders will increasingly need to lead "out there" beyond the school, as well as within it, in order to influence the environment that influences their own work with students (Hargreaves and Fullan, 1998). School leaders in small towns and rural areas have traditionally stood among the most important leaders in their communities. Indeed, Starratt (2004) argues that to be ethical leaders, school leaders are not just leaders of learning but also serve as community leaders, and as citizens within their wider society. Urbanisation, immigration and increases in school size have tended to weaken these relationships between school leaders and their communities, but these and other pressures on families and family life make the wider community responsibilities of the school leaders even more important today. Indeed, leaders of the most successful schools in challenging circumstances are typically highly engaged with and trusted by the schools' parents and wider community (Harris *et al.*, 2006; James, *et al.*, 2006). Policies that try to improve achievement and wellbeing for children in disadvantaged communities are increasingly requiring leaders to become more involved with other partners beyond the school such as local businesses, sports clubs, faith-based groups and community organisations (PricewaterhouseCoopers, 2007), and by integrating the work of the school with welfare, law enforcement and other agencies, sometimes on the school site (Epstein, 2001).

School leadership is also increasingly calling for what Michael Fullan (2006) and David Hargreaves (2004) describe as more *lateral leadership* across schools. Top-down policy strategies that turned leaders into managers, or tried to bypass leaders and teachers altogether through mechanical forms of tightly prescribed instruction, have largely reached their limit in raising performance results. At the same time, while the promotion of increased market competition among schools has increased performance in some cases by schools having more control over student selection or staff appointments, subsequent isolation of schools has restricted their opportunities for continuous improvement and professional learning.

Attempts to reduce school isolation and move beyond the limitations of top-down reform have led to the widespread growth of school networks (D. Hargreaves, 2004; Veuglers and O'Hair, 2005) that create improvement gains by schools helping schools, through sharing best practices and "next" practices, especially between the strong and the weak (Shirley and Hargreaves, 2006; Hargreaves, 2007b). More and more educational leaders – principals and teachers – are therefore becoming engaged in lateral, networked leadership that promotes effective participation in networks, while ensuring that the networks remain tied to clear purposes that are connected to improved learning and achievement (Evans and Johnson, in press).

These various leadership engagements go beyond the school, involving partnerships with communities, businesses, social agencies, universities, policymakers and other schools on a local, national, and international basis, through face-to-face and virtual means. They increase professional learning, enhance improvement through mutual assistance, and create greater cohesion among all those concerned with the achievement and wellbeing of every child. These wider engagements focus leadership beyond the people in leaders' own buildings to the welfare of all young people in the city, town or region, and to the improvement of the profession and its work as a whole. They operate in ways that access learning and support from others in order to provide reciprocal benefits for leaders' own communities. This articulation and co-ordination of effort and energy across individuals and institutions and amid common purposes and improvement goals is what Hopkins (2007) defines as system leadership.

Sustainable leadership

System leadership should also be sustainable leadership. Sustainable leadership includes the systemic development and articulation of leadership efforts, capacities and learning processes across space. It connects these to the articulation of leadership actions and effects over time through effective succession management as well as successful co-ordination of short term and long range improvement efforts. In sustainable leadership, the integration of leadership efforts within complex systems across space and time is also anchored in sustaining moral purposes that promote achievement and improvement for all, especially the most disadvantaged, in relation to principles of social justice. Fullan (2005) defines educational sustainability as "the capacity of a system to engage in the complexities of continuous improvement consistent with deep values of human purpose".

In their original definition of sustainable leadership and improvement, Hargreaves and Fink (2003) argued that "sustainable educational leadership and improvement preserves and develops deep learning for all that spreads and lasts, in ways that do no harm to and indeed create positive benefit for others around us, now and in the future".

As a result of studying the nature and effects of educational change over more than three decades in eight innovative and traditional secondary schools in two countries, they set out seven interrelated principles of sustainable leadership and improvement.

- *Depth:* Sustaining what matters in terms of a clear and defensible moral purpose.

- *Breadth:* Ensuring that improvements benefit the many across a system, and not just a few exceptional instances within it; and that they are a shared and distributed leadership responsibility instead of being dependent on heroic individuals.

- *Endurance* over the long term, across and beyond many leaders, not just within snapshot periods under any one leader's tenure.

- *Justice:* Avoiding harm to and promoting active benefit and assistance for others in the surrounding environment.

- *Diversity* so that improvement efforts value, promote and create cohesion within organisational diversity, rather than developing standardised practices that do not allow cross-fertilisation of learning and are neither adaptable nor resilient to change.

- *Resourcefulness* through prudent use and deliberate renewal of people's energy so leadership initiatives and improvement efforts do not burn them out.

- *Conservation* which builds on and learns from the best of the past in order to create a better future.

These principles of systemic, sustainable and successful leadership and improvement provide a set of orientating concepts. They guide our analysis of the system-wide relationships between leadership and continuous school improvement in one of the world's most remarkable, recently improved and highest performing national educational and economic systems: Finland.

4.3 Exploring the Finnish approach

The Finnish example is an interesting and unusual one for the study of system leadership and improvement. It provides a context for recent specific innovations in system change, which we shall outline later. At the same time, the entire country, its culture and its educational system constitute a particular, prominent and high performing instance of system leadership and improvement. Its distinctiveness includes departure from the predominant global educational reform movement of the past 15 years, which has emphasised testing and targets, curriculum prescription and market competition. High performing Finland might in this sense be regarded as one of a number of outlier examples of *positive deviance* from which other nations can learn as they rethink their own reform strategies.

High performing Finland might be regarded as one of a number of outlier examples of positive deviance from which other nations can learn.

One way to analyse social and educational systems is through different, interrelated "frames" (Bolman and Deal, 2003) or perspectives. Six such frames are moral, learning, cultural, political, technical-structural and leadership (Louis, Toole and Hargreaves, 1999). The *moral frame* encompasses the vision and purposes of a society or organisation. The *learning frame* embraces the forms of learning that are valued within organisations and societies, as well as the processes by which people, organisations and societies improve over time. The *cultural frame* concerns the way of life of a people, their attitudes, belief and practices, and the ways that individuals treat one another. The *political frame* concerns the arrangements and distributions of power in relation to the moral vision and the means to achieve it. The *technical/structural* frame refers to the policies and procedures, roles and responsibilities, and uses of time and space that express the politics and address the vision. Last, the *leadership frame* addresses the processes of influence and responsibility through which valued goals and identified changes are achieved.

Finland's distinctiveness and effectiveness as an economic, social and educational success cannot be found in "silver bullets" – in particular practices that can be readily transposed to other countries so they too could experience Finland's "miracle" of educational and economic transformation. Rather, it is the intersection and integration of the moral, political, structural, cultural, leadership and learning-based aspects of Finland within a unitary whole that define and explain the nation's success.

For instance, while one of the keys to Finland's success appears to be high quality of its teachers, efforts to improve teacher quality in other countries through public relations and enhanced pay miss the point. Finnish teachers are drawn to the profession because of the regard in which it is held in helping bolster and build a wider social mission of economic prosperity, cultural creativity and social justice. These are central to the Finnish identity. The calibre of Finnish teachers is, in this sense, directly related to the compelling and widely shared nature of their nation's broader vision.

The Finnish model cannot be copied wholesale, for it is a model or strategy that arises out of alignment between and integration of a deep set of cultural and social values, a particular kind of social and economic state, and a distinctive approach to educational reform. However, the political and cultural differences that characterise Finnish society along with other elements such as relatively small size or ethnic composition should not be used to excuse its relevance and importance for other settings. Equally, the temptation to cherry pick particular parts of the Finnish strategy for transference to other nations is problematic if any preferred element is not seen in relation to all the others. The challenge, rather, is to promote mutual learning and interaction across countries about the deeper principles and practices that underpin Finland's educational model - and adjust these through thoughtful adaptation within different cultures and contexts. These processes of intelligent interaction rather than direct transplantation are at the heart of *positive deviance.*

A clear and common purpose: competitiveness, creativity, and social justice

Finland is a country that has undergone a profound economic and educational transformation in the past half-century and particularly since a major banking crisis pushed unemployment up to 18% and public debt over 60% of GDP in the early 1990s (Sahlberg, 2007). From being a rural backwater economy, Finland has transformed itself into a high performing economic powerhouse. In the few short years of the 21st century, Finland has already been ranked as the world's most competitive economy by the World Economic Forum (Porter *et al.*, 2004). Educationally, in OECD's 2003 and 2006 PISA results (OECD, 2004 and 2007), Finland's 15 year olds ranked top in reading, mathematics and science, while in equity terms displaying the lowest variance between schools – just one tenth of the OECD average (OECD, 2004 and 2007).

At the core of Finland's remarkable transformation is the nation's longstanding but recently reinvented struggle to develop and be guided by clear objectives that bind its people together. Visiting and interviewing students, teachers, principals, system administrators, university researchers and senior ministry officials, the authors of this paper found a remarkably unified narrative about the country, its schools and their sense of aspiration, struggle and destiny.

Finland is a nation that has endured almost seven centuries of control by two nations (Sweden and Russia), between which it remains sandwiched – and has achieved true independence only within the last three generations. In the context of this historical legacy, and in the face of a harsh and demanding climate and northern geography, it is not surprising that one of the most popular Finnish sayings translates as "It was long, and it was hard, but we did it!"

Yet it is not simply stoic perseverance, fed by a Lutheran religious ethic of hard work and resilience, that explains Finland's success as a high performing educational system and economy. At the core of this country's success and sustainability is its capacity to reconcile, harmonise and integrate those elements that have divided other developed economies and societies – a prosperous, high performing economy and a socially just society. It has also done this in a way that connects the country's sense of its history to the struggle for its future destiny. While some say that the knowledge economy is associated with a weakened welfare state in many other societies, in Finland a strong welfare state is central to supporting and sustaining a successful economy.

At the core of this country's success and sustainability is its capacity to reconcile, harmonise and integrate a prosperous, high performing economy and a socially just society.

In *The Information Society and the Welfare State*, Castells and Himanen (2002, p. 166) describe how "Finland shows that a fully fledged welfare state is not incompatible with technological innovation, with the development of the information society, and with a dynamic, competitive new economy. Indeed, it appears to be a decisive contributing factor to the growth of this new economy on a stable basis."

They also contrast the Finnish approach to other market oriented models, stating: "Finland stands in sharp contrast to the Silicon Valley model that is entirely driven by market mechanisms, individual entrepreneurialism, and the culture of risk – with considerable social costs, acute social inequality and a deteriorating basis for both locally generated human capital and economic infrastructure." (Castells and Himanen, 2002, p. 167)

At the centre of this successful integration is Finland's educational system (Aho, Pitkanen and Sahlberg, 2006). As the respondents interviewed by the OECD team indicated at all levels, Finns are driven by a common and articulately expressed social vision that connects a creative and prosperous future to the people's sense of themselves as having a creative history and social identity. This is epitomised by the use of networks and participation by the Nokia telecommunications company, whose operation and suppliers account for about 40% of the country's GDP (Haikio, 2002). And the visual, creative and performing arts are an integral part of children's education throughout and beyond their secondary school experience.

Technological creativity and competitiveness, therefore, do not break Finns from their past but connect them to it in a unitary narrative of lifelong learning and societal development. All this occurs within a strong welfare state that supports and steers (a favourite Finnish word) the educational system and the economy. A strong public education system provides education free of charge as a universal right all the way through school and higher education. Science and technology are high priorities, though not at the expense of artistic creativity. Almost 3% of GDP is allocated to scientific and technological development and a national committee that includes leading corporate executives and university vice chancellors, and is chaired by the Prime Minister, steers and integrates economic and educational strategy.

All this educational and economic integration occurs within a society that values children, education and social welfare; that has high regard for education and educators as servants of the public good; and that ranks teaching as the most desired occupation of high school graduates. Entry into teaching is demanding and highly competitive, with only 1 in 10 applicants being admitted (Aho, Pitkanen and Sahlberg, 2006; Salhberg, 2007).

These interrelated emphases in Finland's educational and social vision were evident at all levels in the interviews we held with Finnish educators. Directors at the National Board of Education described how educators were "willing to cooperate for national goals" and that this was "a way for them to …really have their voice heard at the national level." In forging future directions, while the National Curriculum Council is "very future oriented", it also tries to determine "what is the best we can learn from the past, (in order to) try heavily to look into the future and what is happening in the world and then analyse the present".

Staff in an upper secondary school we visited emphasised how both "culture and innovation are important for our kids nowadays". The district's leader stressed the importance of Finland's historic creativity as being essential to its goals and vision. Indeed, Finland has the highest number of musical composers per capita of any nation in the world. This is part of, not separate from, the country's embracing of technological innovation and creativity. The upper secondary school students showed commitment to innovative graphic design as well as traditional visual artwork within and outside scheduled school time.

This bringing together of past and future, of technological innovation and traditional creativity, occurs in part through the setting of a strategic vision at national and local levels. Through consultation and discussion, the National Board develops guidelines that provide the support and strategic thinking which, in the words of its director, promote "intensive co-operation all the time". With the support of educational research, the National Board provides a "steering system" for educational policies in an evidence-based way, through small funding, evaluation, and curriculum content. Within this generally understood social vision, the state steers the national curriculum but does not prescribe in detail. Trusted teams of highly qualified teachers write much of the curriculum together at the level of the municipality in ways that adjust to the students they know best.

The state steers the national curriculum but does not prescribe in detail. Trusted teams of highly qualified teachers write much of the curriculum together at the level of the municipality in ways that adjust to the students they know best.

There is also strategic thinking and planning at the district level. Helsinki, for example, is setting a new vision for 2012 (with benchmarks after three years), with every school discussing what the vision along with desired objectives might mean for them. Emphasising the principle of vision being developed in a participatory rather than imposed way, this municipality uses the "balanced scorecard" method of including different participants and assessment perspectives (Kaplan and Norton, 1996). Another municipality has similarly set its vision and values that inspire learning and creativity, and undertakes a system-wide analysis of strengths, opportunities, weaknesses and threats. One of the district's principals pointed out: "the vision here is so close to the national view. Only a few things have been added on in the history of Jarvenpäa (famous artists, for example), so kids have some idea of roots and can be proud of the town."

Adherence to vision and goals is often implicit and shared through daily co-operation, rather than explicitly developed through a strategic plan.

A district director argued that within the national steering system, "we just pick things up, not in a systematic way. These values are easy to find at the national level – we are taking part in many seminars, etc… working together, managers and directors. (While our) values are quite similar, we have freedom in how we organise."

An educator at a school in Tampere put it this way: "every teacher asks, what can I do to make this place better for the teachers and the pupils …. Why are we here?"

To sum up: Finland has defined and defended a particular value system that connects contemporary innovation and traditional creativity within a strong welfare state that structurally and culturally supports high economic competitiveness. In doing so, Finland reconciles the information economy and the welfare state and links the country's history to its future destiny through a delicate balance between change and stability.

Improvement and development are achieved through shared values, high participation and widespread co-operation within a financial, legislative and curricular steering system. Public education is seen as vital to the country's growth and security, so highly qualified candidates are attracted into the teaching profession. The high quality and performance of Finland's educational system cannot be divorced from the clarity, characteristics of, and broad consensus about the country's broader social vision. Finland's *system leadership* is in this respect a *moral leadership,* which means much more than raising the bar and closing the achievement gap (Fullan, 2006; Hopkins, 2007). There is compelling clarity about and commitment to inclusive, equitable and innovative social values beyond as well as within the educational system.

A commitment to learning: in depth and in breadth

Finland is a puzzling paradox of learning performance. This country – the world's leader in measured student performance – places no emphasis on individual testing or measurement driven accountability. Though its scores are outstanding in reading and mathematics, it has no regular national tests for reading and mathematics achievement, it does not consume large parts of the curriculum with the separate teaching of these skills and subjects, and it does not inflict structured reading and mathematics programmes on younger age groups to enhance skill development.

Finland places no emphasis on individual testing or measurement driven accountability. Though its scores are outstanding, it has no regular national tests and it does not inflict structured programmes on younger age groups to enhance skill development.

Finland's high performance seems more attributable to a conceptualisation, commitment to and widespread culture of learning in school and society more widely. Learning, and especially literacy, begin early, if somewhat informally in the home and in preschool within a society where learning and teaching are highly valued and where play as well as talk are emphasised. It was this that the Head of Jarvenpää's Education Committee attributed to success in PISA: "The whole society is respecting teaching and schools. People are reading a lot (for instance, through) fairy tales. Mothers (with generous parental leave benefits) can be home for three years. There is a good library system. All teachers are studying in universities, so are highly educated."

With formal school starting in children's seventh year (later than all other developed countries), and then extending for nine years, Finland exemplifies the principle of *slow schooling* described by Honoré (2004) as leading patiently to sustainable success, compared to the rush to raise test scores quickly. (See also Hargreaves and Fink, 2006.)

Valuing lifelong learning in the way that is characteristic of all Nordic countries, Finland has no system of standardised or high stakes testing and therefore does not expend time and resources on test development and test preparation (Sahlberg, 2006). Rather, it has a broad curriculum that is not preoccupied with tested basics. Maths and sciences are important for business and economic development, but so too are artistic and other forms of creativity that have long contributed to the Finnish identity – as we witnessed in Jarvenpää's upper secondary school.

Interestingly, Finnish teachers have a reputation for "pedagogical conservatism" (Simola, 2005). In some classrooms we visited we did indeed see children listening to their teachers, undertaking individual work and engaging in whole class question-and-answer. We did not see explicit examples of, for instance, attending to students' multiple intelligences or learning styles; nor did we see sophisticated strategies of co-operative learning where children are allocated precise roles in their group work. However, we did observe group work of a different kind – in a middle school lesson where student groups were quietly and gently cooperating on researching and producing reports on different Finnish towns and regions in an informal manner. Thus, even co-operative work seems to be quietly conservative rather than technically complex or dramatic.

> One school principal captured the essence of this seeming pedagogical conservatism in these terms: "We have many, many good practices but we are not describing it and its theoretical basis and we just do it, in Finland. Unlike the USA, we just do, we don't make publications."

In bright and well equipped schools with small classes of less than 30 students, teachers care for their students and appear to know them well without the assistance of complex technologies of individual assessments or a sophisticated array of disaggregated test score data. Caring for children and for one another, especially for those who have the greatest difficulty, is a prime societal and professional value. Educators at one school we visited explained that Finland performs well not by creating geniuses but by lifting up each child from the bottom. Their goal is for there to be "no social exclusion in (their) school, so that nobody is forgotten". In their own school, they observed, if a child began to behave differently or unusually, the teacher would immediately ask the child why, talk to their parents perhaps, then swiftly converse with other teachers who taught the same child to share perceptions and strategies. There are teams that meet three times each week to discuss how to help children with problems. This somewhat informal but highly insistent pattern of early intervention then extends to the welfare committee if necessary, where teachers, administrators, nurses and counsellors address individual student problems before they escalate into major crises (Grubb *et al.*, 2005).

This unhurried yet insistent culture of lifelong learning and attentive care is enhanced by high quality teaching. Other nations are experimenting with ways of rewarding differential performance within the teaching profession. Teaching is already an attractive and desired profession in Finland. It has high status in a learner-centred society where it contributes to the wider social mission. In a society with high taxation and relatively modest income differentials, teaching is paid quite satisfactorily. Working conditions and resources are supportive, schools are well equipped, and like other professionals teachers enjoy considerable trust and autonomy. Teaching is highly competitive; professional entry requires Masters' degrees. Teacher training blends theoretical and practical components, and continuing professional development is becoming more integrated into the collective life and needs of the school.

Teaching is an attractive and desired profession in Finland. Teachers enjoy considerable trust and autonomy. Teaching is highly competitive; professional entry requires Masters' degrees.

Thus, in Finland performance and quality issues and needs are addressed at the point of professional entry through mission, status, rewards, respect and conditions. As a result, resources and energy do not have to be directed at rectifying poor performance later on.

The culture of learning that underpins Finnish school performance is also evident in the pervasive and increasing attention that educators pay to self evaluation as a way to improve their schools. A group of Helsinki principals described themselves as "a learning organisation", working together to "share good ideas and practice". An evaluation process, using teams of one principal and two teachers, helped them to achieve this.

System administrators repeatedly referred to the method and importance of giving schools resources to solve their own problems. A small group of principals in Helsinki was beginning to use more quantitative data within self evaluation processes, finding that teachers are "sometimes surprised by the data". We will return to the use of self evaluation in our later discussion of political accountability.

To sum up: learning rather than measured performance defines the focus and form of system leadership in Finnish education. Learning and teaching are valued throughout schools and society, learning starts early but is unhurried and untested, and learning is broad and lifelong rather than concentrated on test preparation. Teacher quality and performance are addressed by establishing the appropriate conditions to attract high level professionals through good working conditions, clear purpose, status, autonomy and reward. Improvement of schools that employ these highly capable and trusted professionals is achieved by processes of self evaluation within learning organisations that are allocated national and local government resources so they can solve problems for themselves. System leadership, in this sense, is leadership for learning, leadership by learning and leadership as learning – not leadership for performance and testing.

Culture: trust, co-operation and responsibility

System leadership is also cultural leadership (Deal and Peterson, 1999). It involves inspiring, stimulating and supporting people to strengthen commitment, raise aspirations and improve performance through shared beliefs and purposes expressed in common practices and ways of life (Leithwood *et al.*, 2006). Organisational cultures can be strong or weak, collaborative or individualistic, trusting or suspicious (Hargreaves, 1994). A key task of leadership is to create strong and positive cultures that motivate and mobilise people to achieve the organisation's purpose.

At the heart of the human relationships that comprise Finland's educational system and society is a strong and positive culture of *trust, co-operation* and *responsibility*. From the classroom to the Ministry of Education, this trinity of terms was reiterated to our visiting team many times as the key factor that explained performance, problem solving, improvement and accountability.

Finland's highly qualified teachers have a palpable sense of responsibility to all students and their welfare. This responsibility is not just that of Lutheran hard work and diligence, but a concern for the welfare of individuals and the community. We have already described the authentic emphasis on leaving no child behind, and on there being "no exclusion", as one principal put it. Teachers are concerned about the welfare of not only their own children during the time they see them, but of all students in the school. The principals who meet together in the city of Tampere work to benefit students in the whole city rather than concentrating on giving a competitive edge to the children in their own school.

Problems are solved through co-operation. As a ministry official explained, "if you give resources to them, they find a way to solve the problem". Teachers work together to support students experiencing difficulty. If a school has a weak or ineffective principal, then, as one school explained, "the vice principal or some of the other teachers take responsibility for curriculum work at the school level". If people in a school are not leading well, the strategy is not to fire them but, in the words of a Tampere administrator, to "try to develop them, actually".

Problems are solved through co-operation. As a ministry official explained to the OECD team, "if you give resources to them (teachers), they find a way to solve the problem".

Principals are required to have been teachers, and all principals, even those in large secondary schools, do some teaching every week. With these preceding and continuing connections to teaching, along with affiliation to the same union, leaders do not see themselves as "the boss" – nor are they perceived as such by the teachers. Relationships are not very hierarchical, and in schools it is often difficult to distinguish teachers from support staff. Good leadership is shared leadership creating "an environment at school where people are happy doing their work (but not just what they want)".

> One principal with considerable comparative experience explained that relationships between principals and teachers are closer in Finland than in the rest of Europe: *"(They are) not so theoretical but practical (in) working with teachers."* In that respect, *"PISA success depends on school climate and classroom climate, rather than on authoritarian intervention".*

Team structures and processes, as we witnessed in our school visits, enact and enhance these principles of co-operation. In one of the schools we visited, long-term teams were concerned with issues of syllabus, planning and scheduling, professional development, subject organisation, information and communications technology, theme days, and recreation/welfare. A key theme of co-operation and interpersonal communication within schools is the teaching-learning process itself, with special attention to those needing extra support and special care. Special needs educators, who have a distinct position in regular school life play a key role in this area. Short-term teams were concerned with festivals as well as counselling, immigration and the role of school support staff. Team membership was rotated every three years or so to increase learning and understanding across boundaries.

However, although a Ministerial Yellow Book written four years ago emphasised the importance of shared leadership, people commented that co-operation was not always put to the best use. A key member of the National Board of Education expressed it as follows: "We are individualistic people in schools. We make a team but it's not real collaboration. We are responsible people, we go to a team and make use of it but still need to learn real collaboration…. We are still working (at) collaboration."

At a school we visited, for instance, co-operation was restricted to affairs affecting the managerial work, welfare and the school's social functions. Teacher leadership seemed to involve delegation of managerial tasks rather than working together to inquire into and improve student learning. One or two teachers were distinctly unhappy about how these new managerial responsibilities infringed on their teaching time. They saw these as creating additional workload that did not help their classroom teaching – a classic case of what is termed *contrived collegiality* (Hargreaves, 1994). Although co-operation might improve effectiveness, continuous improvement and dramatic transformation in teaching and learning require more thoroughgoing within-school collaboration than currently seems evident in Finland. As long as current effectiveness remains high, this may not be an important issue, but if changes threaten existing effectiveness, this limitation in *collaborative* rather than merely *co-operative* capacity could prove serious.

Yet beyond the school, as well as within it, co-operation and responsibility are part of a powerful culture of trust. There is increasing evidence that high trust educational systems produce higher standards (Bryk and Schneider, 2004). The National Board both expresses and attracts high trust. According to a representative, "We trust the expertise of our principals and teachers. We respect that expertise and we try to understand what is happening in the everyday life of schools and what questions have to be worked with. We try to combine that with issues, interests and needs of the future at the national level."

In return, as academics from the Centre for Continuing Education put it, "People in the field don't hate people in this (Ministry) building. It's more co-operative. It's an informal way of distributed leadership." A local authority committee chair emphasised that they "want(ed) staff to feel they have respect and have opportunities for training and to learn more".

Administrative staff in another local authority echoed arguments we heard elsewhere about the importance of trust, especially in conditions of failure and difficulty. At these times, instead of removing staff, exerting control or imposing interventions, the local authority asks: "How can we help the school? What were the things that went wrong? ... The knowledge (of how to solve the problem) is in the school and we have very capable principals. You have to trust. Trust is the first thing. We try to help rather than count the budget. If there's a problem, we are sitting together and thinking 'what can we do?' Principals are highly valued in our society. We don't want to fail. We want to support, give more training."

Principals and teachers are trusted, to a degree, because of their high qualifications, expertise and widespread commitment and responsibility. This trust is actively built through deliberately created structures and initiatives. This is evident in:

- *Networks:* Adapted from business ideas and companies like Nokia as ways to spread knowledge and improvement across schools. National projects always have "very strong and big networks" for cooperating with national authorities, in forums where people "learn with and work from each other". Municipalities stressed the importance of all teachers participating in local and school-based processes as well as in curriculum development. Some commentators argue that networks spread good practices through disease-like processes of infection (D Hargreaves 2004; Hopkins, 2007). But networks really spread ideas through deliberate though not linear processes of learning and experimentation – more like the spread of good health practices than of infectious disease.

- *Targets:* Shared at the local level through action plans rather than imposed by political or administrative means.

- *Self evaluation:* As the key to continuous improvement rather than imposed inspections or test-based accountability that rank schools competitively on the basis of their test scores.

To sum up: Finland exhibits a pattern of system leadership in strong cultures of lateral and vertical teamwork, networking, participation, target setting and self evaluation. Hierarchies are not feared, and interventions (as compared to co-operative problem solving) are virtually unknown. There are signs that co-operation may not yet have fully developed into more rigorous and challenging processes of collaboration focused on teaching and learning, and this could prove problematic if Finland's system is placed under stress. But for now, high performing Finland rests on a culture of high trust, actively engaged and co-operative professional relationships.

Finland exhibits a pattern of system leadership in strong cultures of lateral and vertical teamwork, networking, participation, target setting and self evaluation. Hierarchies are not feared, and interventions (as compared to co-operative problem solving) are virtually unknown.

Politics: subsidiarity and participation

The politics of system leadership in Finland involves a particular kind of subsidiarity, participation and empowerment. This empowerment is not contrived, but it is fundamental to the way participatory politics is undertaken in Finnish society. In conjunction with the culture of trust, co-operation and responsibility, these forms of political participation strengthen senses of involvement and security while encouraging people to innovate and take risks. Risk and security are therefore integral to rather than opposites of one another and are essential to the Finnish form of leadership.

> As one of the principals put it, "If there is good leadership and strategy, people feel better, and if people feel better, leadership becomes better."

Since the 1970s, Finland's strong reform impetus has always carried with it strong public and professional consensus (Aho *et al.*, 2006). From being a centrally planned and hierarchical system in the 1970s, the Finnish educational system has been transformed, following the economic collapse of the early 1990s, into a highly decentralised system of governance. The National Curriculum steers overall policy direction and sets a broad curriculum framework – for instance specifying a syllabus of 75 courses and 18 different subjects including six compulsory courses – at the national level. Within this broad steering system, considerable decision-making power is devolved to the country's trusted municipalities.

There are 416 local education authorities in Finland, most of them small communes, though the largest encompass whole cities. These municipalities have great powers, including allocating budgets between education, health and social services; designing and distributing curricula specific to the schools and the municipality; determining the appointment criteria for principals; and conducting self evaluations.

This means that municipal leadership takes on extraordinary importance, in the words of the department staff, as it "tries to support every school to be successful." Social, health and education authorities have to work together within municipalities. Indeed, co-operation within municipalities is on the increase, as we will explain in the next section. According to the background report for this study (Ministry of Education Finland, 2007*)*, in their own curriculum documents, schools are obliged to present how they cooperate with other schools. Exactly how they do so varies, however, as there are different approaches across municipalities. In the city of Javenpää, for example, all comprehensive schools follow the municipal level common curriculum which has been created in a city-wide co-operative effort with the participation of several hundreds of teachers, led by the municipal department of education. In other cases, such as Helsinki and Tampere, although the municipality plays a very active role in supporting the preparation of school level curricula as well as encouraging intensive co-operation in this area among schools, this does not go as far as planning a common city-level curriculum.

Among education leaders, the heads of the departments of education in municipalities can exert strong influence on educational development in Finland, in general, and on the development of school level leadership, in particular. While there is a national requirement in selecting principals (management training qualifications or equivalent experience), municipalities for example can refine the criteria to choose whether principals should have managerial power or rather be pedagogical leaders. Some of the municipal leaders have explicit and pronounced concepts about how school leadership should be organised and improved, and take effective steps to achieve these ideas. We saw, for instance, a very strong commitment by the head of the education department of a municipality in favour of school-level collective leadership. She demands that all schools establish and operate *executive teams*. When meeting the leaders of the schools in order to discuss questions related to their work, she prefers to meet the whole team rather than just the principal. In this municipality, professional development is provided and purchased for all members of the executive teams. Leadership at municipal level is shared, among others, between professional administrators (*e.g.* the head of the educational section of the mayor's office) and elected politicians (*e.g.* the head of the municipal education committee). Through this linkage, education is connected to broader community affairs. This connection is reinforced by the integration of educational administration into overall local administration including urban planning, local economic development, health and social care, housing and culture. Educational leadership in this context is strongly influenced by the broader reforms of state administration or municipal governance. This includes economic and business reforms.

The municipal educational leaders we met in Helsinki, Järvenpää and Tampere all used notions and applied procedures coming from business management, such as the use of purchasers and providers and the *balanced score card* approach. This openness towards the world of business and its management approaches seemed to be in harmony with their commitment to pupils' welfare and to the improvement of learning. Being efficient public managers and playing the role of pedagogical leaders did not seem to create role conflicts for them. Compared to many other countries, Finnish forms of educational and social thinking view efficiency and competitiveness as in synergy with education, co-operation and creativity.

Because of the decentralised nature of the system, leadership practices vary between the different municipalities in Finland. In the municipalities we visited, system leadership rests on principles of subsidiarity: within a broad vision, legislative arrangements and funding structures, decisions are made at the level of those most able to implement them in practice. This approach is also evident in Finland's distinctive approaches to assessment, accountability and intervention.

Within a broad vision, legislative arrangements and funding structures, decisions are made at the level of those most able to implement them in practice.

Finland does not have a system of standardised testing or test-based accountability. It does not have systems of competitive choice between schools or order its schools in public performance rankings. In the words of school leadership training providers we met, "all schools must be good enough and there is no reason to have elite schools and bad schools". If schools have difficulty, the government does not intervene punitively but opts for self-correcting systems of support and assistance.

There is an emphasis on evaluation for improvement, especially through school self evaluation which is incorporated into national evaluations. Through this system of self evaluation, networking, participation and co-operation, the system is able to "build co-operative structures and hear the weak signals". The system then responds to these through training, support and assistance from the municipality and other schools in ways that are calmly co-operative rather than dramatic or crisis-driven. In terms of complexity theory, Finland, like its emblematic corporation, Nokia, is a self-correcting, complex system in which negative deviance is rectified through participation and interaction rather than public exposure and intervention.

There is a cost to this, for where those who are failing do not respond to being developed, or teachers do not cover adequately for ailing or failing leaders, there is almost no provision for rapid intervention and it can typically take two years, we were told, to remove incompetent individuals from the profession. But, in line with the OECD statistics on equity and school differences in Finland, these instances seem rather rare and the country is prepared to endure such a small number in order to maintain the overall high standards of learning and performance in its high trust system.

To sum up: system leadership in Finland and its educational system rests on political principles of subsidiarity and decentralisation, along with widespread participation. Improvement is achieved within complex systems of support and networking by self-correcting evaluation and interaction rather than punitive intervention.

Leadership: systemic but not yet sustainable?

Principals in Finland are required by law to have been teachers themselves. Most continue to be engaged in classroom teaching for at least 2-to-3 hours – many up to 20 lessons per week. This lends them credibility among their teachers, enables them to remain connected to their children, and ensures that pedagogical leadership is not merely rhetoric but a day-to-day reality. How is it, we asked, that principals could still teach as well as lead in their high performing educational system? "Because", one said, "unlike other countries, we do not have to spend our time responding to long lists of government initiatives that come from the top." Indeed, principals and national government officials each explained to us their concern for moderating the number, pace and range of reforms so that schools did not spend excessive time reacting to initiatives from the outside.

These combined factors help explain how, at this time, distributed leadership is an endemic feature of Finnish schools, rather than something which individual actors assign or delegate to others as a way to get policy implemented. In the conception of key writers in the field, distributed leadership here is not a set of practices initiated and handled by principals or senior officials. Leadership, rather, is already distributed throughout the culture and organisation of the schools (Crowther *et al.*, 2002; Spillane, 2006).

Principals and teachers are regarded by many in Finland as a "society of experts". In one municipality, the upper secondary school was described as "an organisation of experts who know their subjects and teach them well". This evokes one of the classic categories of the typology of organisations by Mintzberg (1979): the one in which operations are based on the autonomous personal decisions of professionals who might follow various protocols and standards but typically make independent judgments.

> In the words of a member of the national Principals' Council: "Working in schools is easy because we don't have principals acting like a big manager. It's more like a society of experts. We really share things because principals also have pedagogical understanding and that's important. They have to know how to do the job and they still teach during the week. You really know how the work is. You are not just sitting higher and acting like a big manager."

The operation of this "society of experts" is seen as being neither authoritarian, nor especially academic, but a co-operative and (according to Finland's long-standing cultural traditions), practical craft-like activity. The system gets "good results from good people". Innovations, we were told, emerge from almost anywhere – not just from government strategy, but also often from among the "society of experts" itself. One principal, for example, described how innovations can come from the principal, the teachers, or government projects – and principals and teachers then sit down together to discuss what to do about it. As a member of the National Board of Education explained, when teachers or principals have a "very devoted idea" they "get an idea, compose a group, develop an initiative and ask, is that ok in our school?" As many educators testified, there is not a big gap between teachers and principals. As we saw earlier, teachers could, if necessary, assume the running of the school if for some reason, such as illness or crisis, the principal was no longer capable of doing so.

At an upper secondary school, we saw how this seemingly effortless, informal and endemic approach to distributed leadership also encompassed the students. The school operates an efficient network of student tutors. Learning is organised on a course basis, with students having great autonomy to determine their own learning paths according to their individual interests – including courses provided by other upper secondary schools. The student tutoring process allows the organisation to maintain the high levels of diversity and complexity that are favourable for change and adaptation.

The distributed leadership with and among students is not just a structural matter of roles and responsibilities, but a cultural issue as well. Leadership, these confident yet quietly spoken students said, was "shared". They "always cooperate", "can be relaxed and calm", find the principal "easy to talk to" and regard some teachers "like friends" in a community where there is "always someone who can help you". Yet, as is true of Finnish schools from the earliest years (Honoré, 2004), within their culture of distributed leadership students also have to "learn to be responsible" themselves.

Increasingly, however, while this informal, endemic approach to distributed leadership remains dominant, it is being supplemented by formal systems of teamwork and decision-making. Staff are cooperating together on self evaluation, setting targets related to the school's action plan, working on welfare issues with nurses and social workers, and spending time on students identified with special educational needs. We have already described how these systems are being extended into elaborate systems of team decision making in one school (Linnainnaa) to deal with social events, children's welfare, management of the school timetable and related issues. It is the principal's task to assemble many of these teams, steer their work and pull them together.

In contrast to the widely articulated views of principals being one more contributor to a "society of experts", these developments help explain why another view was represented with equal strength. For some, the principal is "responsible for nearly everything" – budget allocation (which is devolved to the school except in small municipalities), interpretation and implementation of legislation, staff appointments, human resource management, professional development provision, action plans and target setting, and the "soft skills" of teamwork and team building. Principals are also responsible for dealing with parent requests and complaints in a system where parents are regarded as having considerable power. As one principal wryly observed, schools have to have a principal because "someone has to be guilty!" The extent of these responsibilities and associated influence varies according to school size – with leaders in small schools having to "do everything" themselves, while those in larger schools are more able to exercise leadership of and among colleagues.

Whether principals are becoming more prominent or whether they remain part of the "society of experts", it is clear that pressure on principals and extensions of their responsibilities include:

- *Declining enrolments* requiring increased co-operation with other schools to provide curriculum or share other resources.

- *Declining resources* due to the burden that impending retirements of the baby boom generation are already placing on Finland's social state and its available expenditure for public education.

- *Increased attention to special educational needs* in a society that compared to other OECD nations categorises and includes greater proportions of special education students, and that will see increases with rising rates of immigration affecting the schools.

- More emphasis within schools and municipalities on *integrating educational provision with health and social services.*

- *Self evaluation and auditing* responsibilities that characterise Finland's distinctive approach to quality assurance (rather than standardised tests).

- Continued emphasis among principals on their teaching contributions as well as on their increased leadership *responsibilities.*

The result of these pressures on the existing leadership role of principals is a feeling that the job entails "more and more work and responsibilities". Shortage of time, increased pressure, expanded scope and accumulating senses of overload – these are the mounting burdens of the Finnish principalship. And, these problems are taking place within a growing crisis of generational succession among Finnish school leaders. Four factors are responsible for this succession challenge.

- *Demographic turnover:* In line with patterns in many other educational systems and in common with other work sectors, around 60% of Finnish principals are due to retire within the next few years. Ministry staff and senior members of the principals' association agree that there seems to be no coherent national strategy to address the serious problem of leadership succession.

- *Increased overload:* The autonomy of Finnish principals and the comparatively modest amount of reform demands to which they are subject may be the envy of counterparts in some countries. Yet the increasing demands of self evaluation, auditing, action planning, special educational provision, and collaboration with health and social services – and now leadership of teacher teams – are seen as more onerous than in the past. This increased scope of principalship along with existing duties and teaching responsibilities (especially in smaller schools), means that the traditional supply line of successors from within the school may be drying up because potential successors do not perceive the principal's job as attractive. The current challenge of principal succession in Finland may be that the queues for the exit far outnumber those for the entrance.

- *Insufficient incentives:* Existing principals maintain and ministry staff acknowledge that the current pay structure does not offer salaries attractive enough to entice teachers into principalship. Teachers in hard-to-staff subjects or in smaller schools (principals' pay is linked to school size) can earn more than their principal. In these cases, movement into principalship can at first carry a financial disincentive. Local authorities make appointments within national collective bargaining frameworks on salaries. However, participation of principals and teachers in the same union and collective bargaining process decreases the likelihood of preferential salary awards for principals, even though this might improve career paths, recruitment and succession. The longstanding ethic that diminishes differences between the two groups who are seen as all being members of a "society of experts" also works against such change.

- *Inadequate training:* Most principals have passed the national qualification for principalship. This provides training in policy planning, budget preparation, managing self evaluation and leadership issues in terms of managing and developing relationships with parents, pupils and teachers. For existing principals, though, there is not a "strong tradition of good leadership training", so national officials told us, because the high trust system of working with quality teachers largely enabled principals promoted through their schools to develop their own roles and their skills on the job. But falling rolls and school closures mean that leadership cannot always now be learned on the job. High turnover will necessitate greater mobility and more open recruitment processes, so the incidence of learning to lead and manage one's existing school is likely to decrease. Last, the increased management responsibilities in self evaluation and working with other agencies, for example, call for new knowledge and skill sets that cannot just be acquired internally. External provision of in-service training however, is currently uneven at best. The "universities are very independent", though they are cooperating more with the National Board. Some larger local authorities like Helsinki and Tampere are also developing partnerships with and purchasing services from local universities, but these opportunities are not nearly so accessible in smaller or more isolated municipalities. As a result of these inadequate and uneven forms of existing leadership support, National Board officials remarked that "principals call all the time to the Board" because the support system is insufficient.

A number of strategies for tackling this disturbing succession scenario were raised by the many educators we interviewed. Drawing on them and our comparative experience elsewhere, there appear to be at least seven possibilities.

- *Work longer and harder:* The national default strategy at the moment is to get existing principals to work longer, beyond the expected retirement age. This stop-gap solution is obviously unsustainable. Many principals of retirement age are capable of offering only a few more years at best. The experiences of overload will increase as the aging process affects them, and they will be poor exemplars of effectiveness as their performance starts to decline. A better use of principal experience as leaders reach the end of their careers is not to extend it, but transfer it through processes of mentoring younger and beginning principals.

- *Lighten the leadership role:* One way to increase leadership capacity, as in the case of water capacity, is to reduce demand (Hatch, 2002). This argument makes eminent sense in reform contexts that accelerate and intensify the pressures on principals. Less initiatives and leaner bureaucracy make sense (Fullan, 2006; PricewaterhouseCoopers, 2007). But by principals' own admission, Finnish educational reform requirements have increased only modestly compared to many other countries, and scaling them back might arguably undermine existing improvement efforts as well as adaptation to change.

- *Improve training support:* In an era of increasing change, it is no longer viable for teachers to learn how to be principals mainly by watching, and then replacing their own principals in their own schools. Nor is a national qualifying course sufficient to carry principals through the subsequent, shifting complexities of their work. The unevenness of the predominantly localised forms of in service training for leaders suggests a need to create a stronger, more coherent national system of leadership preparation, training and development. This might be achieved through the National Board, the principals' and teachers' associations, a confederation of local authorities or a newly created organisation. But the need for a national strategy of training and support for existing school leaders now seems evident.

- *Increase the strength of leadership roles:* The Finnish principalship appears paradoxical. Principals are widely viewed as pedagogical leaders, but this role is exercised in a largely practical and informal way rather than a result of information about pedagogical science, or evidence of pupil achievement. Likewise, while principals are seen as part of a society of experts, they are also the ones who have all the guilt and who shoulder most of the school-wide responsibilities. In times of relative stability, this paradox is sustainable. Principals can be first among equals, working with and representing the community they have been part of and within which they have risen. But when the pace of change quickens, scrutiny becomes more serious, immigration increases and special needs expands, then some individuals, especially principals, need to lead more decisively. Members of the Centre for Continuing Education explained this is already occurring to some degree – since the budget crisis of the 1990s called for strong leadership to orchestrate planning, set priorities and reaffirm values. Teachers, they explained, increasingly recognise that "when one really has to push things", one needs stronger leadership.

- *Redistribute leadership:* The demands on the principalship can be eased if responsibilities can be shared around among other adults in the school. The existing culture of informal co-operation in Finnish schools provides fertile ground for deepening and widening the process of distribution to include other tasks and responsibilities. The team management structures at Linnainnaa were designed in part to ease the internal workload of principals at a time when external demands were increasing. Some teachers welcomed the opportunity, feeling the new system "gave a chance for every teacher to be heard". One very experienced teacher conceded that she learned much about her school and the development of her own skills by participating in the team management process. Many teachers on these committees found themselves leading for the first time. Equally, though, other teachers complained of shortages of time, of responsibilities that drew them away from their own children and classes, and of tasks that seemed disconnected from the core responsibilities for teaching and learning. Such instances of contrived collegiality (Hargreaves, 1994) can create cynicism about the co-operative process. They serve as a warning that distributed leadership needs to extend beyond allocation of tasks to teams, and more into shared responsibilities for improving teaching and learning where everyone, not just the principal, becomes a pedagogical leader.

- *Improve pay incentives:* Many of the foregoing measures can turn the principalship into something that is achievable and is seen to be so. At this point, the disincentives of the existing pay structure, where some teachers earn more than their principals, need to be eliminated. Establishing separate bargaining units for principals might help achieve this, but should not do so at the cost of the co-operative "society of equals" that makes the existing system work so well. Linking rewards to criteria other than school size is also worthy of consideration. The challenge is not so much to increase the financial incentives that might draw people into the principalship, but to remove the disincentives that discourage them from taking this path.

- *Develop systemic, cross-school leadership:* Last, leadership and improvement effects can be increased if leaders cooperate, share resources, provide mutual support and inquire into improvement together across schools, within and beyond their municipalities. Such innovative forms of lateral, systemic leadership are the subject of new initiatives in Finland, and the focus of the next section.

Some conclusions on the Finnish success story

As societies move beyond the age of low-skill standardisation, Finland contains essential lessons for nations that aspire, educationally and economically, to be successful and sustainable knowledge societies. Here are just some of the signs about possible reform pathways to high performance beyond low-skill standardisation that can be taken from Finland's exceptional economic and educational journey:

- Building a future by wedding it to the past.

- Supporting not only pedagogical change but also continuity.

- Incorporating education and educational reform into a common and compelling social mission.

- Fostering strong connections between education and economic development without sacrifice to culture and creativity.

- Raising standards by lifting the many more than pushing a privileged few.

- Connecting private prosperity to the public good.

- Developing a highly qualified profession that brings about improvement through commitment, trust, co-operation and responsibility.

- Embracing principles of subsidiarity that maximise local freedom and responsibility within a broad national steering system.

- Embedding and embodying principles of accountability that are professional and community-based rather than managerial or market based.

Finland itself, we have seen, is a large scale example of an experiment in educational performance. No single part of the overall innovation can or should be extracted or transposed from this society-wide example, since the components are mutually reinforcing parts of a complex system. It is hard to imagine how Finland's educational success could be achieved or maintained without reference to the nation's broader system of distinctive social values that more individualistic and inequitable societies may find it difficult to accept. In this respect, one of Finland's lessons for other nations may be that successful or sustainable educational reform comes with widespread social and economic reform.

Leadership currently contributes to Finnish high performance not by concentrating on measurable performance outcomes, but by paying attention to the conditions, processes and goals that produce high performance. These include a common mission; a broad but unobtrusive steering system; strong municipal leadership with lots of local investment in curriculum and educational development; teachers who already are qualified and capable at the point of entry; informal co-operation and distributed leadership; principals who stay close to the classroom, their colleagues, and the culture of teaching; and (from the principal's standpoint) being first among a society of equals in the practice of school-based improvement.

The success of Finland's distinctive and innovative social and educational system is substantial and rightly deserves its international acclaim. But Finland is facing changes that threaten the sustainability of this system. In line with the literature on organisational learning (Senge, 1990) it is therefore perhaps at the very moment of its stellar success that Finland and its educational system might most need to change.

The success of Finland's distinctive and innovative social and educational system rightly deserves its international acclaim. But Finland is facing changes that threaten the sustainability of this system.

In an intuitive and informal way, Finnish teachers know their students well including the progress they are making in their learning, and they achieve more success than teachers in other nations in quietly and calmly raising all students to the level of the best. They appear to be able to do this without an apparatus of external intervention, inspection and disaggregation of performance data. Informally and practically, leaders also seem to be able to concentrate on knowing their schools, colleagues and communities well – unencumbered by external initiatives – and often promoted from among the people with whom they have taught.

But following EU membership, increased immigration that is already having an impact on Finnish schools (Sahlberg, 2007) will make empathy with pupils less easy or automatic. Other kinds of data (including diagnostic test data) and skills of interpreting it may be needed to identify learning difficulties and track performance as effectively as teachers have been able to do by more informal methods up to now. In future, change may need to be pushed through the culture a little more and not just pulled from it. At the same time, increased interaction with welfare agencies and the special educational needs services is widening, and is adding to the responsibilities of principals, while the pension burdens arising from the society-wide retirement of the baby boom generation are already forcing economies and reducing capacity within education and the wider welfare state. The consequences for sustainable leadership and improvement are significant.

- *Pedagogical leadership* for learning may need to become more informed by research and ongoing evidence of achievement and to have more strength and direction if schools are to help their increasingly diverse learners in the future.

- *Leadership succession* will require a coherent national strategy of recruitment, reward and support if the retiring generation is to be succeeded by eager and effective replacements.

- *Distributed leadership* can lighten the load of the principalship but it must be chiefly focused on learning and teaching rather than managed tasks if it is not to be dismissed as contrived collegiality.

- *System leadership* across districts or regions can provide lateral means for principals to share common resources and to help, support and learn from each other, as they learn to lead together. Such system leadership is a relatively new departure in Finland and the subject of the next section.

4.4 Redistributing leadership in a local community

The final frame of analysis, as outlined in Section 4.3, is the structural-technical frame. This concerns the organisation of personnel, roles, responsibilities, time, space and procedures within systems. Whenever there is an intention to bring about a deliberate change within an organisation, it is activity within this frame along with the political one that is most prominent – either creating new structures with the goal of achieving different purposes, or fulfilling existing purposes more effectively, by establishing new patterns of interaction and culture, through altered distributions of authority and responsibility.

Changes and challenges affecting Finnish society and its educational system are initiating structural efforts to respond in the form of reorganisations of the structures of municipal services and of the leadership arrangements for delivering these services. Four such changes and the structural means of responding to them are key to sustaining the success of the high performance of Finland's educational system and economy. To recapitulate, these are:

- *A pensions and social services challenge:* Due to the impending retirement of the baby boom generation, creating increased pressures on the financial viability of the existing welfare state. This is leading to measures to rationalise and make economies in public services through reducing costs, sharing resources and integrating services.

- *Rural emigration:* To the cities, leading to loss of cost-effectiveness and a growing need to share curriculum offerings, school provision and related leadership responsibilities across shrinking municipalities.

- *Increased immigration:* As a result of joining the European Union and of the need to increase the taxpayer base to relieve the pensions crisis and support the welfare social state. This is leading to increased demand to serve the needs of many immigrant families in terms of special education services and co-ordination of education with health and social service provisions.

- *The challenge of leadership succession:* (Discussed in the previous section) and the pressures this puts on leadership recruitment, continuity and renewal.

One way of responding to these changes and challenges in Finland has been to develop deliberately distributed, system leadership on a city-wide or municipality basis. We were able to examine a particularly innovative example in one Finnish city, Tampere. We are aware, however, that the approach to leadership taken by this particular municipality is one among many others. In recent times, we have been informed by Finnish Ministry officials, variations of these systemic approaches have been adopted in other Finnish municipalities.

One of the main features of educational leadership in Finland (similar to other Nordic countries following decentralisation) is the strong role played by local municipalities. The more than 400 municipalities (or, in the case of upper secondary vocational education, their consortia) are the owners of the majority of schools, they finance their schools (to a significant degree from their own revenues) and they are the employers of teachers (including school leaders). Furthermore, as we have seen, they also play a key role in curriculum planning and development.

The city we visited had adopted a new management model, apparently influenced by business management approaches. The municipal leadership, for instance, has defined the role of the local community (or its elected delegates) as the *purchaser* of services that may be offered by either public or private *providers*, depending on which is more efficient. In the case of schools, the city management reform recognises that there is no significant customer demand for a range of alternative providers, but also stresses that *service contracts* with the providers will include both cost and learning outcome indicators. Here, leadership of the local school management reform is more in the hands of the *educational development manager*, who implements municipal governance reform, than in those of the director of the education department in the city.

The management reform Tampere adopted is part of the broader national reform process that aims to prepare the country to face the challenges of social, economic and demographic change. A background document to the Ministry of the Interior's (2006) project to "restructure municipalities and services" stresses that due to demographic changes, some resources will have to be transferred from the education sector to health and social care. As a result, the expenditure on comprehensive schools in 2010 will reach only 93% of 2005 funding levels. This makes it necessary to reorganise local public services. The reform of management structures and the strengthening of leadership in the city are strongly linked with this process. In the words of the leader of the city management reform, "good leadership is needed when we are changing things". The school leadership reform we looked into – with its allocation to some school leaders of new district-wide co-ordination responsibilities and its associated development of new managerial functions within these leaders' own buildings to counterbalance and compensate for their own wider duties – is directly linked to the effort to meet these challenges.

The municipal reform redistributes school leadership at several levels and in several directions. The overall strategy is to share acting principals at the municipal level: five school principals were working as district principals, with a third of their time devoted to the district and the rest to their individual schools. This redistribution implies the following:

- First, leadership is redistributed between the municipal authority and the schools. Those principals who have been invited by the municipality to share their leadership activities and energies across their own schools in their areas are now taking on roles and functions that were previously dispatched directly by the municipal authority. Beyond leading their own schools, they now co-ordinate various district level functions such as planning, development or evaluation. In this way, the municipality shares some leadership functions with them that extend beyond the boundaries of their own school unit.

- Second, the new district heads are part of a municipal leadership team. Instead of managing alone, the head of the municipal education department now works in a group, sharing problems and elaborating solutions co-operatively.

- Third, district heads now distribute their leadership energies, experiences and knowledge between their own schools and others. While co-ordinating activities like curriculum planning, professional development or special needs provision in their area, they exercise leadership at both the institutional and local district levels.

- Fourth, leadership within the largest schools (which are also led by the district heads) has been redistributed internally between the principal and other staff in the school. This releases the principal for other area-based responsibilities and enables increased leadership experience and capacity within the schools.

All these forms of distributed leadership reinforce each other in the attempted transformation of Tampere's educational and wider public services at a time of profound external change.

Redistributing leadership within the municipality, between municipal authorities and schools, between schools and within schools, all at the same time, significantly changes the way leadership functions throughout the local system. Everyone finds themselves in a new space of more intensive communication, receives new information, and interacts with new people in novel situations. This broadening of communication and the new forms of interaction necessarily lead to changes in behaviour. Municipal leaders start to depend more on the behaviour of district heads as their success in solving local problems is increasingly influenced by what the latter do. District heads also increasingly depend on other principal colleagues in their area, as the evaluation of their work is based not only on what they achieve in their own school but also on what the community of the schools in their area achieves. Principals start to consider and address broader community needs rather than competitively defending the interests of their own organisation. This interaction across schools opens new windows for mutual learning. In addition, as they devote less time and energy to their own school, they are obliged to delegate various management tasks to other staff, which leads to more open lateral leadership within the school, stronger development of distributed leadership capacity and therefore a more constructive approach to leadership succession and sustainability.

> *Redistributing leadership within the municipality, between municipal authorities and schools, between schools and within schools, all at the same time, significantly changes the way leadership functions throughout the local system.*

This local and institutional web of new interdependencies is systemic in several senses.

- Leaders' attention shifts from just the school unit to include the broader local system.

- Boundaries between the various parts of the local educational system and the internal parts of the schools become more permeable.

- The strengthening of mutual interdependencies and interactions then pushes the system towards emergent principles of development and change. What the district heads do in their own schools has an effect on other schools. Actions in each district affect others. For example, in the particular municipality we visited, when a district head developed a new computerised system of information about the resources available to schools in the area, this led to increased transparency throughout the municipality. Similarly, when one school applied a new approach to deal with pupils who had particular learning difficulties, this could quickly be transferred to other schools through the mediation of the special needs coordinator who is also a member of the team of district heads.

- The inter-institutional communication created by the particular reform made it impossible for institutions to hide their resources from each other and exerted moral pressure to share them with those most in need. As one principal explained, "if one of the schools needs to do something but doesn't have enough resources, the principal will phone the other principals and one of them will say, 'we have a little extra – would you like some of ours?'." This management model is also used as an instrument to co-ordinate the curriculum in terms of interpreting national and local strategic goals and also creating coherence among the different curricula developed across the city's schools. This is achieved through the new mechanism of district headship. Part of the job description for this position is "guaranteeing an adequate coherence of the curriculum in the district" and "a smooth school path for the pupil".

- More frequent interactions, stronger mutual interdependencies, increased communication and more permeable organisational boundaries not only improve problem-solving capacities but also generate space for further development. As the education development manager of the municipality explained, the new management model is expected to "create new personal resources for basic education, which will also promote Tampere's ability to take part in nationwide development work and policy discussions" in harmony with the ambitions of the region to be a flagship in Finland's knowledge economy. With the mobilisation of the new network of district heads, the municipal leadership hopes to acquire improved access to schools and to involve them more in implementing its future-oriented strategy. In the words of the municipal development manager: "This way we want to keep alive the future orientation of schools". Accordingly, area principals have been assigned a number of key developmental tasks – for example promoting the sharing of good practice, enhancing evaluation practices as sources for mutual learning, and supporting the professional development of teachers.

Redistribution of leadership across schools has been closely connected with redistribution of leadership within them. In the absence of the principal, the staff has to take matters more into its hands. The creation of the post of the vice-manager has doubled the management posts at the level below the principal. In one comprehensive school we visited, the new vice-manager, the old deputy principal and the principal charged with district affairs comprised the management team of the school. When the group presented the school to us, it was the vice-manager who played the leading role, rather than his principal who also served as district head. The school has operated several teams and every teacher has been a member of one of them. All the teams address whole school affairs, focusing on areas that have been perceived as crucial for the development of the school: recreation, educational development, special education, immigrant education, information and communication, and multicultural education and continuous development.

As other nations and jurisdictions might consider transferring some of the principles or practices described in this system-wide case, it is important to make some clarifications about the politics of this Finnish style of redistributing leadership. In other approaches, decentralised management has often taken the shape of increased responsibility combined with decreased authority. This is because measures to centralise authority over curriculum, standards and assessment in a context of often insufficient resources are coupled with devolution of responsibility and indeed blame to front-line managers for implementing or failing to implement policies adequately (Hargreaves, 1994; Whitty, Power and Halpin, 1998). In the case we examined, however:

- The dangers of moving overwork and overload lower down the system may be less because Finnish educators don't have many external initiatives and requirements to react to, as can be the case for their counterparts in other countries.

- While rationalisation of resources through co-operative activity is one purpose of the Tampere system leadership initiative, there did not seem to be feelings of austerity or resource depletion that have occurred in similar approaches.

- Although, as we saw in the previous section, some teachers can experience their new responsibilities as being a form of contrived collegiality, which distracts them from their core purpose of teaching and learning, the clarity of and common commitment to Finland's wider educational and social vision reduces this risk.

- The market competitiveness that has characterised local management of schools in other jurisdictions appears to have been replaced in Finland by common local commitments to justice, equity and helping one's neighbouring schools.

- Instead of individual interest and isolation characterising the leadership work of locally managed schools and systems, Finland's system leadership is grounded in principles of trust, co-operation and responsibility.

Lessons and conclusions on systemic reform within Finland

The systemic reform in educational leadership and improvement that we analysed, while in its early stages, has already produced some positive results, with greater co-operation and co-ordination between administration and practice. It shows early signs of fulfilling the key principles and purposes of:

- *Rationalising resources* within a financially challenged social state.

- *Integrating services* as a way of accommodating more diverse populations.

- *Increasing transparency* of power and resources within the local system.

- *Improving problem-solving* through intensified processes of interaction, communication and collective learning.

- Enhancing a culture of trust, *co-operation and responsibility* in the pursuit of increased effectiveness and greater equity.

- *Developing leadership capacity* and attending to succession and stability by increasing the density of and opportunities for local leadership in the school and municipality.

This particular systemic innovation we analysed is inextricably embedded in the educational and social innovation that is contemporary Finland. Attempts to increase international understanding of and learning from this case therefore need to avoid the extremes of either transferring particular elements of Finland's systemic reform without regard for the social, political or cultural systems in which they are embedded; or dismissing the relevance of the Finnish case (or indeed any other) because it seems too different and may be perceived as politically or economically inconvenient. The municipality's and the nation's approach to and success in system leadership and improvement in education is significant precisely because it demonstrates the importance of connecting educational to societal improvements across multiple, and internally consistent as well as integrated frames of concern and action – moral, cultural, political, structural/technical, learning related and leadership oriented. This ethical and organisational commitment and consistency within a coherent system appears to be an essential and broadly transferable lesson of systemic educational reform.

4.5 Food for thought

Across OECD countries, Finland represents an example of success in educational outcomes. The Finns have managed to marry past and future, to adapt to change while maintaining traditions, to care for equity while ensuring quality of education outcomes. All of this has been done in a context where leadership is shared across the board to ensure that goals and objectives are common across the country. There is a common purpose for teachers, for school principals, indeed for all those participating in the education process that ensures high quality. These features make Finland the focus of international attention to try to understand what lies behind this educational success. Below is a list of considerations or recommendations of features found in the Finnish approach to education for systemic improvement that may be able to be adapted and adopted in other countries or settings:

- A broad and inspiring social as well as educational mission beyond the technicalities of achievement gaps and beyond lofty but vague goals like "world class education".

- Recognising that the most important point of exercising quality control in relation to performance is the point of professional entry where the motivating incentives of status, reward and professional as well as social mission should be most emphatic.

- Increasing professional capacity by limiting and rationalising unnecessary demand in terms of the pace, scope and intrusiveness of external initiatives and interventions.

- Addressing the development and exercise of professional and social responsibility as an alternative way of securing quality assurance compared to the widespread emphasis on bureaucratic and market driven forms of accountability.

- Developing political and professional leadership that can build trust and co-operation as a basis for improvement.

- Building greater lateral leadership not merely through loose and geographically dispersed professional networks but through area-based co-operation that is committed to the welfare and improvement of children and citizens within the town or the city.

- Narrowing inequalities of opportunity and achievement by integrating strong principles of social justice into system leadership: the strong helping the weak within and beyond schools' immediate communities.

- Clearly articulating the relationship of and continuation between needed progress and valued heritage.

- Devolving sufficient core responsibilities such as considerable degrees of curriculum development to the local municipal level so that lateral leadership and co-operation become pedagogical and professional engagements, not merely administrative tasks.

- Extending leadership teams and distributed leadership within schools to increase leadership capacity across them.

- Paying detailed attention to learning (curriculum and pedagogy) as a basis for high performance, rather than priming measured performance in the hopes that it will serve as the main lever for improving teaching and learning.

- Challenging the necessity for expensive and extensive systems of high-stakes testing.

- Exploring ways to integrate business principles in educational reform and the development of knowledge societies, with principles that preserve and enhance a strong and inclusive social state.

Recommendations for Finland

But Finland's success needs sustainability. Even the Finns continue searching for ways to constantly improve their education system. They are themselves sometimes surprised about their PISA results and the interest these have generated around the world; they too want to understand what the key features to their success are and what they can do to improve. Their systemic approach of sharing and distributing leadership at different levels is a way to counteract some of the problems that are reaching Finland in the coming years: reduced education budgets due to population ageing, a shortage of school leadership due to retirement, and a less unified population due to immigration. Some suggestions below may help Finland to address these issues more effectively:

- Develop a clear national strategy for leadership development and succession.

- Deepen principal leadership and lateral leadership so they move beyond administrative and social co-operation to encompass improvements of pedagogical practice. Support experimental projects aiming at organisational and leadership development focused on enhancing learning and based on co-operation between schools, local communities and teacher training institutions.

- Employ current principals now nearing retirement not by extending their service and contracts in relation to their existing jobs, but by enabling them to develop increased leadership capacity via coaching and mentoring and by releasing others to engage in this work together.

- Enhance school level evidence creation through diagnostic testing so the development and performance of an increasingly diverse student body will not be managed only by intuition and interaction, but also monitored to detect early on those moments when intuition within the context of cultural difference may fall short.

- Articulate and share hitherto tacit knowledge about Finland's educational and economic success so that others can learn from it and it is organisationally more transferable.

Final reflections

The struggle for improved educational equity and achievement is essential and urgent across countries. Organisations increase their capacity for improvement when they promote internal learning about achievements as well as errors. Likewise, nations and states can also increase their opportunities for improvement when they open themselves to learning from others' successes, struggles and setbacks. Teachers do not get better merely by copying the ones who taught them – especially when their own schools, subjects and students may be completely different. Acknowledging the successes of others, engaging with them, then intelligently adapting and continuously adjusting them to one's own situation – these are the ways in which we improve through learning.

Finland's success and its continuing struggles provide the opportunity for others' improvement. We have articulated our understanding of the Finnish experience to be treated as a source of open and intelligent engagement that might lead to adaptive improvements in a number of other national and state settings. At the same time, even if Finland heads many of the world's rankings of educational and economic performance, its present success and the means it has used to achieve it should not undermine its capacity to adapt to face the changing circumstances of the future. Finland cannot settle with its existing success if its development is to be sustainable in the future. Ideological allegiance must not impair the ability and necessity to learn continuously, interactively and internationally if the educational and economic systems of OECD nations are to transform successfully into knowledge societies.

In the quest for improved educational equity and achievement, no one holds all the ultimate answers, but we can learn from each other as we strive to move further forward. With intelligent and open engagement, as well as sensitivity to varying cultural contexts, cross-country learning from cases such as this can lead to successful knowledge transfer, circulation and application that might benefit many jurisdictions. It is in that spirit that this report and its findings has been written.

Annex 4.A1
Case study visit programme
16-19 January 2007

Tuesday 16 January 2007, Helsinki, Ministry of Education

Time/place	Name	Post	Specialisation
10.30-11.00	Mr Aki Tornberg	Ministry of Education Counsellor of Education	Statistics and Research Analysis
11.00-12.00	Mr Heikki Blom	Ministry of Education Counsellor of Education	General Upper Secondary Education
	Mr Jari Rajanen	Ministry of Education Counsellor of Education	Basic Education
12.00-13.00	Lunch		
13.00-14.00	Mr. Jorma Kauppinen	National Board of Education	Head of the Upper Secondary School Unit, General
	Mrs Irmeli Halinen	National Board of Education	Head of the Basic Education Unit
	Mrs Sirkka-Liisa Kärki or other person	National Board of Education	Head Of the Upper Secondary School, Vocational
14.00-15.00	Mrs Outi Salo	Town of Helsinki Director, Basic Education	
	Mrs Eija Säilä	Principal of Oulunkylä School	Principal of Primary Education School
	Mrs Mervi Willman	Principal of Helsingin Kuvataidelukio	Principal of General Upper Secondary School, Fine Arts
15.00-16.00	Mr Gustav Wikström Mr Vesa Laine	The Association of Finnish Local and Regional Authorities:	Mr Wikström: Director, Swedish-speaking Mr Laine: Educational legislation Mr Lempinen: Director
	Mr Jorma Lempinen	The Finnish Principals' Association	
16.00-17.00	Mrs Eeva-Riitta Pirhonen	Ministry of Education Director of Basic and General Education Division	Director

Wednesday 17 January 2007, Tampere

Time/place	Name	Post	Specialisation
09.30-11.00	Mr Hannu Suonniemi	Director of Education in Tampere	Director
	Mr Veli-Matti Kanerva	Executive Director	Director of Basic Education
	Mr Jaakko Lumio	Executive Director	Director of Welfare services
11.00-12.30	Mrs Sirkkaliisa Virtanen	Deputy Mayor	Deputy Mayor, Chair of Education Committee
Lunch			
12.30-14.00	Meeting with principals, teachers and students and school visits (principals work in action) Arto Nieminen deputy mayor Tero Suni Head Teacher (north-eastern) Virva-Leena Masar deputy head teacher		
14.00-15.30	Mr. Erkki Torvinen Mr. Esa Parkkali Mr. Markku Valkamo Mr. Tero Suni Mr. Petri Fihlman	Principals	

Thursday 18 January 2007, Järvenpää, General Upper Secondary School

Time/place	Name	Post	Specialisation
09.30-11.00	Mrs Marju Taurula	Director of Education, Järvenpää	Director
	Mr Seppo Rantanen	Executive Director	Basic Education
	Mr Atso Taipale	Principal	Principal of General Upper Secondary Education
	Mrs Helinä Perttu	Chair of the Education Committee	
11.00-12.30	Meeting with principals and viceprincipals: Mrs. Marja Yliniemi, Mrs Hanna Saarinen, Mr Atso Taipale, Mr. Jukka Ottelin		
12.30-14.00	Meeting with students at Upper Secondary level: Eevi Huhtamaa, Emma Åman, Johanna Halla, Heidi Leinonen, Nelly Jaakkola, Leena Nousiainen		
14.00-15.30	Meeting with teachers: Members of Upper Secondary School's Leadership team: Jukka Ottelin Deputy Principal, teacher, maths and computing Aino Härkönen teacher, Finnish language and literature Seija Aarto, teacher, philosophy. Antti Mattila teacher, religion and psychology Maija Mäntykangas, teacher, chemistry. Tuija Haapala, teacher, translator, English		

Friday 19 January 2007, Helsinki, Ministry of Education

Time/place	Name	Post	Specialisation
08.00-09.00	Mr. Kauko Hämäläinen	Director	Director of Continuing Education Center PALMENIA
	Mr. Antti Kauppi	Executive Director	Executive Director of Continuing Education Center PALMENIA
	Mr. Jukka Alava	Director	Institute of Educational Leadership, University of Jyväskylä
	Mrs Elise Tarvainen	Head of Division	Institute of Educational Leadership, University of Jyväskylä

09.00-14.00 Conclusion: OECD review team meeting.

References

Aho, E., K. Pitkanen and P. Sahlberg (2006), *Policy Development and Reform Principles of Basic and Secondary Education in Finland since 1968*, World Bank, Washington, DC.

Berliner, D. (2006), "Our Impoverished View of Educational Reform", *Teachers College Record*, Vol. 108, No. 6, pp. 949-995.

Bolam, R., L. Stoll and A. Greenwood (2007), "The Involvement of Support Staff in Professional Learning Communities", in L. Stoll and K. S. Louis (eds.), *Professional Learning Communities: Divergence, Depth and Dilemmas*, Professional Learning, Open University Press, Maidenhead, pp. 17-29.

Bolivar, A. and J. M. Moreno (2006), "Between Transaction and Transformation: The Role of School Principals as Education Leaders in Spain", *Journal of Educational Change*, Vol. 7, No. 1-2, pp. 19-31.

Bolman, L. G. and T. E. Deal (2003), *Reframing Organisations: Artistry, Choice, and Leadership*, Jossey-Bass, San Francisco, CA.

Bryk, A. S. and B. L. Schneider (2004), *Trust in Schools: A Core Resource for Improvement*, Russell Sage Foundation, New York.

Castells, M. and P. Himanen (2002), *The Information Society and the Welfare State: The Finnish Model*, Oxford University Press, Oxford.

Crowther, F., S. Kaagan, M. Ferguson and L. Hann (2002), *Developing Teacher Leaders: How Teacher Leadership Enhances School Success*, Corwin Press, Thousand Oaks, CA.

Deal, T. E. and K. D. Peterson (1999), *Shaping School Culture: The Heart of Leadership*, Jossey-Bass, San Francisco, CA.

Dodd, D. and K. Favaro (2007), *The Three Tensions*, Jossey-Bass, San Francisco, CA.

Epstein, J. L. (2001), *School, Family, and Community Partnerships: Preparing Educators and Improving Schools*, Westview Press, Boulder, CO.

Evans, M. and C. Stone-Johnson (in press), "Internal Leadership Challenges of Network Participation: The Experiences of School Leaders in the Raising Achievement/Transforming Learning Network", *International Journal of Leadership in Education*.

Fink, D. and C. Brayman (2006), "School Leadership Succession and the Challenges of Change", *Educational Administration Quarterly*, Vol. 42, No. 1, pp. 62-89.

Fullan, M. (2003), *Change Forces with a Vengeance*, Routledge, London.

Fullan, M. (2005), *Leadership and Sustainability: System Thinkers in Action*, Sage Publications Ltd, Thousand Oaks, CA.

Fullan, M. (2006), *Turnaround Leadership*, Jossey-Bass, San Francisco, CA.

Giles, C. and A. Hargreaves (2006), "The Sustainability of Innovative Schools as Learning Organisations and Professional Learning Communities during Standardised Reform", *Educational Administration Quarterly*, Vol. 42, No. 1, pp. 124-156.

Gronn, P. (2003), *The New Work of Educational Leaders: Changing Leadership Practice in an Era of School Reform*, Sage Publications Ltd., Thousand Oaks, CA.

Grubb, N., Jahr, H. M., Neumüller, J., and S. Field, (2005), "Finland Country Note for OECD Equity in Education Thematic Review", available at *www.oecd.org/edu/equity/equityineducation*.

Haikio, M. (2002), *Nokia: The Inside Story*, Edita, Helsinki.

Hargreaves, A. (1994), *Changing Teachers, Changing Times: Teachers' Work and Culture in the Postmodern Age*, Professional Development and Practice, Teachers College Press, New York.

Hargreaves, A. (2003), *Teaching in the Knowledge Society: Education in the Age of Insecurity*, Teachers College Press, New York.

Hargreaves, A. (2007a), "Sustainable Professional Learning Communities", in L. Stoll and K. S. Louis (eds.*), Professional Learning Communities: Divergence, Depth and Dilemmas*, Professional Learning, Open University Press, Maidenhead, pp. 181-195.

Hargreaves, A. (2007b), "The Long and Short of Educational Change", *Education Canada*, Vol. 47, No. 3, p. 16.

Hargreaves, A. and D. Fink (2003), "Sustaining Leadership", *Phi Delta Kappan*, Vol. 84, No. 9, pp. 693-700.

Hargreaves, A. and D. Fink (2004), "The Seven Principles of Sustainable Leadership", *Educational Leadership*, Vol. 61, No. 7, pp. 8-13.

Hargreaves, A. and D. Fink (2006), *Sustainable Leadership*, Jossey-Bass, San Francisco.

Hargreaves, A. and M. Fullan (1998), *What's Worth Fighting for Out There?*, Teachers' College Press, New York.

Hargreaves, A. and I. Goodson (2006), "Educational Change over Time? The Sustainability and Nonsustainability of Three Decades of Secondary School Change and Continuity", *Educational Administration Quarterly*, Vol. 42, No. 1, pp. 3-41.

Hargreaves, D. (2004), *Education Epidemic: Transforming Secondary Schools through Innovation Networks*, Demos, London.

Harris, A. (2001), "Building the Capacity for School Improvement", *School Leadership & Management*, Vol. 21, No. 30, pp. 261-270.

Harris, A., D. Muijs, C. Chapman., J. Russ and L. Stoll (2006), "Improving Schools in Challenging Contexts: Exploring the Possible", *School Effectiveness and School Improvement*, Vol. 17, No. 4, pp. 409-425.

Harris, A and A. Townsend (2007), "Developing Leaders for Tomorrow: Releasing System Potential", *School Leadership& Management*, Vol. 27, No. 2, pp. 169-179.

Hatch, T. (2002), "When Improvement Programs Collide", *Phi Delta Kappan*, Vol. 83, No. 8, pp. 626-639.

Hay Group Education (2004), *Distributed Leadership: An Investigation for NCSL into the Advantages and Disadvantages, Causes and Constraints of a More Distributed Form of Leadership on Schools*, Hay Group Education, London.

Honoré, C. (2004), *In Praise of Slowness: How a Worldwide Movement is Challenging the Cult of Speed*, HarperCollins, New York.

Hopkins, C. and D. Jackson (2003), "Building the Capacity for Leading and Learning", in A. Harris, C. Day, D. Hopkins, M. Hadfield, A. Hargreaves and C. Chapman (eds.), *Effective Leadership for School Improvement*, Routledge, London.

Hopkins, D. (2001), *School Improvement for Real*, Routledge, London.

Hopkins, D. (2007), *Every School a Great School: Realising the Potential of System Leadership*, Open University Press, New York.

Hord, S. M. (ed.) (2004), *Learning Together, Leading Together: Changing Schools through Professional Learning Communities*, Teachers College Press, New York.

James, C., M. Connolly, G. Dunning and T. Elliott (2006), *How Very Effective Primary Schools Work*, Paul Chapman, London.

Kaplan, R. S. and D. P. Norton (1996), *The Balanced Scorecard: Translating Strategy into Action*, Harvard Business School Press, Boston.

Kotter, J. (1996), *Leading Change*, Harvard Business School Press, Boston.

Leithwood, K., C. Day, P. Sammons, A. Harris and D. Hopkins (2006), *Seven Strong Claims about Successful School Leadership*, National College for School Leadership, Nottingham.

Leithwood, K. and D. Jantzi (2000), "The Effects of Different Sources of Leadership on Student Engagement in School", in K. Riley and K. S. Louis (eds.), *Leadership for Change and School Reform*, Routledge, New York, pp. 50-66.

Leithwood, K., D. Jantzi and R. Steinbach (1999), *Changing Leadership for Changing Times*, Open University Press, Buckingham.

Leithwood, K. and K. S. Louis (eds.) (1998*), Organisational Learning in Schools*, Swets and Zeitlinger, Lisse.

Levin, B. (2000), "Putting Students at the Centre in Education Reform", *The Journal of Educational Change*, Vol. 1, No. 2, pp. 155-172.

Lieberman, A. and L. Miller (2004), *Teacher Leadership*, Jossey-Bass, San Francisco, CA.

Louis, K. S. and S. D. Kruse (1995), Professionalism and Community: Perspectives on Reforming Urban Schools, Corwin, Thousand Oaks, CA.

Louis, K. S., J. Toole and A. Hargreaves (1999), "Rethinking School Improvement", in K. S. Louis and J. Murphy (eds.), *Handbook of Research in Educational Administration: A Project of the American Educational Research Association*, Longman, New York, pp. 251-276.

MacBeath, J. and P. Mortimore (2001), *Improving School Effectiveness*, Open University Press, Buckingham.

MacMillan, R. (2000), "Leadership Succession: Cultures of Teaching and Educational Change", in N. Bascia and A. Hargreaves (eds.), *The Sharp Edge of Educational Change: Teaching, Leading and the Realities of Reform*, Routledge, London, pp. 52-71.

McLaughlin, M. W. and J. E. Talbert (2001), *Professional Communities and the Work of High School Teaching*, University of Chicago Press, Chicago.

Ministry of Education, Finland (2007), "Improving School Leadership, Finland Country Background Report", a report prepared for the Department for Education and Science Policy, Publications of the Ministry of Education 2007:14, Finland, available at *www.oecd.org/edu/schoolleadership*.

Ministry of Interior (2006), *Future Challenges*, a background document of the "Project to Restructure Municipalities and Services".

Mintzberg, H. (1979), *The Structuring of Organisations: A Synthesis of the Research*, Prentice-Hall, Englewood Cliffs.

Mortimore, P., P. Sammons, L. Stoll, D. Lewis and R. Ecoh (1988), *School Matters: The Junior Years*, Open Books, Wells.

Mulford, W. (1998), "Organisational Learning and Educational Change", in A. Hargreaves, A. Lieberman, M. Fullan and D. Hopkins (eds.), *International Handbook of Educational Change*, Kluwer Academic, Dordrecht.

New Commission on the Skills of the American Workforce (2007), *Tough Choices or Tough Times: The Report of the New Commission on the Skills of the American Workforce*, Wiley, San Francisco.

Newmann, F., B. King and P. Youngs (2000), "Professional Development that Addresses School Capacity: Lessons from the Urban Elementary School", paper presented at the American Educational Research Association, New Orleans, 28 April.

Newmann, F. M. and G. Wehlage (1995), *Successful School Restructuring: A Report to the Public and Educators by the Center on Organisation and Restructuring of Schools*, The Center on Organisation and Restructuring of Schools, Madison, WI.

OECD (2001), *Schooling for Tomorrow: What Schools for the Future?*, OECD, Paris.

OECD (2004), *Learning for Tomorrow's World: First Results from PISA 2003*, OECD, Paris.

OECD (2007), *PISA 2006: Science Competencies for Tomorrow's World*, OECD, Paris.

Porter, M., K. Schwab, X. Sala-i-Martin and A. Lopez-Claros (eds.) (2004), *The Global Competitiveness Report*, Oxford University Press, New York.

PricewaterhouseCoopers LLP (2007), *Independent Study into School Leadership*, Department for Education and Skills, Nottingham.

Rosenholtz, S. (1989), *Teachers' Workplace*, Longman, New York.

Sahlberg, P. (2006), "Education Reform for Raising Economic Competitiveness", *Journal of Educational Change*, Vol. 7, No. 4, pp. 259-287.

Sahlberg, P. (2007), "Education Policies for Raising Student Learning: The Finnish Approach", *Journal of Education Policy*, Vol. 22, No. 2, pp. 147-171.

Schmoker, M. (2006), *Results Now: How We Can Achieve Unprecedented Improvements in Teaching and Learning*, Association for Supervision and Curriculum Development, Alexandria.

Senge, P. M. (1990), *The Fifth Discipline: The Art and Practice of the Learning Organisation*, Doubleday, New York.

Senge, P. M., N. Cambron-McCabe, T. Lucas, A. Kleiner, J. Dutton, and B. Smith (2000), *Schools that Learn: A Fifth Discipline Fieldbook for Educators, Parents, and Everyone Who Cares about Education*, Doubleday, New York.

Shirley, D. and A. Hargreaves (2006), "Data-Driven to Distraction", *Education Week*, Vol. 26, No. 6, pp. 32-33.

Silins, H. and B. Mulford (2002), "Leadership and School Results", in K. Leithwood, P. Hallinger, K. S. Louis, P. Furman-Brown, B. Gronn, W. Mulford and K. Riley (eds.), *Second International Handbook of Educational Leadership and Administration*, Kluwer Academic, Dordrecht, pp. 561-612.

Simola, H. (2005), "The Finnish Miracle of PISA: Historical and Sociological Remarks on Teaching and Teacher Education", *Comparative Education*, Vol. 41, No. 4, pp. 455-470.

Spillane, J. (2006), *Distributed Leadership*, Jossey-Bass, San Francisco.

Starratt, R. J. (2004), *Ethical Leadership*, Jossey-Bass, San Francisco.

Stoll, L. and K. S. Louis (eds.) (2007), *Professional Learning Communities: Divergence, Depth and Dilemmas, Professional Learning*, Open University Press, Maidenhead.

UNICEF (2007), *Child Poverty in Perspective: An Overview of Child Well-being in Rich Countries*, Innocenti Report Card 7, UNICEF Innocenti Research Centre, Florence.

Veuglers, W. and J. M. O'Hair (2005), *School-University Networks and Educational Change*, Open University Press, Maidenstone.

The Wallace Foundation (2007), *Wallace's REPORT '06*, The Wallace Foundation, New York.

Wenger, E. (1998), *Communities of Practice: Learning, Meaning and Identity*, Cambridge University Press, Cambridge.

Westbury, I., S.-E. Hansen, P. Kansanen and O. Björkvist (2005), "Teacher Education for Research-Based Practice in Expanded Roles: Finland's Experience", *Scandinavian Journal of Educational Research*, Vol. 49, No. 5, pp. 475-485.

Whitty, G., S. Power and D. Halpin (1998), *Devolution and Choice in Education: The School, State, and the Market*, Open University Press, Buckingham.

Chapter 5

The English approach to system leadership
by
Stephan Huber, Hunter Moorman and Beatriz Pont

This chapter provides information and analysis on the English systemic approach to school leadership for school improvement. This refers to a practice in which schools work beyond their school borders for the benefit of the school system as a whole. England (UK) was selected by the OECD as an example of a systemic approach to school leadership because it has been promoting this vision through a number of policies and practices at national, regional and school level by stimulating school and school leadership collaboration so that "every school is a good school for every pupil". In the past five years, the English have developed a number of different opportunities for schools and school leadership to collaborate for school improvement as a whole. Among the different approaches we can highlight the role of the National College for School Leadership (NCSL) in the development of school leaders who "think and act beyond the school", such as the National Leaders of Education or school improvement partners, the role of an independent organisation which has promoted school networks called the Specialist Schools and Academies Trust (SSAT) and the possibility for schools to develop different degrees of collaboration or partnerships with other schools.

The chapter is based on a study visit to England, organised by the Department for Education and Skills (DfES), now the Department for Children, Schools and Families (DCSF), at OECD's request. The visit included meetings with stakeholders in London and visits to two schools. The chapter sets the English context, defines the systemic approach and provides examples of the two schools, which had improved their results considerably following a systemic approach to school leadership. It then provides some analysis of the practices and ends with recommendations.

5.1 The OECD case study visit to England

England (UK) was selected by the OECD as an example of systemic approach to school leadership because it has been pioneering a number of policies and practices at national, regional and school level by stimulating school and leadership collaboration with the aim of making "every school a great school".

Data collection from the study visit to England included extensive documentation and individual and group interviews during the visit. Documentation for the analysis included material from the DfES (now DCSF), the National College for School Leadership, the Specialist Schools and Academies Trust, the Training and Development Agency for Schools, the Association of School and College Leaders and several other associations. The schools visited provided extensive documentation including evaluation reports, development plans, and school management documents.

The chapter is based on an expert-oriented team effort. The team comprised Professor Dr. Stephan Huber, Professor and Head of the Institute for Management and Economics of Education (IBB) of the Teacher Training University of Central Switzerland (PHZ), as team rapporteur; Mr Hunter Moorman, OECD consultant and expert in leadership, education reform, and organisation development; and Beatriz Pont of the OECD Secretariat. Professor David Hopkins, inaugural HSBC iNet Chair in International Leadership at the Leadership Centre of the Institute of Education, University of London, provided specific expertise and knowledge to the team as an internal country expert.

5.2 The English context

How the English school system has evolved

In England, the responsibility for education policy lies principally with the Department for Children, Schools and Families (DCSF, formerly DfES), though responsibility for implementation and monitoring is shared with the local authorities, formerly called local education authorities (LEA). Scotland and Northern Ireland have autonomy in education policy decision making and therefore differ from what is described here for England. The DCSF holds responsibility for the development, interpretation, implementation, and control of the national educational policy through a framework of Education Acts passed by Parliament. The Department also oversees the National Curriculum, monitoring both the content and the quality of teaching in schools. Through the Teacher Training Agency (now Teacher Development Agency), it has established a framework for the initial training of teachers, and most recently, it has begun to focus on the continuous professional development needs of teachers and head teachers. The Department's role also includes devising formulae for the allocation of budgets to local authorities, and, since 1988, also directly to individual schools. The trend has been towards increasing financial and managerial autonomy at the school level, which has contributed to a decrease in local authority influence.

Under the Education Reform Act 1988, the influence of the LEA was reduced. Originally, schools were given the chance to become grant-maintained (GM schools), and to leave their LEA in favour of direct funding from the government. This meant that they no longer fell under the jurisdiction of the regional education authority, but under the Department for Education directly, and, as a consequence, received their budget directly from London. The amount of the budget, which still depended on the number of pupils, was greater this way, as no deduction to support local educational services was applied. On the other hand, the services of the LEA were no longer available, except on a paid for basis. The schools could buy services on the open market, in which the local authority is one, but only one, of the providers. Schools opting out in this way affected all schools in the district, as the government did deduct the amounts paid to such schools from LEA budgets, making it more difficult for LEAs to maintain services for schools that remained within the local system. The replacement of grant maintained status with foundation schools effectively extended the arrangements to more schools, making the role of the LEA even more difficult to sustain.

The LEAs have recently been incorporated into their local authorities, bringing together local education and children's services. Local authorities remain responsible for the performance of publicly financed schools in their respective districts, and their tasks include ensuring that there are enough school places and school buildings suitable for the education of children living in the district. The regional differences which shape the school system in England can be accounted for by the freedom with which the local authorities can establish schools. However, their capacities to determine the distribution of funds to schools, to develop curriculum locally, to appoint teaching staff and to inspect schools have all been eroded over the past two decades, as the national policy has moved towards a partnership built around strong government and strong schools. There was a high degree of ambivalence in the 1990s as to the local authority role. But with the Education and Inspections Act 2006, their new role of commissioner, champion and challenger is clearly laid out. Although it is a much more limited role than previously it is secure at least into the medium term.

Within the individual school, the school governing body is in charge of the delegated budget, and of the management of the school. Members of this body include the school leader, elected representatives of the parents, representatives of the teaching and the non-teaching staff and of the local authority – the latter being representatives of the local political community. Since the 1988 Education Act, school governing bodies have had considerably increased powers, which extend to the selection of teaching staff, the establishment of salary and promotion policies and, significantly, the appointment and suspension of the teachers and of the head teacher. Generally, responsibility for the day-to-day management of the school is delegated by the governing body to the head teacher, who consequently needs to have a close relationship with and the confidence of the school's governors.

For the last decades, the practice of school leaders has been shaped and influenced by changes in the education system, particularly by the reorganisation of selective schools into comprehensive schools and by the subsequent creation of many large schools. The head teachers of these schools were perhaps the first to feel the burden of school management alongside the professional leadership role, as the sheer size of these schools brought new problems of structure and control. For school leadership, this meant a much stronger management orientation within the job, more complex organisational structures and more complex patterns of decision-making and delegation. The pace of change has accelerated within the last decade as devolution and decentralisation have continued to be pursued by successive governments committed to local management. The range of reforms introduced during this period is unprecedented, and includes:

- a national curriculum;

- national, standardised tests for all pupils at the ages of 7, 11, 14 and 16;

- nationwide publication of individual school results in school ranking lists in national newspapers; the so-called league tables;

- increased parental choice of (and so competition between) schools;

- significantly increased powers for the governing body of each school, by which the influence of the parents was to some extent institutionalised;

- annual reports on the school's progress by the head teacher to the governing body;

- annual reports from the members of the governing body, the school governors, to the parents, the community, the ministry or the school authorities and the general public;

- local management of schools (LMS), a formula under which school funding levels are determined by pupil numbers;

- a nationwide accepted assessment procedure for teachers and school leaders;

- regular school inspections (originally at four-year intervals) against national standards of the quality of teaching, learning and management in each school;

- the publication of the results of these inspections;

- the obligation to draw up a school development programme taking into account the recommendations from the inspectors' report;

- the possibility for schools to leave their local authority and to become directly funded (grant maintained) – to receive their budgets centrally from London.

Out of these reforms a number of new responsibilities and additional duties have emerged. The role of head teachers in England has become much more demanding and challenging, as a recent survey to more than 1 000 principals in England and Wales has highlighted (PricewaterhouseCoopers report, 2007).

The accountability of schools towards the parents and to the community in general has also increased and become sharper. It is now one of the central areas of focus for school leaders. Preparing for one of the regular school inspections held by the Office for Standards in Education (Ofsted), for example, means a lot of additional work and creates considerable strain for head teachers and staff alike. During inspection, a team of inspectors can seem to turn the school upside down for anything up to a week, and after their findings have been published, the head teacher is responsible for setting up a school programme within a given time and with a clear timescale, which takes remedial action for any deficiencies stated. In England, inspection reports are made public, that is they are available to parents and extracts from them are frequently published in local newspapers. (This procedure has been described as a name and shame policy.) This additional pressure created is meant to stimulate the school's improvement efforts.

Recent education legislation has transferred a great deal of authority to the school governing body. The head teacher has to cooperate with this body continuously in all major decision-making processes. Yet, in some schools, head teachers questioned the competences and even the availability of governors, as a recent survey revealed. One fifth (21%) of the participating head teachers described their governing body as quite or very ineffective which suggests that there is need for capacity building measures for some governing bodies in order to provide the strategic challenge required (PriceWaterhouseCoopers, 2007).

Due to the changes in the school system and the resulting market orientation (the number of pupils has a direct impact on the size of the budget allocated to the school), there has been intense competition among schools for the last two decades. A good reputation for the individual school is an important aim, to attract gifted and high-achieving pupils, or at least their parents are encouraged to opt for the school under local selection procedures. The ranking by exam results has, therefore, become extremely important to establish and protect. Consequently, schools and their school leaders are very much interested in the performance and image of the school, on which they are dependent for their income.

Many educationalists claim that these ranking lists have had an unfortunate influence on public perceptions. Certainly, the consequences for the individual school, as well as for the individual pupil, are often negative, and it is clear that the construction of the tables favours schools that are already advantaged. Less successful schools have to fight against the following vicious circle: bad reputation, worsening school atmosphere, decreasing identification of the pupils with their school, decreasing number of pupils, reduction of resources, decreasing job satisfaction and motivation among staff, lack of applications of well-qualified teachers for this school, worse quality of lessons, decreasing pupil achievement, worse results in the league tables. Different studies show that most head teachers disapproved of the great competitive pressure open enrolment and league tables had produced, and considered the strong market orientation as educationally misconceived, even harmful.

In England, even in the largest schools, traditionally the head teacher had retained some teaching commitment. Head teachers wanted to take a part in what they saw as the core activity of the school – teaching, for a variety of reasons: "they can give some support where needed, they know about what is expected, know what the pressures are and gain understanding, and they get street credibility" (Huber, 1997, p. 30). Sadly, finding time for such activities had become more difficult as many came to see administrative tasks as the new priority.

It is within this framework that the central government recently established a five year strategy focused on improving standards for all, closing the achievement gap, and promoting choice and opportunity among a diverse student body by preventing dropouts and preparing all students for a successful transition to work or further education. An elaborate body of policy and support mechanisms have been put in place to advance these policies. These include setting national standards, national testing, school inspection, and accountability measures and new programmes like the New Relationship with Schools, Every Child Matters, extended schools and children's centres.

At least two assumptions are at work behind these policies: (1) Given the variability among school conditions and quality, it is necessary to find ways to prompt schools to take responsibility for improving against new accountability requirements, and, (2) schools may not be able to meet their responsibilities unless they work with partners, *e.g.* with another school, a local college, or an employer institution.

Policy and support mechanisms in England include setting national standards, national testing, school inspection, and accountability measures and new programmes like the New Relationship with Schools, Every Child Matters, extended schools and children's centres.

Thus inspection responsibilities have been somewhat shifted to the schools themselves, and school improvement partners (SIPs) have been introduced to help school leaders deal with new mandates and accountability pressures. Support for partnering and school improvement has been provided, among other means, through the Specialist Schools and Academies Trust. By 2008, each comprehensive school is to become a specialist school or an Academy, concentrating on particular academic areas while offering the full national curriculum. Schools facing special challenges or in need of improvement are particularly encouraged to become Academies, independent of their local authority but publicly funded and run. Schools may also seek Trust status to operate with considerable independence as government maintained schools in partnership with outside organisations providing unique expertise and perhaps additional funding.

The central government has established the National Strategies Programme to provide schools with special support to help them raise standards through a focus on improving the quality of teaching and learning and on improving school management and leadership (DCSF, 2007a).

One of the assumptions behind current education policy in England is that schools may not be able to meet their responsibilities unless they work with partners, e.g. with another school, a local college, or an employer institution.

Hopkins (2006) has provided a theoretical framework for the different policy tools available for school reform:

"England has since 1997 taken the opportunity to achieve high standards across an entire system of 24 000 schools and over 7 million school students. In order to move from the evidently underperforming system of the mid-1990s the government put in place a policy approach best described as "high challenge, high support. The way in which these principles of "high challenge, high support" are turned into practical policies to drive school improvement is summarised in the following diagram.(Barber, 2001, p 4)"

Figure 5.1 Policy mix for schools which have attained school improvement

The important point is that the policy mix was complementary and mutually supportive (see Barber, 2001, p. 4). The policies for each segment (see below) are linked:

- ambitious standards: high standards set out in the national curriculum, national tests at age 7, 11, 14, 16;

- devolved responsibility: school as unit of accountability, devolution of resources and employment powers to schools;

- good data/clear targets: individual pupil level data collected nationally, statutory target-setting at district and school level;

- access to best practice and quality professional development: universal professional development in national priorities (literacy, numeracy, ICT), leadership development as an entitlement;

- accountability: national inspection system for schools and local authorities, publication annually of school/district level performance data and targets;

- intervention in inverse proportion to success: school improvement grant to assist implementation of post-inspection action plan, monitoring of performance by local authority (district), less frequent inspection visits for successful schools.

Current school leadership policy in England

In England, school leadership has been a key policy focus for the last decade. At a national level, leadership policy is aiming to ensure that there is the right number of school leaders with the appropriate skills to be effective leaders. In particular, with apparent disparities in leadership across schools in the country, there are different efforts to try to help increase performance of low performing schools by a) promoting the systemic view of school leadership and b) providing schools with tools for improving leadership. The creation of standards for school leadership, the National Standards for Headship, in 1997 and the establishment of the National College for School Leadership (NCSL) in 2000 fall within this remit.

The National Standards for Headship are constantly revised following widespread consultation within the profession but also incorporation of current government thinking and guidance. This catalogue of requirements for the qualification and for assessing candidates consists of two sections: a short section on the core purpose of headship (Box 5.1) and a more detailed section on the key areas representing the role of head teachers.

Box 5.1 What is the core purpose of the head teacher in England?

For the DfES (now DCSF), "the Core purpose of the head teacher" is "to provide professional leadership and management for a school" as this "will promote a secure foundation from which to achieve high standards in all areas of the school's work" (DfES, 2004, p 4; Ref: 0083/2004).

The standards claim:

"To gain this success a head teacher must establish high quality education by effectively managing teaching and learning and using personalised learning to realise the potential of all pupils. Head teachers must establish a culture that promotes excellence, equality and high expectations of all pupils.

The head teacher is the leading professional in the school. Accountable to the governing body, the head teacher provides vision, leadership and direction for the school and ensures that it is managed and organised to meet its aims and targets.

The head teacher, working with others, is responsible for evaluating the school's performance to identify the priorities for continuous improvement and raising standards; ensuring equality of opportunity for all; developing policies and practices; ensuring that resources are efficiently and effectively used to achieve the school's aims and objectives and for the day-to-day management, organisation and administration of the school. The head teacher, working with and through others, secures the commitment of the wider community to the school by developing and maintaining effective partnerships with, for example, schools, other services and agencies for children, the local authority, higher education institutions and employers. Through such partnerships and other activities, Head teachers play a key role in contributing to the development of the education system as a whole and collaborate with others to raise standards locally.

Drawing on the support provided by members of the school community, the head teacher is responsible for creating a productive learning environment which is engaging and fulfilling for all pupils."

Source: DfES, (2004).

The NCSL has the responsibility for co-ordinating and further developing head teacher training and development programmes. Hence, the college's purpose was to create, for the first time in the UK, a co-ordinated and structured approach to leadership progression.

In 2001 the NCSL produced its Leadership Development Framework. It set out the five "key stages" around which school leader development activities should be targeted in the following years. These are:

- emergent leadership: when a teacher is beginning to take on management and leadership responsibilities and perhaps forms an aspiration to become a head teacher;

- established leadership: comprising heads of faculty, assistant deputy heads who are experienced leaders but who do not intend to pursue headship;

- entry to headship: including a teacher's preparation for and induction into the senior post in a school;

- advanced leadership: the stage at which school leaders mature in their role, look to widen their experience, to refresh themselves and to up-date their skills;

- consultant leadership: when an able and experienced leader is ready to take on training, mentoring, inspection or other responsibilities.

Under the college umbrella, various training and development schemes have been implemented across the country, *e.g.* the National Professional Qualification for Headship (NPQH), the Leadership and Management Programme for New Headteachers (HEADLAMP), Leadership Programme for Serving Heads (LPSH), New Visions, and Leading from the Middle. The NCSL now runs around 25 individual leadership development programmes, various strategic initiatives, some research projects and online learning possibilities. Hence, England is taking significant steps towards a comprehensive provision of school leader development.

Following these measures, a number of positive developments can be observed, according to the DCSF:

- As of April 2004, all new candidates for headship must have gained or be working towards the National Professional Qualification for Headship (NPQH). Since 2001, over 16 500 candidates have passed NPQH.

- The recent report from the Public Accounts Committee on "Poorly Performing Schools" acknowledges that the NPQH and other leadership programmes have contributed to the increased professionalism of school leaders.

- Over 90% of heads enjoy and feel confident in their role (MORI, 2005).

- Over 55% of deputy head teachers and over 85% of NPQH candidates want to become a head teacher at some stage in the future (MORI, 2005).

- Yet, at the same time, the DCSF admits that some particular difficulties remain:

- There is a need to improve how the right people for headship can be identified, trained and encouraged, because a number of deputies and middle leaders are not interested in promotion to head teacher and some candidates see the NPQH as a stepping stone to less senior roles.

- Although head teacher vacancy rates in maintained schools in England have remained low and fairly stable (0.8% in 2005 and 2006), some schools in some areas are facing great difficulties in recruiting, *e.g.* small primary schools, rural schools and faith schools.

- The number of head teachers reaching retirement age each year is set to increase. In 2005, an estimated 60% of head teachers in the maintained sector were aged 50 and over, compared to 40% in 1997.

- The school landscape continues to evolve and we have to be sure that training and development for today and tomorrow will equip school leaders with the skills required to improve standards, ensure equality of opportunity and narrow attainment gaps through initiatives such as the Every Child Matters agenda and the 14-to-19 reforms.

- While workforce reform is having a positive impact overall on the teaching profession, it is a concern that the latest Office of Manpower Economics (OME) survey of the teaching workforce (October 2006) indicates that the average number of hours worked per week by secondary heads has risen from 60.8 hours in 2000 to 65.1 hours in 2006, and for primary heads there was a downward trend from 58.9 hours in 2000 to 52.9 hours in 2005, but then a slight increase to 53.5 hours in 2006.

- Reasons often cited as a disincentive to becoming a head are work-life balance, stress, initiative overload, and less contact time with pupils.

For the DCSF, to strengthen school leadership ranks high among the tools for improving schools and the education system. Within the five-year strategy focused on raising standards for all, closing the attainment gap and improving 16 and over staying on rates, the Department sees the need to strengthen school leadership to make "every school a great school" through the leadership development actions spelled out in the schools white paper "Higher Standards, Better Schools for All". These include: effective succession planning; a new and better mix of school leaders; more tailored provision of leadership development programmes; leaders for challenging schools; and national leaders of education.

However, national policy reach is more strategic than action oriented, given the role of local authorities. The 150 local authorities in charge of local administration of state education services show a wide range of performance.

With this view in mind, the policy reforms that are relevant for effective leadership include:

- the introduction of clear standards for school leaders, teachers, pupil achievement and schools in general;

- Ofsted reports and publication of school results;

- the promotion of schools' self evaluations;

- the provision of subsidies, strategies and programmes that schools can access to improve their leadership.

DCSF's reform initiatives and schemes launched during the last couple of years are unusually extensive compared to other countries worldwide. The quantity of individual initiatives, however, does not necessarily say much about their implementation and the effect they have to the quality of schooling for the benefit of the pupils. Obviously in a system with local management of schools, it depends a lot on school leaders' knowledge of these opportunities and their ability to tap this variety of public subsidies and make them work to their benefit. While some school leaders make full use of the initiatives, others see their number and complication as overwhelming and distracting from schools' core mission.

5.3 Defining and conceptualising system leadership in England

According to David Hopkins, a proponent of the concept of system leadership in England, system leaders are those head teachers who are willing to shoulder system leadership roles: who care about and work for the success of other schools as well as their own. If the goal is "every school a great school" then policy and practice has to focus on system improvement. This means that a school head has to be almost as concerned about the success of other schools as about his or her own school. Sustained improvement of schools is not possible unless the whole system is moving forward.

In England, there appears to be an emerging cadre of head teachers who are following this approach and beginning to transform the nature of leadership and educational improvement.

Recent research on system leadership has begun to map the system leadership landscape (Hopkins and Higham, 2007) and identified significant amount of system leadership activity in England, far more than previously expected.

According to Hopkins (2006), some of the key aspects of system leadership are:

- the moral purpose of system leadership;
- system leadership roles;
- system leadership as adaptive work;
- the domains of system leadership.

At present, in England, there are many possibilities for schools and principals to work with others, at individual and institutional level. Many of these strategies have been developed in recent years in the search for system-wide school improvement, and the National College for School Leadership has played an important role in this area. These roles can be divided into formal roles which have developed through nationally supported programmes; and more informal roles that are locally developed and are far more fluid, ad-hoc and organic. Flexibility is often an important factor in the development of these system leadership roles.

Among the different system leaders' roles are:

- Educational partnerships: Developing and leading a successful educational improvement partnership between several schools, often focused on a set of specific themes that have outcomes reaching beyond the capacity of any one institution. These include partnerships on curriculum design and specialisms; 14-to-19 consortia; behaviour and hard to place students. While many such partnerships are in what is commonly referred to as "soft" organisational collaboratives, some have moved to "harder" more fomalised arrangements in the form of (con)federations (to develop stronger mechanisms for joint governance and accountability) or education improvement partnerships (to formalise the devolution of certain defined delivery responsibilities and resources from their local authority).

- Choosing to lead and improve a school in extremely challenging circumstances and change local contexts by building a culture of success and then sustaining once low achieving schools as high valued added institutions.

- Partnering another school facing difficulties and improving it, either as an executive head of a federation or as the leader of a more informal improvement arrangement. Earlier research on executive heads for the NCSL led to the College's advice on complex schools to the Secretary of State: "there is a growing body of well-documented evidence from around the country that, where a school is in serious trouble, the use of an executive head teacher / partner head teacher and a paired arrangement with that head's successful school can be a particularly effective solution, and is being increasingly widely applied" (NCSL 2005, p 3).

- Acting as a community leader to broker and shape partnerships and/or networks of wider relationships across local communities to support children's welfare and potential, often through multi agency work. Such system leadership is rooted firmly in the national Every Child Matters (ECM) and children agendas.

- Working as a change agent or expert leader within the system, identifying best classroom practice and transferring it to support improvement in other schools. This is the widest category and includes:

  – heads working as mentor leaders within networks of schools, combining an aspiration and motivation for other schools to improve with the practical knowledge and guidance for them to do so;

  – heads who are active and effective leaders within more centrally organised system leadership programmes, for instance within the Consultant Leader Programme, School Improvement Partners (SIP) and National Leaders of Education (NLE), trained through the NCSL;

  – heads who with their staff purposely develop exemplary curricula and teaching programmes either for particular groups of students or to develop specific learning outcomes in a form that is transferable to other schools and settings.

The formal and informal roles hold a very significant potential to effect systemic educational improvement. If a sufficient cadre of system leaders were developed and deployed, there would be:

- a wider resource for school improvement: making the most of leaders to transfer best practice and reduce the risk of innovation and change focused on attainment and welfare;

- an authentic response to failing schools (often those least able to attract suitable leaders);

- a means to resolve the emerging challenge of, on the one hand, falling student rolls and hence increasingly non-viable schools and, on the other hand, pressures to sustain educational provision in all localities;

- a sustainable and internal strategy for retaining and developing head teachers as a response to the current and projected shortage (a survey by the General Teaching

Council in 2006 warned that 40% of head teacher posts would be filled with difficulty in the coming years).

Ultimately, the test of system leadership is whether it is having an impact where it matters. There is now growing evidence in the English secondary school system that this approach to system leadership is having a positive impact, with a number of schools having improved their examination results under new school leaders (see for example Hopkins and Higham, 2007).

5.4 System leadership in practice: Two particular school approaches

In the course of the OECD study visit, we visited two particularly inspiring schools demonstrating systemic approaches to school leadership. School leadership is distributed throughout the school and there are different forms of collaboration with other schools and other partners. Moreover, both schools had achieved improved outcomes. This case study provides the basis for a model of how collaboration, federation and system leadership might improve schools.

Description of the schools' systemic approaches

A federation of two schools (school setting A)

School A1 in this recently formed federation had overcome challenging circumstances and transformed itself into a high value-added school, now supporting other schools in similar transformations. It has recently federated with school A2, a school "causing concern" following Ofsted inspection. Before federating with school A1, it was in remedial status and is now in serious weaknesses, somewhat improved but still not achieving expected results. During this four year period there was no progress in the quality of learning, and progress in raising pupils' aspirations and pupil achievement was disappointingly slow. Consequently, school A2 willingly enlisted school A1's support in its development and transformation into a federation.

School A1 has worked to raise the academic achievement of all pupils by developing a successful school leadership and management approach. This includes leadership distribution across the school, the alignment of standards and a particular model of monitoring and support for student and teacher performance (analysed in the following section). Since 2001, school A1 has supported a number of schools facing challenging circumstances. School A1 is the lead regional school and the local delivery group school for the national school-centred initial teacher training (SCITT).

Their profile

School A1 is an 11-to-18 mixed comprehensive school with Specialist Technology College status, which includes a sixth form college and also provides traveller education. There are over 1 800 pupils (some 200 in sixth form), with 7% of minority ethnic backgrounds, and 54 pupils have English as an additional language. School A1 serves a low socio-economic student body with high levels of underperformance. The school area has been designated for social intervention through programmes such as Excellence Cluster, Interlok, Low Attainers Pilot or BIP (listed below). The performance of pupils in the primary sector has required literacy, numeracy and behaviour management strategies to ensure access to learning. The presence of a sixth form on site has allowed students and parents to raise their aspirations for 11-to-18 education and given students opportunities to follow pathways into post-16 and higher education.

School A1 has been extremely active in reform, combining pedagogical and managerial reforms to respond to its particular challenges. It has adopted different learning models and is developing personalised learning. A monitoring and support system has been quite successful, through a particular use of data that allows for monitoring and interventions to support pupils whose behaviour is affecting their achievement. It has developed an ICT information system that enables the school to promote electronic home/school links. The school is supported by an education welfare officer, among other non-teaching staff.

In addition, school A1 has developed into an "extended school" with integrated services including educational psychologist, nurses, mental health care personnel, specialist teachers, 40 learning and behaviour support assistants, school-based attendance officers, and more. The school now manages the region's local services delivery group, providing extended school services to 23 other schools.

It has made recruitment and retention of high quality staff a priority by:

- creating a teacher training centre to counter the lack of qualified teachers in the area;

- providing professional development during the week to all staff;

- assessing a number of classroom support assistants for the higher level teaching assistant (HLTA) status;

- capacity building at the senior level by participating in the DCSF Trainee Head/ Deputy Programme.

Looking to benefit from different public support and for improvement, the school has engaged with and launched a number of initiatives that focus on collaboration with other schools and with the school system as a whole (Box 5.2).

This school's results have turned around; key stage 4 (age 14-to-16) results have moved from the lowest quartile in 1988 to the upper quartile in 2006. It is now a "high value-adding school", ranking in the top 5% in GCSE results among schools serving similar areas. The results are at key stage 4 (examinations at the end of compulsory schooling, usually taken at age 16): 48% of students achieved five "good" GCSEs (A*-C) in 2006 (the national average was 50%), 5+A*-G 88%, 1+A*-G 98%. This school has a strong, well organised and supportive governing body, which has helped develop its role with school A2 and its ambitions to deliver broader local services.

Box 5.2 School improvement and system leadership initiatives in a particular school

- Specialist Technology College status: schools with or aspiring to specialist status can receive a wide range of support and partnership links through the Specialist Schools and Academies Trust.

- Leading Edge School: the school is recognised for innovative practice and part of the national and regional forum for innovative and "next" practice support for other schools.

- Enterprise Pathfinder School: there is a strong vocational curriculum; the school pilots for new accreditation and assessment systems; and there are links to and involvement with the local business community.

- Leadership Incentive Grant (LIG) school: the school seeks to stimulate collaborative working between strong and underperforming schools.

- Behaviour Improvement Partnership (BIP) lead school: the school is developing new practice to raise attainment.

- Excellence Cluster (now EiC) lead school: the school works with community schools for pupils age 5-19 to raise aspirations and performance across the region.

- Local Delivery Group (LDG) management: the school promotes partnerships with public services and the voluntary sector to support children and families in need.

- Team around the Child (TAC): the school models good practice from the LDG for the county.

- Low Attainers' Pilot (LAP – school A2 only): targeted support is provided for English and mathematics in key stage 3 to improve attainment and promote active learning.

- School Centred Initial Teacher Training (SCITT): the school has gained accreditation as a training centre to counter the lack of qualified teachers in the area.

School A2 is an 11-to-16 comprehensive school with leisure facilities on site. There are 826 students, 4% of whom belong to minority ethnic groups, and 16 students with English as an additional language. Pupils are drawn largely from two of the wards with the highest indices of deprivation for the region and many pupils and their families have English as an additional language (EAL), special educational needs (SEN) or social services support. The students show the full range of ability but there is a higher proportion of underachievement and SEN than in other schools within the town. Pupil aspirations are low, as are outcomes in recent years.

School A1 is a high value-added school; school A2, which is officially described as having serious weaknesses, willingly joined a federation with school A1.

Ofsted inspections had placed the school in "special measures" and then "serious weaknesses" in recent years because of underperformance, inadequate teaching and learning, and a curriculum not suited to learners' needs. Its reputation had diminished, and with that its recruitment. As a result the school suffered from overstaffing and budget deficits, staff absence and malpractice, and poor student behaviour and attendance.

Schools A1 and A2 are now managed through one governing body, an executive with a principal responsible for both schools, and an associate principal on the site of school A2.

The federation

Schools A1 and A2 federated and are now managed through one governing body, an executive with a principal responsible for both schools, and an associate principal on the site of school A2 to lead the transformation agenda. The management team, including a trainee head teacher and a former trainee head teacher and vice principals, has joint site responsibilities.

The management and pedagogical model developed in school A1 has been adapted for school A2. In addition, to improve understanding and increase skills, continuing professional development for middle leaders was given a priority. As well as targeted professional development in-house, a large group of staff were identified to undergo training in effective classroom observation. Performance management is more rigorous and sets measurable targets against accountability for the future. Middle leaders' motivation, initiative and commitment have all improved.

The single governing body has focused on monitoring teaching and learning by meeting regularly with designated heads of department and visiting department activities. Governor training ensures they are aware of new initiatives and school development priorities.

Some results

- With federated status, progress at school A2 has been strikingly good in this short time. Student achievement has improved, behaviour is better, and the teaching force has been stabilised. In just one year, academic results have increased. At key stage 4, the percentage of pupils at 5+A*-C is 28% in 2006, up from 16% in 2005; while 5+A*-G is up to 86% in 2006 from 69% in 2005, and 1+A*-G 94%.

- The individual reviews for senior managers and restructuring of departments following the curriculum review and staff departures have generated a more effective team and have been cost effective, according to the Teaching and Learning Responsibility (TLR) review.

- Cross-site management has provided expertise and vision at a time of significant change for the school.

Developing system leadership in one school (school setting B)

Another school the OECD team visited presented showed how school leadership focuses on school improvement by strengthening internal and external leadership, reaching out into the wider community and focusing on system-wide school improvement.

The school profile

School B is one of the largest schools in the county, with over 2 000 students, 118 teaching staff and 82 support staff. It is an 11-to-18 co-educational mixed comprehensive school. It was awarded specialist technology college status in September 2002, which means that it offers the whole National Curriculum but with an added focus on the technological, scientific, mathematics and ICT curriculum. It has undertaken an extensive and far-reaching refurbishment programme which benefits almost all curriculum areas, and includes a new sixth form block. This has allowed the sixth form numbers to grow to 450.

Around 95% of students are of white British background. Several Asian minority ethnic groups account for the remaining 5%. Students' attainment on entry to the school is slightly higher than the national average. The proportion of students with learning difficulties and/or disabilities, or with statements of special educational need is below average.

Systemic programmes and initiatives

The school has developed a particular leadership management model based on a six week cycle of evaluation which allows for individual monitoring and support of all students and teachers. Leadership is distributed across a wide range of staff. Specific teams cater to the different needs: supporting, mentoring and guidance for students and teachers; specialised support in information technologies; and support on reforming the workforce (*e.g.* modifying individuals' and teams' responsibilities).

School B uses a six week cycle of evaluation which allows for individual monitoring and support of all students and teachers.

The school takes part in a number of initiatives:

- Training School: It provides initial teacher training, courses for new entrants into the teaching profession, as well as middle leaders and established leaders. This role also allows the college to recruit talented new teachers as they enter the profession.

- Raising Attainment and Transforming Learning (RATL): It is a support school for this Specialist Schools and Academies Trust project, which involves it in working with other schools and colleges to share good practice. It offers a number of access days each year where colleagues from other schools can visit to see, discuss and compare different approaches to raising pupils' achievement.

- National Leader in Education Support School (NLE): It is a support school designed to allow leading schools and colleges to work with other schools identified by Ofsted inspections as requiring special measures. As a result of these changes many of its aspiring leaders now find themselves with significant development opportunities.

Leadership and management structure

The school's leadership team has recently been restructured to take into account that it is no longer a single entity which could be managed by a head teacher and staff working solely within the confines of the buildings. The new structure creates an executive principal who is supported by vice principals and assistant principals, which enables the school to pursue its external agenda and allows more scope for career opportunities for a wider range of staff.

The vice principals are responsible for ensuring that the school's standards are maintained and improved. They will also develop international links and take over NLE Support School/RATL roles.

Staff from various levels in the school are involved in deepening and improving its approach to learning, experience, support and leadership (Figure 5.1). It is considered crucial that some staff members take part in more than one of these activities, to encourage complementarity (the exchange of ideas and themes between areas).

Figure 5.2 Leadership and management structure in case study school B

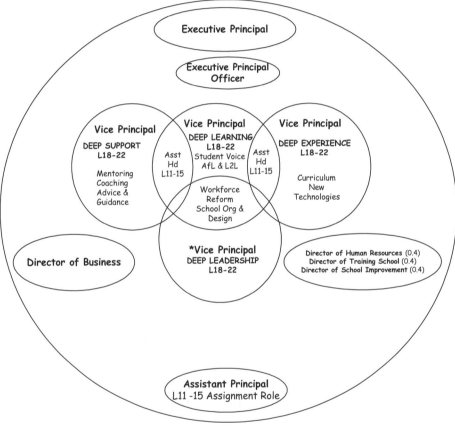

*Plan for succession
Involved in external work of Principal
Represent college at official events, meetings, Trust Status etc
They will experience the pressures of the role in a safe environment

The terms Principal and Vice Principal are intended to reflect the global understanding of the role and to signal a change to parents, staff and students in terms of the direction and depth to which we set our new context and future development

Some results

Statistics demonstrate the school's success in achieving national standards. The Ofsted inspection of November 2006 rated the school Grade 1, outstanding in all areas: 90% of the pupils met GCSE standards in 2006, in the top 5% nationally for value added; 60% achieved 5 A* -C (including English and Maths), showing a high value added; A-level (post 16) results also merited a ranking of outstanding.

Since September 2003, the school has been a DCSF Training School. This has enabled staff to access high quality training and develop their expertise. The school is popular with parents, and is over-subscribed. Achieving specialist technology status in 2002 helped to improve facilities and raise standards across the curriculum. Investment in information and communications technology (ICT), and in particular the creation of a "learning zone", where students can work independently during lessons and after school, has supported students' learning very well. These developments, increasing students' independence and collaborative skills, allied to high standards of literacy and numeracy combine to prepare students for life after school.

The OECD review team found that these two school settings illustrate high performance learning communities that are at the heart of system leadership.

Common features of the school settings

These two school settings provide examples of how school leaders and their school communities are responding to the challenges identified in England. The OECD review team found that they illustrate high performance learning communities that are at the heart of system leadership. We provide an overview of these features below because we think that the internal school leadership processes go hand in hand with the role that system leaders play.

Belief in student capacity to learn

Effective leadership and school performance rest on a powerful vision of teaching and learning. Both schools pursue clear visions to ensure that every student achieves to the highest level possible.

Inclusion is as important as achievement. The schools believe that their remit must include all children. School A1 is charged with educating children from lower socio-economic background and a dispirited urban environment. The head of school told us: "What drives us is that we are absolutely committed to inclusion." While he acknowledged that it can have a negative effect on test scores, he will not compromise on this commitment. Both schools not only extend themselves to serve their own students, but also go to great lengths to include children with out-of-school commitments, such as Roma or traveller students who are in and out of town on an irregular basis. Heads and teachers told us that students come first, and that they will do all in their power to guarantee their students' success.

Administrators, teachers, and staff seem to be confident of their ability to deliver. They get the best personnel through hires or internal development. One head noted that every leader in his school is first and foremost a highly qualified teacher: "It's the connoisseurship in the classroom that has led to the transformation." They have put systems in place to focus and manage their efforts: "Praising Stars" and the "Management Matrix" described below are two of these.

Student achievement is not just about cognitive gains. Both schools have comprehensive programmes giving students opportunity for self-expression and development in a wide variety of ways. Sports, drama, community service, and other extra-curricular activities appear to have the same emphasis on commitment and excellence as academic studies. When asked if the focus on learning reduced time for other dimensions of student growth, teachers responded that they did not concentrate solely on cognitive development but on the whole student. "Not to focus on the whole student is to open the door to decline in academic achievement," is the way one department head put it.

The school leadership teams established targets, measured student and teacher performance, adjusted curriculum and instruction, reallocated teaching resources, provided remediation and support and set new targets.

Alignment of standards, curriculum, instruction, and assessment

National performance standards, curriculum, instruction, and assessment are aligned in each school's programme. With the national standards in view, we were explained how schools set realistic but challenging performance targets for each student, at each level, in each subject. To do this, schools have considerable flexibility in adapting curriculum to align it with standards in ways most suitable for their students.

To ensure correct alignment, the leadership teams follow rigorous management systems. For the longer term, the school year or beyond, layered leadership and management teams with perspectives crossing year groups, subject areas, and ability groups orchestrate the curriculum, instruction, and testing programme to achieve performance goals. Within the course of the year, these same teams closely monitor student and teacher performance. In a succession of six-week evaluation cycles running through the year, the school leadership teams established targets, measured student and teacher performance, adjusted curriculum and instruction, reallocated teaching resources, provided remediation and support and set new targets. Where schools are joined in partnerships or federations the same management processes are applied.

Members of the school communities used terms like "autonomous" and "self-managed" to describe themselves. They had internalised the school performance and accountability culture, its values and exemplary practices. Each of them was able to take initiative, to act on their own to maintain the alignment between performance goals and the school programme intended to produce them. Thus adjustments and corrections in the linkages across standards, curriculum, instruction, and assessment were made daily in countless small, independent decisions that needed no outside direction.

Reliable monitoring and support for student and teacher performance

Student learning and development are the core purposes of these schools, and carefully developed management processes concentrate the schools' resources to this end.

School B is described as "driven by data". Through the school's data-based monitoring system, the head can track and pay attention to each one of the 2 000-plus students in his school. Student (and teacher) progress is monitored regularly. Every six weeks modifications are made in each student's curriculum and instruction. Students showing exceptional progress are helped to develop further; students in need of help are given extra work and instruction in areas of need. Teachers too receive support and professional development where data show they need it (Box 5.3).

Box 5.3 Effective school monitoring and support processes

Both schools visited during the OECD review had very effective processes for monitoring and support of student and school performance using an IT package that allowed it to monitor individual student, classroom, teacher or grade performance. Both schools have teams that follow performance and teams that support the results with appropriate interventions either with students or teachers.

In school B, the data management and monitoring system is called "Praising Stars". For each student, specific performance goals are identified for each six-week period, and weekly performance data monitor progress and identify areas of success and need for improvement. A team of non-teaching "learning managers" spend 60% of their time monitoring students and managing instruction. Their findings are discussed every week in meetings of the senior leadership team, which take decisions on adapting curriculum and instruction and developing strategies for learning for the individual student and for student groups and classes. The school has planned flexibility into the curriculum and teacher assignments so special lessons and additional teacher support can be shifted to help students who are not keeping up. Teacher effectiveness is also assessed. Special help is directed at the individual teacher or department that falls below expected results, and more formal professional development can be arranged.

With such a structure in place, the school head told us that his team is capable of massive intervention, observing every classroom teacher using the analysis to push for excellence in every category that is measured.

A similar tool for managing learning and teaching at school setting A is the "Management Matrix". The matrix is an elaborate but accessible depiction of a set of relationships across staff roles and responsibilities, functions (curriculum, teacher training, health, and finance, etc.), and strands covering key ways of managing teaching and learning. The entire school operates according to a comprehensive, clearly spelled out understanding of goals and objectives, responsibilities, and core functions. The matrix is the foundation for an ongoing, systematic dialogue about performance data, analysis, and actions for improvement. It is the framework for a pervasive culture of achievement, inclusion, and distributed leadership enacted in every part of the school.

Clearly defined roles are assigned to the different staff to monitor student learning and development, assess teacher effectiveness, allocate curriculum and instruction where it is most needed for each student, and provide or procure teacher professional development. Each member of the leadership team has responsibility to link with a particular group of teachers and year group, and the entire team works together on areas of special urgency.

- School B's leadership team has three priorities: to direct student performance, to remediate underperforming teachers, and to conduct two day a week interventions with subject-area departments. The head of school reviews progress with the senior leadership team for one half-hour one day a week and for three hours each Thursday. The head and his team also each week do a "walk around" to observe classroom practice, identifying teachers for praise or help and gauging the impact of instruction on student learning. Individual staff meetings are scheduled as needed.

- At the heart of the support structure are the seven learning managers, who report to the leadership team. Learning managers spend 37 hours a week working in the classrooms with teachers and students identified from the Praising Stars data in the most recent six-week cycle. After analysis of the performance data, they prepare a focused sequence of interventions for those students or teaching groups who are not reaching target grades. A "learning to learn" programme provides remediation for students underachieving in core subjects, and the "behaviour for learning" programme helps students whose behaviour is causing concern and interfering with their learning.

- Middle leaders are department heads. While they used to play a rather managerial role, now they are leaders responsible for maintaining and raising standards. They monitor pupil performance data, observe teachers (and are themselves observed), give teachers feedback and support, and serve as coaches and mentors.

- Five teachers are given extra pay and reduced teaching loads to serve as assistant head teachers serving on the team. They are supported by four associate assistant heads, usually department heads who rotate on one- or two-year assignments.

These processes contribute to align quality teaching standards, evaluative criteria, feedback, and professional development. This means a shared understanding of what constitutes good teaching and outcomes.

Flexible curriculum, classroom instruction, and personalised learning

These schools offer flexible, targeted curriculum and instruction. Both the content of the curriculum and the structure of the school day can be modified to meet emerging needs. Though the environment seems to be highly structured and stable, there is much flexibility and openness to opportunity.

School B, for example, has enhanced student learning opportunity by:

- condensing Key Stage 3 to two years and extending Key Stage 4 to three years;

- revamping its schedule, starting the school day later in response to parental urging and opening up a two-hour block on alternate Tuesdays for curriculum and instruction meetings;

- giving staff an extra three days holiday per year,

- focusing on underperforming students by developing after-school classes and homework clubs, providing help from classroom support assistants, creating a "learning zone" resource centre, night clubs to provide support instruction, and better communication with parents;

- creating further choice and individualisation in the curriculum through four distinct "curriculum pathways" and a personalised learning agenda with nine "gateways" (Hargreaves, D.H., 2004);

- broadening its supply through the Trust Status partnership among several schools in the region, which gives students in that community access at one of the participating schools to special studies and specialised diplomas that any one school could not provide.

School A also highlighted that it is always looking for ways to serve students "on the cusp of disengagement". It seeks to identify students prone to criminality, dropping out, misbehaviour, and underperforming and to provide challenges and support to engage them. A network supports all students, ensuring that they attend regularly, feel a part of the community, and are engaged in their classes. Intervention teams mentor students or provide additional study out of class. The integrated services of the "extended school" meet a range of special needs. Prevention is emphasised; the school tries to create a culture where asking for help is "OK". School staff told us that they are "creating the maximum amount of flexibility for the child who could not cope with the standard or regular classroom or programme".

Flexibility in curriculum and instruction is supported by observation of classroom practices, which seemed to be widespread. At school setting A, we were told that an open door policy ensures that there are frequent visitors to each classroom for observation and comment. A three-member team observes teaching, learning, and behaviour in the classroom.

School A seeks to identify students prone to criminality, dropping out, misbehaviour, and underperforming and to provide challenges and support to engage them.

Teachers and department heads at school B described to us the change in teachers' attitudes toward observation that had taken place in the past five or six years. Once, the idea of being observed would have raised their hackles. Now teachers are open to it; they expect and want to be observed. Teachers are observed by their head of department at least once every half-term, and are also seen by their mentors. Classrooms are also observed weekly by the touring senior leadership team. Where observations indicate the need for help, peer observers, coaches, and Advanced Skills Teachers can provide constructive intervention.

Once, the idea of being observed by colleagues or school leaders in class would have raised teachers' hackles. Now teachers are open to it; they expect and want to be observed.

Leadership development and leadership distribution

Leadership in both schools is provided through a richly textured fabric of formal and informal roles and responsibilities. In fact, leadership development in these schools is not a separate activity but an essential element of the school's work to promote students' achievement and well-being. The schools had different structures for organising and focusing the work of leaders and for identifying, developing, and making best use of leadership talent among teachers, staff, and administrators.

In school setting B, for example, leadership and management tasks are distributed across an estimated 30 individuals serving on the senior leadership team (SLT), middle managers, learning managers, and the management team. These are augmented by teacher leaders serving as Advanced Skills Teachers and others who teach in the Training School and who volunteer to serve on school inspection teams and bring back valuable knowledge and experience. Some heads of department are invited to serve on the SLT, bringing important contributions and taking valuable leadership experience. These roles are rotated so many are given exposure and opportunity to develop.

The school takes risks and reaches far to identify and create opportunity for leaders to develop. When the learning manager role was established, the head gradually promoted non-teachers from other roles, including classroom aides and parent volunteers. Some in the school said this approach wouldn't work but it has been a success. The two assistant head teachers we interviewed described how they matured in other roles in the school, were given increasing levels of decision-making responsibility in lesser roles, and then grew into the assistant head role from which they were invited to serve a rotating term on SLT. Cross-training and shared responsibilities are a valuable result: "We know each other's business. We can step in for each other and not lose a beat. In our environment with the momentum and urgency of the press for achievement, this is essential."

Promising teachers and staff can be developed through the Developing Leaders Programme. Participants stress that the leadership is distributed in a structure that evolves as circumstances dictate. One person described it as cone-shaped, smaller at the top and bigger at the bottom but all the time expanding at both ends. One assistant head teacher was at one time also a head of year and had the job of managing the heads of year. These were difficult roles for her and for them, as both had both teaching as well as management duties. The school's response was to eliminate the heads of year and create the team of seven learning managers described above.

A variety of training programmes help foster leadership capacity in teachers and staff who show promise or inclination at different levels: aspiring heads, developing leaders, middle leaders and established leaders.

These schools are the victims of their success, seen by other schools as training grounds for their own future leaders. However, they see losing staff promoted to positions in other schools as a source of pride rather than distress, and the benefits in reputation and morale and effectiveness are said to outweigh any loss.

System leadership in practice

It is the English government's view that achieving its core education priorities requires meeting key systems conditions. First, each school must work with partners such as another school, a local college, or an employer institution. Second, because projections show that there will not be enough well-qualified heads in the coming years, the most effective school leaders will have to share their expertise with other schools. Heads committed to serving in a system leadership capacity can use a number of government programmes designed to foster school improvement through partnering arrangements and shared leadership of various sorts. School A and school B have done this.

Partnering and the sharing of leadership come in many forms. Here we describe several kinds of school collaborations and partnerships – often in combination – involving school A and school B.

Under the federation between school A1 and school A2, school A1's leadership and proven systems were extended to school A2. School A1's head teacher first assumed authority over school A2. School A2's head welcomed the help and signed on as deputy. Over several challenging months, the new leadership duo introduced school A1's vision of change, adopted its management matrix, replaced low performing teachers, and built up small successes creating a "can-do" culture. The leadership team at school A1 was able to cope with its head's absence at school A2. The governing bodies have been merged, and soon the schools will be reorganised as two Academies, one serving ages 11 to 14 and the other 15 to 19. Leaders from both schools point out that school A1 surrendered any superior or dominant role and left room for its partner to blossom. This was made possible by the shared understanding and support for common vision across both schools.

Additional testimony for the efficacy of federations came from our meeting with a director of children's services at a local authority, which showed that federations allow for pooling and broadening of curricula. Systems and leadership can be transferred from one school to another without reinventing the wheel or imposing outside change on the school. A federation is more attractive to candidates than a single struggling school, so teacher recruitment is easier. Tackling tough gaps in achievement can be helped by aggregated data and joint strategies. Such collaboration can also be accomplished in "soft" federations involving no formal budgetary or governance integration; over time as they succeed and the relationship grows, federations that bring in new partners and funding will help institutionalise the partnership and sustain change.

School B had also taken advantage of a number of opportunities for working and collaborating with other schools. A special grant enabled the head and four other school heads to meet regularly, to share students in immersion programmes offered by the schools, and even to share staff. A structure called Learning Gateways provides the means for identifying places and opportunities for the schools to collaborate.

Box 5.4 Benefits of collaboration

The collaborating head teachers spoke enthusiastically about the benefits of collaboration. They told us that it makes no sense to operate as islands, when they can pool resources for the benefits of their students. Sharing resources and ideas helps them face the many demands on their time and energy, as mutual support helps them cope with hard times. Their varied perspectives are useful in finding ways to work through complex problems. One of the heads "loves data"; another "hates it", and leans on her colleague for help with statistics. In exchange, she offers expertise in workforce development. Such collaboration cannot be forced; it must grow voluntarily as trust and common vision develop. Because the success of collaboration rests on trusting relationships developed over time, it's important that heads remain in their positions long enough to build those relationships.

A special grant enabled the head of school B and four other school heads to meet regularly, to share students in immersion programmes offered by the schools, and even to share staff.

Five schools in the region also collaborate in the Leading Edge Partnership. Each of these schools is a specialist school, meaning that each has adopted a particular academic focus in which it has specialised. School B, for example, has developed technology as its specialism. Trust Status is conferred by the government on schools that create partnerships with foundations or other private and public entities (businesses, universities) to operate as independent state schools. State funding is the same as for other schools but Trust schools have the long-term benefits of sustained partnership with a particular focus such as school improvement. School B and its school partners are considering applying for Trust status to help all of them to take advantage of the individual school specialisms, contributing higher levels of expertise and resources in areas like business studies or technology, and permitting students to cross-register in courses across the partnership.

Both schools are recognised for their leadership practices and are able to share and transfer experience as lead schools in different areas (Box 5.2), such as Excellence

Cluster lead schools, Raising Attainment and Transforming Learning (RATL) schools, or as National Leader in Education support schools.

Interviewees, but also research and experience from other school contexts, give evidence of numerous advantages of collaboration. Among them are: reduction teachers' feelings of isolation; shared responsibility for students´ learning, development, and achievement; effective learning processes; the awareness of being part of a teaching and learning community; greater acceptance of continuing professional development; greater professional satisfaction; and motivation to contribute to school development processes.

Federations can also save costs through sharing of equipment and of personnel, *e.g.* in cleaning and catering, and teaching staff (*e.g.* supply teachers expert staff in specific subject areas). Students benefit from specific courses that could not have been offered by the schools individually (*e.g.* evening sessions). Collaboration among schools sometimes enables them to benefit from funded programmes that they would not have had access to individually. Finally, by creating knowledge pools through the collaboration of experts, and by creating a culture of exchange and feedback, their practices help improve quality.

Benefits of federations include: cost savings through sharing of equipment and personnel; access to a wider range of courses for students; and a culture of knowledge exchange and feedback, which can help improve quality.

However, fruitful collaboration has a number of pre-requisites. Among them are the participation of staff in decision making, a feeling of ownership, suitable timetables (offering time for communication and exchange), the voluntary involvement of the stakeholders, the willingness of the individual to get involved in change, and above all, mutual respect and acceptance of each other's competences.

Different layers of leadership: individual, distributed, and system

These cases demonstrate ways in which school leaders can shift from management to leadership. We see in them concrete illustration of the practices and characteristics identified formally in the research literature on leadership in the UK (PriceWaterhouseCoopers, 2007; Matthews, undated; HayGroup, 2002) and more broadly.

Professional leadership

The leaders of both schools we visited were professional leaders. Each had a strong vision of the school – its purpose and outcomes, values, and character — and had managed to persuade others to follow. At the same time, they demonstrated a commitment to distributing leadership through empowerment, trust, sharing, delegation, and creating opportunities for development of others. Our visits provided examples of the pursuit of their goals and seemingly endless supply of energy. Both were advocates for their visions and remarkable change agents.

In both schools we saw extensive groupings of leaders reaching well down into the school, opportunities for formal professional development, and a strong emphasis on the development of a deep cadre of formal and informal leaders from within.

These leaders practised what researchers have defined as strong leadership (Leithwood and Riehl, 2003). Their visions are achievable and motivating, they *set direction*. Then the leaders go beyond inspiring and motivating; they *develop people*. They expend a great deal of their time and energy helping others grow professionally by creating opportunity, delegating, giving feedback, coaching, and providing formal training. Recognising the synergy that must exist between workers and organisation, they have worked hard to *redesign the organisation*. Both *core technology*, the technical processes concerning effective teaching and learning, and the *structure and processes*, the framework of roles and responsibilities, time and space, and standard operating procedures, have been reshaped to support the goals of student learning.

A further characterisation of the principal's role emphasises strategic leadership. Their work is strategic in two dimensions:

- working with the school community to delineate a clear vision and mission for the school and to align the operation of the school to serve the vision and mission;

- managing the school's relationship with its environment (school district or municipality, other schools, parents and community, business community, research and knowledge resources, and sources of external funding and technical assistance), primarily through collaborations to obtain or align with resources in the larger environment to help the school achieve its mission.

Strategic leadership in this sense is directed at obtaining from the environment those resources and support that are necessary for the school's success. The more systemic dimension of leadership that aims to export the school's expertise and resources to support the larger system will be explored below.

Distributed leadership and internal leadership development

It does not seem possible to have effective system leadership without a foundation of effective leadership distributed throughout the school. By distributed leadership we mean the allocation of formal and informal leadership roles and responsibilities to members of the school community (teachers and staff primarily, but parents, community members and students as well) to take advantage of expertise in the pursuit of the school's mission. Thus in both schools we saw extensive groupings of leaders reaching well down into the school, opportunities for formal professional development, and a strong emphasis on the development of a deep cadre of formal and informal leaders from within.

In school B, for example, leadership and management tasks are distributed across an estimated 30 individuals serving on the SLT, middle managers, learning managers, and the management team, as described in the previous section. There seemed to be a striking density of leadership throughout the organisation. Staff were integrally involved because they appreciated that they were important in the organisation. The effects of this approach to distributed leadership seem to include a reduction of workload and stress for the individual, a fostering of quality through the feedback systems in place, and engagement to create everyone's commitment.

Heads of school and others stressed the importance of respect and support for those taking leadership risks in their own leadership and in developing it in others. At the same time, all were held accountable, expected to do their best at all times and to learn from mistakes. Failure was tolerated as a necessary part of learning.

System leadership

System leaders are said to find that it is not possible to be fully effective if they do not treat their school as one part of a larger system. The larger system includes the parents and community the school serves and other schools in and beyond the community, as well as the Ministry and other organisations aiming to inspire and support school improvement. To judge from school settings A and B, each school and its leader(s) take an approach to system leadership that draws on its particular strengths and abilities. While there is no single formula for success at system leadership, there are common ingredients.

A school is part of a larger system which includes the parents and community the school serves, other schools in and beyond the community, the Ministry and other organisations.

The Hay Group's (2002) study of system leadership (which includes school setting A) identifies leadership qualities and systems that account for successful partnerships. One set of characteristics seems to speak especially to the notion of system leadership:

- Continually promote the vision of successful education.

- Think beyond the immediate canvas (of school A1 and school A2).

- Believe that anything is possible.

- Respect the system but do not be limited by it.

- Grow staff and involve them on this larger canvas.

System leaders appear to exhibit many of the same qualities and practices they exercise in their own schools. However, they apply them on a larger scale.

System leaders have a view of the way their schools fit into and are affected by the larger system. The principals of school A1 and school B are teachers and coaches of change. As transformational leaders (see Leithwood and Jantzi, 1990; 2005), they are dedicated to supporting the community in the quest to reach a vision for that community. Seeking to create collaborative school cultures, they teach, or arrange for others to teach, the skills and dispositions needed for the community's new work. They create the supportive emotional and intellectual environment and provide the coaching the community needs.

System leaders have achieved success in their own schools, and their results and methods have been vetted against benchmarks and research-based practice. No two systems are identical, and no one system can be successful simply by adopting another school's successful practices (see Berman and McLaughlin, 1978; McLaughlin, 1990). Successful practices must be adapted in and to the receiving context. More than the skill of replication, then, the system leader needs what Portin and colleagues (2003) have identified as a particular form of contextual literacy and problem-solving capacity, as well as skill in transformational and adaptive practices. The OECD team was struck by the comprehensive, fully elaborated systems in use at school A1 and school B not only for their own operation but also for managing their partnerships with other schools.

As a final observation about system leadership, it seemed to the team that the principals we met with were dedicated to what Elmore (Chapter 3) has termed "the practice of improvement". School heads occupy a lonely position; practitioners frequently mention the physical, emotional, and mental isolation of the job. It can be easy to seek refuge in the certainties of given structures and long-established practices. Heads reported to us that their partnerships helped them to challenge assumptions and set aside things that didn't work. The new perspectives and emotional support of partnerships can thus help in rethinking the work of schools and leadership and bringing new mental models and approaches, sometimes posing uncomfortable threats to current practice, to bear.

5.5 Food for thought

In England, there have been many changes for schools in recent years. Much responsibility has been transferred to them framed in a system of standards, assessment, evaluation and accountability. The recent government five year strategy focuses on improving standards for all, closing the achievement gap, and promoting choice and opportunity among a diverse student body by preventing dropouts and preparing all students for a successful transition to work or further education. To attain these objectives, many different programmes and approaches have been set into motion for schools. A focus on leadership has also been at the core of reform. The creation of the NCSL and the different training and development programmes available for all levels of leadership have contributed to a more professional culture of school leadership. Many opportunities for co-operation and collaboration are working towards ensuring that "every school is a great school".

The creation of the NCSL and the different training and development programmes available for all levels of leadership have contributed to a more professional culture of school leadership.

Strengths

The systemic agenda has been permeating the English school system and from what the OECD team was able to see, it is having a positive impact on leadership and on school performance.

A broad policy framework guides large-scale reform in education

Levin (2001) has observed that three strategies typically constitute contemporary large-scale, governmental reform programmes: decentralisation, increased testing and centralised curriculum, and public choice and other market mechanisms. However effective such strategies may be on their own, additional elements are needed. A balanced reciprocal relationship must exist between accountability and support for reform (Elmore, 2000; see also Chapter 3), which implies that support for the change process as well as efforts to learn from it are essential (see Berman and McLaughlin, 1978). Education policy must originate in the practice of teaching (Elmore and McLaughlin, 1988).

The English approach combining decentralisation and accountability, supporting infrastructure, and incentives for local innovation and leadership supported by targeted funding seems to the visiting team to exemplify much of the best of current wisdom about large-scale school reform. A comprehensive policy framework grounded on state-of-the-art research provides coherent direction, incentives, capacity building and support for broad-based, systemic change. Refinements in policy based on cycles of implementation and feedback seemed to have produced increasingly sophisticated and responsive practices. This comprehensive reform framework should be continued in its present broad outlines.

System leadership is an effective mechanism for reaching key policy aims

System leadership is helping to boost school performance, support reforms across schools, spread leadership expertise more broadly, and provide for leadership succession. System leadership seems to be an especially effective tool for managing in environments of overload and fragmentation that are characteristic of all contemporary complex social systems. Our observations of the system leaders confirm Fullan's (2000) description of the three "stories" describing how coherence is brought to a disjointed system. Effective schools change their internal dynamics by functioning as collaborative schools (the "inside story"), deal with the forces that press on them from outside by forming partnerships (the "inside-outside story"), and benefit from the organisation of an "external infrastructure of reform" among agencies beyond the school (the "outside-inside story"). These stories are vividly portrayed in our two case schools' workings as high performance learning communities, in their extensive relationships with their environments through partnerships and networks, and their interactions with the extensive infrastructure of support for reform comprising the SSAT, NCSL, other organisations, and a variety of targeted funding and other initiatives. System leadership succeeds by co-ordinating three domains — the high performance learning community of the school, the school's immediate environment including community, other schools, and corporations, for example, and the larger "external reform infrastructure" (see Fullan, 1999, 2000).

When we refer to system leaders or leadership, we should emphasise that we mean less the actions of individual leaders than the combination of the actions of individuals and groups of leaders in the context of a highly supportive infrastructure.

The schools visited had achieved impressive results in student and school performance, fostering improvement in federated schools, and transferring skilled personnel and innovative practice to the broader system. We saw evidence that these results have been substantially facilitated by recent English policy initiatives. Such anecdotal evidence is echoed more solidly in a variety of evaluations and reports brought to the visiting team's attention (see for example Matthews, undated; Matthews *et al.*, 2006; PricewaterhouseCoopers, 2007; Specialist Schools and Academies Trust, 2008).

System leaders seem to portray the characteristics of high performing leadership

System leadership seemed to the OECD team to characterise not just a cadre of leaders "willing to shoulder system leadership roles" but rather to define the ideal of practice for all school leaders. The attitudes and values, the skills and dispositions, and the collaborative, systemic practices of "system leaders" are required of all school leaders who will work in the system that is intended to be put in place under the current reforms.

The attitudes and values, the skills and dispositions, and the collaborative, systemic practices of "system leaders" are required of all school leaders.

The common positive characteristics we found in the case studies we visited were:

- *Core purpose of school:* Both schools have a clear focus on the core purpose of school, namely teaching and learning. Every effort made by people involved in the school is expected to fit this focus.

- *Outcome- and performance orientation:* Both schools are focused on school outcome and pupils' attainment. They aim not only at cognitive achievements but at more holistic outcomes, as cognitive, emotional and social outcomes are interdependent and only achieved in a reciprocal process in addressing them comprehensively. Both schools focus on high performance using a challenging learning-centred model based on a strong and shared belief that every pupil can learn.

- *Individual approach to improve learning outcomes through intensive use of data:* Both schools have a pervasive use of data; they use a rigorous approach of systematically and regularly collecting data from all pupils across all subject areas. In both, information is revisited every six weeks. The database provides the possibility to analyse individual developments and to identify needs of action.

- *Evaluation and assessment:* The schools have a culture of constant assessment. In both schools classrooms are open for collegial and senior visits. Teachers are ready to be observed and to get feedback. Assessment in these schools does not stop with the pupils but includes the teachers' teaching/instruction. There is a feedback system about the work of management and leadership, too. Both schools seem to have established a system of monitoring and feedback involving the whole school.

- *Resource-oriented approach:* The schools aim to use evaluation and assessment as a basis for positive reinforcement of the individual achievements of both pupils and staff, leading to further improvement. This positive resource-orientation seems to be a necessary requirement for learning and change processes.

- *Professional development:* In both schools, professional development of staff is high on the agenda. The professional development is most often needs-oriented in-house training. They also try to develop and enlarge the school's leadership capacity through leadership experiences linked to training and development opportunities. This mixed approach of development and practical experience seems to have sustainable effects.

- *Co-operation and collaboration:* In both school settings, "co-operation and collaboration" seem to be very important. The schools' leaders aim to empower people within the school, supporting work in teams, among the pupils as well as the staff.

The reforms are contributing to build different types of leadership capacity across the system

In order fully to appreciate the effectiveness and potential of the English policy framework, it is necessary to understand two broad conditions of contemporary social systems. First, leadership operates in a complex social system characterised by overload and extreme fragmentation (Fullan, 1999; 2000), in a strategic environment characterised by volatility, uncertainty, complexity, and ambiguity (Knowlton, 2003). Second, the nature of the work of education systems is intensive (Thompson, 1967) and self-organising (Fullan, 2000). Each leadership act or pedagogical decision produces a new set of conditions for which a new set of responses is needed, much as the rock climber's choice in solving one problem presented by the rock face creates a new situation with new problems to be worked out. Such systems can only be controlled to a limited extent. Beyond that, incentives, capacity, and support are needed to engender innovation and improvement and in particular to link them in ongoing cycles of learning and improvement.

System leadership can ensure a distribution of leadership throughout school and larger system levels and by stimulating the development of the schools' and system's learning communities.

Systemic reform can be thought of as a form of distributed leadership carried out at the systems level. A considerable list of new roles is developing for system leaders, and many parts of the system have roles to play and the expertise and capacity to carry them out. A shared understanding of the direction of the whole system and the place of individual parts in the overall system fosters a process of ongoing co-ordination of efforts characterised by initiative, distributed decision-making, local experimentation, pervasive and timely communication, and self-organised improvement.

The particular power of system leadership is that it ameliorates or overcomes the "overload and extreme fragmentation" characteristic of complex social systems including education. Only strategic leadership can manage systems volatility, uncertainty, complexity, and ambiguity.

One implication of seeing system leadership as a powerful form of distributed leadership at the systems level is that both additive and concertive dimensions (Gronn, 2002) should be nourished. Most emphasis currently seems to be on the additive side, that is, on defining and fitting leaders for new roles as system leaders. Over time, the emphasis should shift to the concertive side, that is, to creating widespread common understanding of the system purpose and direction, encouraging initiative and experimentation, promoting communication and feedback throughout the system, and strengthening the skills and capacity of all leaders potentially to serve as system leaders.

System leadership also implies learning communities. A learning community may be thought of as a setting that makes "deliberate use of individual, group, and system learning to embed new thinking and practices and continuously renew and transform the organisation in ways that support shared aims" (Collinson and Cook, 2006, p. 8). Elements of a learning community encountered in this case include leadership as the "practice of improvement" (Elmore, Chapter 3), based on a disposition to challenge regularities of schooling; professional norms of collegiality and experimentation (Little, 1982), professional community (Louis *et al.*, 1996; 1997); communication and continuous improvement around progress in reaching objectives; and a balance of accountability and support (Elmore, Chapter 3). The distribution of leadership that orchestrates the learning is both a cause and consequence of the functions of the learning community.

System leadership fosters initiative, distributed decision-making, local experimentation, pervasive and timely communication, and self-organised improvement.

New paradigms of leadership and schooling

Not only do system leadership, distributed leadership, and learning organisations promise more effective forms of leadership, but implicit within these leadership and school practices is to be found a new logic of school effectiveness and social innovation.

Contemporary education must respond to a new set of requirements in which ongoing and rapid change replaces sameness, individualisation and personalisation supplant uniform programmes, and teacher autonomy yields to professional teacher community. The new pedagogy of deep learning, development of higher order thinking skills, and teaching for understanding requires flexibility, creativity, and inspired experimentation in teaching and learning (Sims, 2006). Resources and work processes formerly managed through hierarchical control systems must now be directed through shared vision and organisational learning. According to systems thinker Peter Senge (2000), this change has occurred along four dimensions, from:

- organisations as machines to organisations as living systems;

- fragmentation to relatedness;

- deficit to developmental thinking;

- acceptance of what is to questioning of what is, why, and what else could be.

Contemporary education is characterised by ongoing and rapid change, personalisation and professional teacher community.

Distributed leadership is intrinsic to these new dimensions and modes of schooling. While the elaboration of formal roles is one aspect of distributed leadership, its more powerful aspect is to embody and enable collective, emergent activity at the core of school learning communities. System leadership may start in the individual school but extends to broader levels of the education system including other schools and governance levels.

Learning organisations like the schools we visited show that where shared understanding of mission and goals, distribution of work, and abundant communication are at play, quality of decision-making and co-ordination of teaching and learning far surpass what is possible under a control regime.

Finally, system leadership implies the transference of capacity rather than scaling up of products and innovations. Because "going to scale" runs headlong into the same conditions of overload and fragmentation, that limit centrally mandated reform, what must be moved from one place to another, from the more to the less successful sites, is capacity and not products or particular innovations. Capacity means understanding the objectives, values, and principles of effective practice, of relevant knowledge, skills and dispositions, and of distributed work within a learning community, all supported by resources to help the system through the adaptive process. System leadership is a powerful tool for building and distributing capacity in the system.

System leadership is a powerful tool for building and distributing capacity in the system.

Towards further progress

The visiting team also identified several topics where further attention may lead to greater sustainability of the systemic approach to school improvement.

Balance continuous improvement and maintenance

The government of the English education system has a strong framework for large-scale education reform, which appears to be working. At the same time, the sheer number of initiatives and programmes and the speed at which schools are expected to implement them may be counterproductive. True improvement results from a balance of making best use of innovative ideas and concepts on the one hand and maintaining proven ones on the other.

Focus should be on making improvements to the current framework on the basis of experience and feedback. Care should be taken to limit introduction of new initiatives that increase the overload and fragmentation experienced by school leaders and communities. For the schools themselves, an important task is to carefully consider what they should maintain in order not to run the risk of losing something valuable and effective while making efforts to keep up with all these innovations.

Continue to adjust the balance between accountability and school autonomy

It is important that reform support complements standards, testing, and accountability; experience will suggest ways in which the balance needs to be adjusted. For example, introducing school self-evaluation and improvement planning has been greeted as a positive development. Greater emphasis on systematic self-evaluation and less on external Ofsted evaluation, and continuing to refine the targeting of external evaluations seems to be warranted.

Strengthen the capacity of governing bodies and local authorities to support school improvement

School governing bodies are of uneven capacity and appear to have a mixed record of success in supporting school improvement. Training, capacity building, and networking can improve their ability to meet national policy goals as well as local priorities.

Local authorities have lost some of their traditional roles and gained broad new responsibilities for school improvement planning and extended services, among others. While there is need to respect the authorities' distinct regional character, there is also a need to reduce variations in quality and capacity, and to ensure that all agencies can carry out their remits at a high level of performance.

Emphasise leadership development at the school level

The visiting team was impressed at the two case study schools' success in developing leadership internally. These new leaders fuel local school improvement, and also contribute to improvements in partnered or networked schools; many then serve as higher-level leaders in yet other schools. Some of this school-level leadership development is conducted in collaboration with the NCSL and/or SSAT. These evidently highly effective forms of leadership development have the potential to ameliorate the anticipated leadership succession problem.

Make more explicit use of principles of high performance learning communities

The case study schools exemplify high performance learning organisations. Learning communities combine strong formal leadership, distributed leadership, powerful systems focusing the work of the organisation on quality teaching and learning, teacher professional community, and modes of communication and continuous learning that foster steady improvements in performance. These factors interact to create capacity for high performance. The job of the leader and the focus of the larger system should be to develop such capacity. Teachers, governing bodies, local authorities, and community leaders as well as school leaders should understand the principles and operation of high performance learning organisations and have the knowledge, skills, and dispositions to make their schools function as high performance learning organisations.

Balance the sense of urgency for reform with a realistic understanding of the time needed for successful change

Some UK experts told the visiting team that individual underperforming schools can be turned around in one year. Fullan (1999) states that reform of an elementary school ordinarily takes about three years and that, depending on size, around six years are needed at the secondary level. Large-scale, second-order system change, where fundamental values and beliefs must change, may take a full generation. While some successes can be achieved in the short term, there will be harder nuts to crack that resist short-term results. Levin (2001) encourages system leaders to acknowledge the magnitude of the task and to work for small, achievable wins that buoy spirits, confirm policy directions, and generate learning needed for cracking the harder cases.

Include training for system leadership in the different stages of teacher and leadership training

Training for system leadership should start with teacher education and continue in school leader preparation and training and thereafter during professional development for teachers and other leaders. System leaders, distributed leadership, and learning organisations accomplish levels of performance that are not possible in settings where these elements are lacking. Training programmes should be redeveloped: reorganising their conventional content under these newer concepts; and introducing new behaviours, skills, and dispositions entailed in these processes.

Develop new forms of accountability and financial support for system leadership.

Modes of accountability and financing suited to conventional leadership and schooling may not be suited to system leadership. Where the efforts of more than one leader and indeed an entire school community are responsible for the successes (and failures) of the school or federation, accountability must be shared. Incentives and rewards for performance, as well as sanctions, will be most effective and fair when they apply to all who are responsible for school performance.

By the same token, methods of supporting system leadership may need to be reconsidered both to ensure that those who bear greater burdens or take greater responsibility are suitably compensated and that systems that share and benefit from the contributions of system leaders are paying fairly.

Use system leadership to enhance the move to collaboration instead of competition?

The times of an extremely competition-oriented relationship among schools seem to be over. The rather market-driven competition in the education sector typical of England for some time was disapproved of by many practitioners and educationalists. There are challenges in converting a competitive culture to one of collaboration. But a new widening of perspective and a focus on mutual responsibility and collaboration among schools are most welcome from an educational point of view and can contribute to change the educational landscape to make "every school a great school".

A new widening of perspective and a focus on mutual responsibility and collaboration among schools can help to make "every school a great school".

Annex 5.A1
Case study visit programme
30 October - 2 November 2006

Monday 30 October 2006, London, Department for Education and Skills

Time	Name	Post	Notes
10.00-11.00	Laura Cunningham	Team Leader Leadership Policy Team, DfES	
11.00-12.00	Peter Wanless	Director School Standards Groups, DfES	Wider view of system reform on improving standards
12.00-13.15	Lunch		
13.15-14.00	Peter Mathews	Ex Ofsted Inspector and Consultant (London Challenge, Primary Strategy)	
14.00-15.00	David Crossley	Specialist Schools and Academics Trust	
	Sir Ian Hall	Headteacher Training and Future Leaders Programme	
15.00-15.45	Toby Salt	Strategic Director for School Leadership Development, NCSL	Overview of NCSL. Different things to influence leadership
15.45-16.30	John Dunford	General Secretary, Association of School and College Leaders	
16.30 - 17.15	Ralph Tabberer	Director General Schools Directorate DfES	Delivering strategies for improving education.

Tuesday 31 October 2006, Outwood Grange College, Wakefield, W. Yorkshire

Time	Post
08.30 – 09.30	Headteacher
09.30 – 10.30	Headteachers of Wakefield Schools
10.30 – 11.00	Assistant Heads
11.00 – 11.30	Heads of Department
11.30 – 12.00	Associate Assistant Heads
12.30 – 13.00	Parent Governors. Student council members
13.00 – 13.30	Developing young leaders (SSAT)
13.30 – 14.00	Community representatives
14.00 – 14.30	Chair of Governors. Vice-Chair of Governors
14.30 – 15.15	Head of Training School. Consultant to Senior Leadership Team

Wednesday 1 November 2006, Federation of Chalvedon School and Sixth Form College and Barstable School in Basildon, Essex

Time	Post
08.30	Introductory presentation and discussion with Principal
09.15	Tour of Chalvedon with retired VP
09.55	Discussion with pupils and students
10.15	Principal's leadership behaviours –discussion with Management Consultant
11.00	Early collaboration; Trainee Heads Programme; Local Delivery; EEBP – presentation and discussion by/with Associate Principal
11.45	The Matrix – presentation by the Federative SMT
12.30	Governance – discussion with the Chair of Governors
12.50	Lunch
13.20	LEA perspective – discussion with a School Improvement Partner
13.40	Teaching and non-teaching staff. – discussion with retired VP, partner company representative, caretaker, catering employee
14.00	Travel to Barstable. Tour of Barstable with Associate Principal
14.50	Discussion with pupils
15.10	Academies Programme

Thursday 2 November 2006

Time	Post	
8.15 - 9:15	Frankie Sulke, Director of Children Services for Lewisham Local Authority	Combined post of Director of Education and of Children Services: to clarify innovation at the local authority level and system reform.

Annex 5.A2.
List of abbreviations

ARU	Anglia Ruskin University
EAL	English as an additional Language (provision for children whose first language is not English)
ECDL	European Computer driving License
ECM	Every child matters
EWO	Education Welfare Officer
FFT	Fisher Family Trust
GT	Graduate Trainee
HLTA	Higher Level Teaching assistant
LAP	Learning Assistant Programme
MA	Multi Agency
MidYIS scores	Middle Year information system scores (a test to develop ability, a measure which relies on pupils general experiences and their ability to acquire knowledge and solve problems rather than what they are been taught at school)
NVQ	National Vocational Qualification
PANDA	Performance AND Assessment
PGCE	Post Graduate Certificate in Education
QL	Quantum Learning
SEN	Special Education Needs
SSCo	School Sports Coordinators

References

Barber, M. (2001), "Large-scale Education Reform in England: A Work in Progress", paper prepared for the School Development conference, Tartu, Estonia.

Berman, P. and M. McLaughlin (1978), *Federal Programs Supporting Educational Change, Vol. VIII, Implementing and Sustaining Innovations*, R-1589/8-HEW, report prepared for the US Department of Health, Education, and Welfare, Rand Corporation, Santa Monica, CA.

Collinson, V. and T. Cook (2006), *Organizational Learning: Improving Learning, Teaching, and Leading in School Systems*, Sage Publications, Thousand Oaks, CA.

DCSF (Department of Children, Schools, and Families) (2007a), *The Standards Site, The National Strategies Primary*, viewed 14 September 2007 at *www.standards.dfes.gov.uk/primary/about/*.

DCSF (2007b), *The Standards Site, The National Strategies Secondary Key Stage 3*, viewed 14 September 2007 at *www.standards.dfes.gov.uk/primary/about/*.

DCSF (2007c), *Statutory Guidance for Schools Causing Concern*, viewed 15 July 15 at *www.standards.dfes.gov.uk/sie/documents/2007SCCGuidance.doc*.

DCSF (2007d), *Support for Schools Causing Concern: Contributions from National Strategies Programmes*, 2006-2007, viewed 15 July 15, 2007 at *www.standards.dfes.gov.uk/sie/documents/nssup.doc*.

DfES (Department for Education and Skills) (2004), *National Standards for Headteachers*, reference 0083/2004, Department for Education and Skills.

Elmore, R. (2000), *Building a New Structure for School Leadership*, The Albert Shanker Institute, Washington, DC.

Elmore, R. and M. McLaughlin (1988), *Steady Work: Policy, Practice, and the Reform of American Education*, Rand Corporation, Santa Monica, CA.

Fullan, M. (1999), *Change Forces: The Sequel*, Falmer Press, London.

Fullan, M. (2000), "The Three Stories of Education Reform", *Phi Delta Kappan*, April, pp. 581-584.

Gronn, P. (2002), "Distributed Leadership", in Leithwood, K. and P. Hallinger (eds.), *Second International Handbook of Educational Leadership and Administration*, Springer International Handbooks of Education, vol. 8, Springer, New York, NY, pp. 653-696.

Hargreaves, D.H. (2004), *Personalising learning: Next steps in working laterally*, Specialist Schools and Academies Trust, London.

Hay Group (2002), Maverick, *Breakthrough Leadership that Transforms Schools*, An Exploratory Study by the Hay Group, available at *www.transforminglearning.co.uk/research.*

Hopkins, D. (2006), "Realising the Potential of System Reform" in Daniels, H. , J;Porter and H. Lauder (eds.), *Companion in Education Series*, Routledge / Farmer, London.

Hopkins, D. (2007), "Sustaining Leaders for System Change", in B. Davies (ed.), *Developing Sustainable Leadership*, Paul Chapman Publishing, London, pp. 154-174.

Hopkins, D. and R. Higham, R. (2007), "System Leadership: Mapping the Landscape", *School Leadership & Management*, 27(2), pp. 147–166.

Huber, S.G. (1997), *Headteachers' Views on Headship and Training: A Comparison with the NPQH,* School of Education, University of Cambridge, Cambridge.

Knowlton, W. (2003), *Developing Strategic Leaders: Executive Assessment and Development*, PowerPoint presentation, Industrial College of the Armed Forces, National Defence University, Fort McNair, Washington, DC.

Levin, B. (2001), *Reforming Education: From Origins to Outcomes*, RoutledgeFalmer, London.

Leithwood, K. and D. Jantzi (1990), "Transformational Leadership: How Principals Can Help Reform School Cultures", *School Effectiveness and School Improvement*, 11 (4), pages 249-280.

Leithwood, K. and. D. Jantzi (2005), "Transformational leadership", in B. Davies (ed.), *The Essentials of School Leadership*, Paul Chapman Publishing and Corwin Press, London, pp. 31-43.

Leithwood, K. and C. Riehl (2003), *What We Know About Successful School Leadership*, Laboratory for Student Success, Temple University, Philadelphia, PA.

Little, J. (1982), "Norms of Collegiality and Experimentation: Workplace Conditions for School Success", *American Educational Research Journal*, 19 (3), pp. 325-340.

Louis, K., H. Marks and D. Kruse (1996), "School-Wide Professional Community", in Newmann, F. and Associates (eds.), *Authentic Achievement: Restructuring Schools for Intellectual Quality*, Jossey-Bass, San Francisco, CA.

Louis, K., H. Marks and D. Kruse (1997), "Teachers' Professional Community in Restructuring Schools", *American Educational Research Journal*, 33 (4), pp. 757-798.

Matthews, P. (undated), *Attributes of the First National Leaders of Education in England: What Do They Bring to the Role?*, National College for School Leadership, Nottingham.

Matthews, P., P. Scammons, Q. Gu, C. Day and P. Smith (2006), *Supporting Leadership and Securing Quality: An Evaluation of the Impact of Aspects of the London Leadership Strategy*, National College for School Leadership, Nottingham.

McLaughlin, M. (1990), "The RAND Change Agent Study Ten Years Later: Macro Perspectives and Micro Realities", paper based on address given at the Annual Meeting of the American Educational Research Association, San Francisco, CA, March 27-30, 1989, Center for Research on the Context of Secondary School Teaching, Report No. CRC-P89-108.

MORI (2005), *The State of School Leadership in England*, DfES Research Report 633

NCSL (2005), *Leadership in Complex Schools: Advice to the Secretary of State*, National College for School Leadership, Nottingham.

Portin, B., P. Schneider, M. DeArmond, L. Grundlachet (2003), *Making Sense of Leading Schools: A Study of the School Principalship*, Center on Reinventing Public Education, University of Washington, Seattle, Washington.

PricewaterhouseCoopers (PwC) (2007), *Independent Study into School Leadership: Main Report*, Department for Education and Skills, London, England.

Senge, P. (2000), *Systems Change in Education, Reflections*, Society for Organizational Learning, 1 (3).

Sims, E. (2006), *Deep learning – 1*, Specialist Schools and Academies Trust, London.

SSAT (Specialist Schools and Academies Trust) (2008), *The Long and Short of School Improvement: Summary of the Evaluation Report on the Raising Achievement Transforming Learning Project of the Specialist Schools and Academies Trust*, SSAT, London.

Thompson, J. (1967), *Organizations in Action: Social Science Bases of Administrative Theory*, McGraw Hill, New York.

Chapter 6

The Flemish (Belgian) approach to system leadership
by
Christopher Day, Jorunn Møller, Deborah Nusche and Beatriz Pont

This chapter aims to provide information and analysis on the "communities of schools", a particular Flemish approach to school leadership for systemic improvement. These communities are voluntary collaborative partnerships between schools. The government's objective when establishing them was to make schools collaborate to enhance student guidance systems, lessen the managerial-administrative burden on principals to allow more focus on pedagogical leadership, increase the use of ICT, and rationalise resources through collaboration on staff recruitment and course supply. The Flemish communities of schools were selected by the OECD Improving School Leadership activity as an innovative example of school leadership co-operation for improved schooling outcomes.

This chapter is based on a study visit to Flemish Belgium, organised by the Flemish Ministry of Education at OECD's request. The case study visit included meetings with stakeholders in Brussels and two site visits. The chapter outlines the reasons for exploring the Flemish approach to school leadership, describes the broader context within which the communities of schools operate, defines the communities of schools as a systems innovation, analyses the practice in terms of constructs and impact, and ends with some recommendations on how they can be made sustainable.

6.1 The OECD case study visit to Flemish Belgium

The Flemish communities of schools were selected by the OECD as an example of a systemic approach to school leadership, according to the defined criteria (see Chapter 1). From reading the literature and in discussions with Flemish representatives, it seemed that this approach would represent an example of how to develop models of school and school leadership co-operation for the benefit of students and school outcomes.

In Brussels, the OECD study team met with representatives from the Ministry of Work, Education and Training, the Christian Teaching Union, the group of Brussels community schools, the Antwerp City school system, and the umbrella organisation of Jesuit schools. The site visits covered a community of Catholic schools in Louvain and a community of former state schools in Willebroek. We thank all participants for their openness and engagement in discussions.

The study team's four members were: Dr. Christopher Day (Rapporteur), Professor of Education and Director of the Teacher and Leadership Research Centre (TLRC) at the University of Nottingham, UK; Dr. Jorunn Møller, Professor at the Department of Teacher Education and School Development, University of Oslo and Professor at the University of Tromsø, Norway; and two members of the OECD Secretariat, Beatriz Pont (team leader) and Deborah Nusche.

6.2 The Flemish context

Belgium is a federal state with three levels of government: the central state, the regions (the Flemish region, the Walloon region and the Brussels capital region) and the communities (the Dutch-speaking Flemish community, the French-speaking community and the German-speaking community). Education is under the control of the communities. Flanders has merged the Flemish region and community powers so as to create a single Flemish government, with its capital in Brussels. With 58% of the total population, Flanders is the largest Belgian community. It is densely populated and highly urbanised.

System governance

The Flemish education system is based on the constitutional principle of freedom of education, which guarantees every natural or legal person the right to establish and organise schools autonomously. Parents and students can choose any school they want and funding will follow the students. The Flemish Ministry of Education interferes only minimally in the organisation of schooling. It sets final attainment levels for students, provides a legal framework for schooling, and allocates funding for salaries.

Most Flemish schools and educational services are grouped into one of the following three networks (OECD, 2001; McKenzie *et al.*, 2004; Devos and Tuytens, 2006) (Figure 6.1):

- **Subsidised private schools:** Schools founded by private individuals or associations. The vast majority of these schools are linked to the Catholic church. Private schools enrol about 69% of students (OECD, 2001). Most of the school boards are linked to Catholic dioceses. The Catholic school boards are grouped under different umbrella organisations, such as the Jesuit or Salesian umbrella organisations. There are also a small number of non-Catholic private schools, including Protestant schools and schools following a specific educational method, such as Steiner or Freinet.

- **Community schools** (former state schools): Public-authority schools provided by the Flemish community government. These schools are required to be neutral in regard to religious or ideological views. They enrol about 14% of students (OECD, 2001). Within this network, the decision making power is held by school boards representing groups of up to 50 schools. At the central level, the groups of schools are represented by the community education board.

- **Subsidised public-sector schools:** Public-authority schools governed by municipal or provincial authorities. Religious and ideological neutrality is also required. They enrol about 17% of students (OECD, 2001). Within this network, the local authorities act as school boards. The school boards are grouped under two umbrella bodies: the Flemish Towns and Municipalities Education Secretariat, and Provincial Education Flanders.

School boards within each network enjoy far-reaching autonomy. In the Flemish system, a school board can be defined as the natural or legal person or group responsible for one or several educational establishments. The boards devise their own curricula, regulations, educational methods and personnel policies. Board members can be volunteers chosen by the parents or professionals paid by the networks. Schools within one geographical unit, such as a town or village, may be governed by different school boards, which can lead to a costly duplication of structures and a lack of co-operation between schools.

Figure 6.1 Governance of the Flemish education system

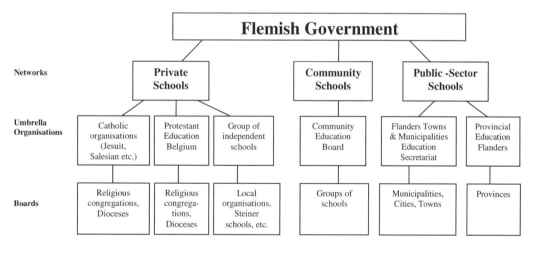

School leaders are in charge of their school under the supervision of the school board. Status, position, job description, selection, and training of school leaders vary according to the education network within which they work.

Funding

The financing scheme for schooling in Flanders is based on parental choice. The government finances teacher salaries according to the same criteria for all recognised (public and private) schools. Funding is based essentially on the number of students enrolled. Parents are treated as clients who choose the best quality school. As funding is calculated according to student numbers, the system favours schools that can attract and retain students. Traditionally, schools have thus competed for students and resources.

Assessment and evaluation

In Flanders, there are no standardised tests of learning outcomes, either in primary or in secondary education. Most people interviewed by us agreed that national testing was unnecessary and could potentially be harmful. School inspections are formative in nature and inspection reports are not written in a way that would allow for inter-school comparisons. There is no systematic evaluation of school leadership, and principals are not held accountable for student performance.

There is a growing emphasis on the principals' responsibility to monitor and evaluate teacher performance. But principals do not receive any kind of training to develop their skills in coaching teachers so as to improve students' learning outcomes. The largest teaching union, among others, suggests that the principals' increased responsibilities for teacher evaluation should be accompanied with increased principal training and preparation. Externally organised assessments such as PISA provide some information on the performance of Flemish students. Flemish PISA results stand out in two ways: on the one hand, students' mean PISA scores place the region within the group of highest performing countries for each subject area. On the other hand, Flanders is also characterised by a very wide distribution of achievement scores.

Equity issues

The 2003 PISA results show that there are very large differences between the strongest and the weakest students in Flanders. Belgium as a whole has the largest performance dispersion of all participating countries. Socio-economic status (SES) and language spoken at home have an important impact on the performance of Flemish students in the PISA tests (De Meyer *et al.*, 2005). The PISA results have raised concern about the tail of underachieving students in Flanders.

One of the factors leading to inequality seems to be the secondary education system, which streams students into three types of schools: academic, vocational and technical. Children with lower SES are overrepresented in vocational and technical schools, and there is an image of lower quality attached to these schools.

In practice, the principle of freedom of choice does not guarantee to parents that their children will actually be enrolled in the school of their choice. In prestigious and high achieving schools, the demand for enrolment often exceeds the schools' capacities, so parents may spend hours or even days at the school hoping to be able to register their children. The coordinator of Jesuit schools regretted that the "first come first served" system does not allow for positive discrimination.

School leadership framework

School leaders are appointed by the school boards. The only community-wide formal requirement for school leaders is to have a teaching qualification. The different school boards may set additional criteria. In most cases, school leaders are selected from the teaching staff in a rather informal way. Vacancies are not widely advertised and recruitment processes seem to lack openness and transparency. As a result, not all interested candidates may get a chance to apply. Many schools, especially in primary education and in "difficult" areas, find it hard to get qualified candidates.

Compared to management positions in other sectors, the working conditions of school leaders are not very attractive. After a 12-month probationary period, school leaders are appointed for a permanent position. They do not have many further career opportunities. Salary differences between school leaders and teachers are small. Remuneration of school leaders is far below the average for management positions in the labour market.

Most stakeholders interviewed agreed that the training and support structures for school leaders are insufficient. Only the network of community education provides mandatory pre-service training for school leaders. The other networks offer some voluntary, mostly in-service training opportunities.

As in many other countries, school leaders in Flanders are faced with a wide range of tasks and challenges. Depending on the boards and networks, they have different degrees of responsibility in administrative, budgetary, pedagogical, personnel and public relations matters. Most of the time, the school boards delegate substantive powers, such as hiring and firing teachers, to the principals. The school leaders' wide-ranging autonomy is not matched with a systematic evaluation or accountability system, and their essential role in school development is not accompanied with central support structures or performance-based remuneration.

> *Depending on the boards and networks, school leaders in Flanders have different degrees of responsibility in administrative, budgetary, pedagogical, personnel and public relations matters.*

Summary: choice, competition and identity

It is clear from this that there are five key components by which we can identify the educational system in Flemish Belgium. These provide a lens through which we may examine the "communities of schools" innovation:

- **Choice:** In principle, parents choose the school their children attend. Thus, as a group, they determine the size of schools by means of their preferences.

- **Competition:** Traditionally because funding follows the students, schools have varied in size because they have competed for resources.

- **Identity and autonomy:** All education is publicly funded but choice and competition have resulted in the formation of three governing networks representing private (mostly Catholic), public (municipal / provincial), and community (former state) schools. Within these, there also exist special groups, for example, the Jesuit schools have their own umbrella organisation, and the public schools are organised differently according to where they are, urban or provincial. Of these, the network of Roman Catholic schools is by far the largest, representing 68.4% of all students (Opdenakker and Van Damme, 2007).

- **Standards and equity:** We have seen that Flemish Belgium scores highly in its PISA results but that it has one of the widest margins between the levels of achievement of the highest and lowest groups. PISA data also shows that the differences in performance between schools are very strong and that a large proportion of between-school variance is explained by differences in students' socioeconomic backgrounds (OECD, 2004).

- **Leadership:** Traditionally, schools have been governed by school boards. These have operated within the umbrella board of each network. The school boards are mostly made up of volunteers and while the principals are accountable to the boards, there is a tradition of principal autonomy. More importantly, there is, according to some research, a, "lack of strong participative professionally-oriented leadership in the majority of Flemish secondary schools" which has meant that principals themselves have not significantly affected school practice (Opdenakker and Van Damme, 2007, p. 196).

6.3 Systems innovation: Communities of schools

> A principal: "We have a tendency to do new things and forget to abolish the old…every decision is part of a complicated negotiation."

In 1999, the Flemish Ministry of Education established "communities of schools" for secondary education, having regard to issues of choice, competition and identity. These were also established for primary education in 2003/04. These communities are voluntary collaborative partnerships between schools. For secondary education, 11 "competencies" were set out through which such communities were charged with consulting about staffing, curriculum and resource allocation. Box 6.1 provides a detailed definition of what these communities of schools entail. For primary schools, the collaboration possibilities are more open.

There are now 118 communities of schools in secondary education, covering more than 95% of schools in Flanders, with an average of 6 to 12 schools belonging to a community. There are 367 in primary education, covering 97% of schools. During the site visits, the OECD team focused on communities of schools in secondary education. Secondary school communities have been operational for long enough for stakeholders to adapt and respond to the new framework. Primary school communities, on the other hand, have been given fewer resources and powers during the 2003-05 pilot years. A revised school community policy was launched only in 2005/06, and its impact on the organisation and management of schooling is not yet very visible (Section 6.6).

The objective of the communities of schools was to make schools work in collaboration by sharing resources, to rationalise supply of courses and to promote cost savings across schools. The government's aspirations were that this new system would enable the enhancement of student guidance systems, particularly in relation to their educational career trajectories; the lessening of the managerial-administrative burden on principals in order that they might become pedagogical leaders; the increased use of ICT; and the rationalisation of resourcing both in relation to staff recruitment, functioning and evaluation and in relation to co-operation in curriculum.

Box 6.1 Definitions of communities of schools in Flanders

Primary education communities of schools (created in 2003/04):

In primary education, a school community consists of several schools which belong to either the same or different school boards and/or education networks. The school communities can decide autonomously to make available resources for a co-ordinating director. They can have decision making powers for specific matters. The school board or school boards to which a school within the community belongs decides whether it transfers powers to the school community or not. The powers that can be transferred are: the use of resources as a stimulus within the school community; the use of a staffing points system for care, ICT and administration, ICT staff within the school community; sharing special education school expertise; or the inclusion of additional schools within the school community. The school community can make agreements about these issues and submits these to the school board/boards of the schools that are part of the community.

Secondary education communities of schools (created in 1999):

In secondary education, a school community consists of one school or a group of schools which belong to either the same or different school boards and/or education networks. A co-ordinating director may ensure that the school community operates smoothly in secondary education. They have the following powers (based on decree):

- concluding agreements on the organisation of rational education provision;

- concluding agreements on objective pupil orientation and support;

- concluding agreements on the staffing policy: criteria for appointing staff, for the overall functioning of staff and assessing staff;

- concluding agreements/making decisions on the distribution of extra teacher hours within its establishments;

- concluding agreements on the determination of the criteria and the use of weekly teacher hours that can be combined at a school community level.

- concluding agreements on the distribution of resources for support staff for its establishments;

- concluding agreements on the use of resources for ICT co-ordination;

- making recommendations about investment in school buildings and infrastructure, with the school board using the investment resources of community education or the education infrastructure agency Agentschap voor Infrastructuur in het Onderwijs (AGIOn) (for the other networks);

- entering into collaborative partnerships with one or several other schools outside the school community.

Source: Devos and Tuytens (2006)

The immediate effects of the innovation were to establish internal markets which regulated competition for students between schools and increased opportunities for collective action to be taken to allocate staffing and other resources, and for student guidance systems and curriculum. While these are important features, it must be acknowledged that the scope for collective decision making was at the margins and did not affect principals' autonomy.

The scope for collective decision making was at the margins and did not affect principals' autonomy.

With only a small number of exceptions, the communities of schools remain nested within the traditional networks structure and depend largely on the traditional leadership of boards and directors within that structure.

While it may be said that the innovation added another layer of bureaucracy to the existing system, in practice schools and systems have responded in different ways. This chapter will give examples of these different responses in Section 6.3.

Because the innovation was centrally initiated, a form of "contrived collegiality" (Hargreaves, 1994) was imposed. Thus, schools have clustered in different ways. They are rather loosely coupled within systems which are in different phases of development and may not yet be said to have become communities. There are three government concerns that are key to understanding this innovation:

- "evening out" and raising what was perceived as variable quality of education in schools;

- closing the equity gap between students which had existed over many decades and which is so evident in the PISA results;

- not to "interfere" with the strong sense of identity and autonomy held by the networks, school boards and individual schools.

Examples of systems innovation in Flemish Belgian schools

Table 6.2 below gives an illustration of the different stages of development of a range of communities of schools in Flanders. It shows the ways in which existing network and board managers, as well as individual schools, have adapted to the innovation. The model presents the different levels of change on a continuum from status quo (no evidence of change) to transformation (development of a community identity). We then provide brief examples of the different practices we observed during the visit, explaining how they fit into the framework of change levels. Section 6.4 provides an analysis of the leadership practices at each level of this multi-layered system.

Table 6.1 Adaptations of networks to communities

Change levels	Catholic Jesuit schools	Community schools, Willebroek	Community schools, Brussels	Public sector schools, Antwerp	Catholic schools, Leuven
1. Status quo No evidence of change to structures, roles and responsibilities, culture. Power remains at the network level	✓				
2. Minimum change Evidence of some change to existing structures but not to cultures or roles and responsibilities. Power remains at the network/group level		✓	✓		
3. Adaptation (early signs) Evidence of change in structures, roles, responsibilities and cultures. Power is distributed				✓	✓
4. Transformation Communities of practice have established an identity which supersedes network identity					

Private (Catholic Jesuit) communities of schools

The coordinator of seven Catholic Jesuit school groups with 800 staff spread across Flanders spoke of preserving the special bond between them. Thus, although the schools had joined communities of schools, it was not perceived as a key development tool. There was some scepticism about the extent to which the quality of education would be improved through such membership. Under the pre-existing system, distributed leadership was practised through school group teams of principals, with one of these taking leadership as *primus inter pares*. The school board leaders met monthly, and the leaders' group met weekly. The school board continued to take final decisions, "on everything" and principals were accountable to the board. They had, "a sense of being responsible together" for the education in their region. The coordinator was responsible for system-wide staffing and administration, and staff and principal training. In effect he acted as a director of education.

Communities of schools in community education

According to the director of the regional group of schools, communities of schools were a "theoretical concept". It was the director together with the school group who decided on policy. Two communities of schools had been created within the group of schools (one for primary and one for secondary schools). Although the communities of schools each had a co-ordinating director, they were accountable to the group director who was accountable to the board. As in the Jesuit school network, and as in the example which follows, the director and his staff led the vision and the policy making. They administered the system and had benefited from the establishment of the internal market, which had led to reduced competition between schools. The director was also clearly responsible for hiring and firing school principals, and for steering policy in the group of schools. Within the group of schools, some principals had already been responsible for the system leadership of more than one school before the establishment of school communities.

Communities of schools in community education (Brussels)

This system was managed from the centre by a general director with 30 staff. Unlike the example that follows, however, leadership had not been widely distributed. There were three communities of schools (primary, secondary and art schools) and principals had responsibilities for hiring and firing teachers (responsibility delegated by the board to the principal). The general director and his staff were responsible for all administrative and financial tasks, leaving the principals to concentrate on pedagogical matters. There was no history of cross school curriculum planning, although the communities (and the network as a whole) were now focusing on developing curricula and teaching pedagogies which would help solve the problems of the 80% of students for whom Dutch was not their first language. Support for this was provided at the level of each community of schools. All principals had job descriptions and there were detailed criteria and procedures governing the recruitment and appointment of all staff. Principals met monthly, and there were in-service competency based training programmes. According to the general director, not all secondary school principals saw the need for a full-time co-ordinating director of their community of schools.

Public (municipal) communities of schools (Antwerp)

The network in Antwerp had established itself as a "learning city" department with five to six "companies", each with its own co-ordinating director under the co-ordination of a director who reported to a single board. In this sense it was similar to Willebroek. However, centrally funded cross school projects were available by application, and social policies for disadvantaged students (50% did not speak Dutch as a first language) were centralised. Within each community of schools, principals were beginning to take specialist cross-school responsibilities (*e.g.* ICT, guidance). Hiring and firing was, as in Willebroek, the responsibility of the director of the school board. Antwerp was in the process of establishing campuses with several schools which would specialise in different fields of study, and there was a long and strong tradition of leadership advice, career counselling and development.

Private (Catholic) communities of schools (Leuven)

This community comprises 14 secondary schools, and one campus of three schools and a teacher training institute which had been established with one director 25 years previously. The community of schools had begun, six years previously, with 11 school boards; these had since reduced to seven. It had appointed a former principal of one of the prestigious, respected and high achieving schools as its full-time co-ordinating director. Under her leadership, the principals from the schools had begun to meet monthly and, though they still described themselves as "scanning, getting to know each other and building trust", they have established a clear agenda. This includes improving individual guidance and counselling services for students, agreeing a common process for selection to reduce competition within the community, negotiating common working conditions for teachers, and creating curricula for students with special educational needs. Teachers themselves were described as being, as yet, "barely aware" of changes and despite a collective "vision for integration", different schools still had "distinct visions and interests". The community had recently agreed to provide targeted support (from the envelope of hours provided to the communities) for one of its members which was finding difficulty in recruitment and staffing.

6.4 Multi-layered system leadership

The management and leadership of this systemic innovation may be identified as being distributed across four levels: the central government of Flemish Belgium; the private and public networks (which also have a legitimate vested interest in survival): the communities of schools themselves; and school level.

Central government level

The management of this innovation by the central government may be summarised in the words of one senior official: "We want them to go their own way towards the goal that we want."

This respect for localised decision making within the watchful eyes of the existing networks characterised the approach at this level. It created opportunities for the establishment and growth of communities of schools but did not and does not provide system leadership. For example, there are no centrally provided training resources for system leadership or leadership of communities of schools, no monitoring and evaluation of the use which communities of schools make of additional centrally provided resources, and no systemic efforts to collect and disseminate examples of practice in communities of schools. There has been one government evaluation of the scheme (Department of Education, 2005a; 2005b). It found that the progress of the systems innovation had been, in the words of government officials, "uneven" and "a little bit slow". They suggested that many boards had, "slowed down the pace, in some instances to paralysis" and that the innovation was now "at a turning point".

Network level

> A stakeholder: "Networks are the sparring partners, defending their position against the ministry and the unions."

Networks responded to the innovation in different ways. As we have seen in Section 6.3, in some instances (*e.g.* Leuven) the number of individual school boards had reduced, but only 19 of the communities of schools in the Catholic system are at present under the governance of one school board. This suggests a resistance to change by many school boards. In community education (*i.e.* former state schools) one school board is the rule. At the network level, also, the variety of leadership models illustrates the different responses to the innovation.

These range from those which have changed minimally, to those which have made some changes but retained existing structures, to those which have made moderate changes to structures of governance and whose culture has begun to change in the direction of becoming a more mature community of schools.

Communities of schools level

No communities of schools are self-governing, independent of the networks to which they belong. The nature of the leadership within the communities depends upon two interacting elements: the extent to which leaders within the traditional network structures distribute leadership; and the vision and strength of leadership in the newly formed communities. Thus, in the public schools networks in municipalities (*e.g.* Antwerp and

Brussels), communities of schools are serviced and led by a general director and his staff under a single board (a parallel would be a local city authority in England). In the case of Brussels, there are three school groups but they are communities principally for the purposes of staff recruitment; in-service training and leadership development; and tackling the problem of significant numbers of non-Dutch speaking students in their schools.

In the case of Antwerp, a different, more distributed leadership model exists. A number of municipal companies (sub systems) have been created, each with their own leadership. Leadership training is strong in both sub systems. The public school network in Willebroek (a province) is based on the traditional leadership of large groups of schools by a director and his staff. However, within the group are two co-ordinating directors (one full-time primary, one part-time secondary). In all three cases the directors and the boards have a clear responsibility for the vision and direction of the groups of schools. The same would be true of the Jesuit network. However, in the case of the Catholic system in Leuven, it is clear that the co-ordinating director, working closely with the principals, has taken this responsibility.

School level

A policy maker: "No one knows about the quality of principals."

While this chapter focuses on system leadership it is, nevertheless, important to discuss briefly the role of leadership at school level. This is for two reasons: the innovation ultimately relies for its success upon principals; and the communities of schools' coordinators are drawn largely from the ranks of existing or former principals. The principals of each school or sub group of schools (which, in the case of Leuven, existed before the innovation) retains responsibility for his/her own schools' direction. Thus, ultimately the impact of the system innovation at school and classroom level depends on the extent to which the principals recognise its benefits and on the quality of their own leadership.

In Flemish schools, although it is the principal who is responsible for pedagogical leadership, in general this leadership does not seem to be exercised. Principals have little time left for pedagogical leadership, as they are increasingly expected to carry out managerial and organisational tasks. In addition to managing relations with students, parents, educational authorities and the local community, they are taking on increasing responsibilities for personnel management, monitoring, evaluating and continuously motivating their staff. A second challenge is for them to ensure student care and well being in environments with growing social and cultural diversity. Finally, as the government is increasingly focussing on the role of individual schools in quality assurance, principals are taking larger responsibility for school self-assessment and evaluation.

Many stakeholders mentioned that middle management is of utmost importance to allow the principal to focus more on the school's educational project. Middle management may also provide opportunities for shared leadership and strengthened policy implementation capacities within the school. During the visit, we observed that some schools (for example the Catholic schools in Leuven) had a well-functioning middle management structure with distributed responsibilities for different aspects of management (ICT, material, student well being). In other schools this seemed to be less present. In a 2005 study, Van Petegem *et al.* (in Devos and Tuytens, 2006) call for middle management to be further developed in Flanders. According to the director of the Jesuit network, such a structure is an essential precondition for the success of communities of schools.

Part of the stated rationale for establishing communities of schools was that the principal could be freed from many bureaucratic tasks in order to spend more time in pedagogical leadership. We did not always observe this. In some cases the communities of schools even seemed to add to the principal's workload. On the other hand, by compelling principals to work together, school communities are beginning to engage them more in pedagogic leadership: regular meetings between principals, exchange of practices, views and understandings, as well as joint training initiatives were found across all the communities of practice.

By compelling principals to work together, school communities are beginning to engage them more in pedagogic leadership.

6.5 Conceptualisation

System leadership conceptualisation

Communities of schools in Flemish Belgium are a systemic innovation to create a more localised structure of relationships, roles and responsibilities. The traditional networks (public and private) had adapted but, essentially, continue to dominate in the leadership of those communities. After creating and providing some resource for the communities of schools, central government has taken no further direct role in their development (for reasons of choice, autonomy and identity). If there is a theory of action, then it is that networks and communities of schools should be free to find their own ways of providing leadership. Based on a tradition of minimal interference by the Ministry of Education, the Flemish community government provides no guidance on what kind(s) of leadership may be more, or less, effective. Nor has it provided support for communities in developing a sense of community vision, leadership, strategic direction or pedagogical advancement.

Hopkins (Chapter 2) proposes that "a school head has to be almost as concerned about the success of other schools as he or she is about his or her own schools", and that, "sustained improvement of schools is not possible unless the whole system is moving forward". This assumes a reality that is not yet in evidence in Flemish Belgium, since the system of communities of schools is neither monitored nor evaluated. It might be the case, but we did not discern any evidence about how the whole system was moving forward. From the evidence presented, it is also clear that moving forward has different meanings for those within the system.

Hopkins recognises, however, that the aspiration of systems transformation being facilitated by the degree of segmentation existing in the system only holds when certain conditions hold. These are, first, there is increased clarity about the nature of intervention and support for schools at each phase of the performance cycle; and second, schools at each phase are clear as to the most productive ways to collaborate in order to capitalise on the diversity within the system.

In the case of Flemish Belgium the responsibilities and power to determine the nature and direction of the communities of schools may be said to be distributed to those communities. However, the result is that neither of Hopkins' conditions for system transformation are met. Communities of schools are not yet clear about the most productive ways to collaborate in order to capitalise on the diversity within the system because there has not been increased clarity about the nature of intervention and support in the process of the innovation.

Not resolving the tensions between respecting the rights of all communities to exercise autonomy and the responsibilities of government to provide leadership guidance and support for the implementation, continuation and institutionalisation phases of the innovation has resulted in systemic development which is slow and uneven.

Not resolving the tensions between autonomy and guidance on system leadership has resulted in slow systemic development.

Power and responsibility

Power is a fluid, interactive and reciprocal process. School leaders at all levels do have power in their formal position, but at the same time they are aware of the relative nature of power. To see power as a relationship means that power relations are always two-way, even if the power of one actor in a social relation is minimal compared to another. Both the actions of subordinates and the actions of superiors influence the structures of domination. As one of the co-ordinating directors said, "We need to have the principals on board in order to succeed." At central level it was emphasised, that "in this country you convince people to follow. It is a country of negotiation."

The configuration of power relationships in the community of schools is shaped by the mutual understanding of the authority and influence of the school boards and the influence of co-ordinating directors and principals. The principal enjoys a high degree of authority but there are constraints which lead to reliance on a wide range of sources of influence.

Both centralisation and decentralisation of the educational system, irrespective of motives, puts in focus the balance between political and professional power over education (Lundgren, 1990). On the one hand, a system change like introducing communities of schools might be interpreted as a form of centralisation within the context of Flanders where the school boards have enjoyed a high degree of autonomy. A new intermediate level is introduced, the drive for change is top-down, and a potential for a change in power relationship has been created. On the other hand, the Flemish approach has allowed for different interpretations in the different communities, aligned with the history and tradition of the country, and the power structure of the school boards is preserved.

The balancing act of introducing an intermediate level like the communities of schools can be framed as "decentralised centralism" (Karlsen, 2000), and it sharpens the question of who has the responsibility. Such a system change may result in contradictory decisions. Universal acceptance of any balance is difficult to achieve because some stakeholders' interests are always compromised (Hoyle and Wallace, 2005). In addition, there will remain a tension between decentralisation efforts and the need for central control (Weiler, 1990).

Similar to the configuration of power relationships, patterns of responsibility are reciprocal. Responsibility concerns the obligations teachers and school leaders have to each other in answering questions about what has happened within one's area of responsibility and in providing reliable explanations about why it has happened. As Elmore (Chapter 3) argues, for each unit of responsibility given, a unit of support must be provided. According to him, the present accountability policy will not increase school performance without a substantial investment in human capital aimed at developing the practice of school improvement in a diverse population of school leaders and teachers.

6.6 Programme effectiveness

> A school principal: "It has been an evolutionary journey of what you hope will become a community in 10 to 20 years. A lot has happened during seven years. Before, we were very competitive. Now we collaborate more, and it is new to work together. It is a small revolution when you look back."

Three broad intended objectives of the communities of schools policy can be distinguished. First, the policy was explicitly aimed at making schools collaborate in order to rationalise and improve the provision of curricula, staffing, facilities, student orientation, administration, care and ICT. Second, a less explicit intention appeared to be to introduce a layer of educational policy implementation based on geographical proximity rather than on affiliation with a board or network. Third, the innovation of communities of schools seems to be ultimately geared towards improving the quality of teaching and learning.

There is little quantitative evidence about the degree to which these objectives have been achieved. The government does not systematically monitor or evaluate its policy of communities of schools, but there have been two evaluations of communities of schools undertaken by the Flemish Education Ministry. One focused on primary school communities (Box 6.2), while a second one evaluated communities of secondary schools after five years in operation.

Box 6.2 Evaluation of primary school communities (February 2005)

After a pilot phase of two years (2003/04 and 2004/05), the Flemish Ministry of Education evaluated a randomly selected sample of 29 primary school communities. The evaluation consisted of a survey questionnaire sent to teachers and principals, and interviews conducted with representatives from each school community. The main findings were:

Usefulness: Overall feedback from respondents was positive. Almost all participants affirmed that school communities were a useful concept, and the great majority believed that the communities helped to increase the schools' capacities.

Positive outcomes: The great majority of respondents (25 of the 29 communities' representatives) considered "co-operation" in itself as the most positive outcome. Others mentioned a "common vision" (4), a common care policy (5), and a better distribution of tasks among schools (4).

Reasons for joining a school community: Sixteen respondents indicated that their major motivation for joining a community was to receive extra resources from the government; 11 respondents stated that the creation of their communities was merely a formalisation of pre-existing school collaboration structures; 8 respondents mentioned pressure from Brussels or from their school boards as a reason for joining.

Domains of co-operation: Material co-operation is very important for the surveyed school communities. Most communities share facilities such as libraries and gymnasiums (19), and combine their schools' purchasing power when ordering materials (17). Many respondents cooperate in ICT (17) and care policy (16). Teacher exchanges take place in only one community. There seems to be very little, if any, pedagogical co-operation: some (9) do not at all cooperate in the pedagogical domain, while some others (9) indicated that they organise common "study days".

Impact: Participants were asked about the perceived impact of school communities on different stakeholders. The majority of respondents agreed that:

- there is no impact on the school personnel (19);

- there is no impact on students (29);

- there is a negative impact on principals because the communities have increased their workload (14).

The results from this evaluation led the ministry to introduce some changes to the design of the school community policy, namely an increase in the amount of resources allocated to the communities. The increased bonus was aimed at allowing primary school communities to appoint a formal co-ordinating director (a principal exempted from some tasks at his/her own school).

Source: Department of Education (2005a).

The evaluation undertaken for secondary school communities shows that some of their objectives have been reached. Communities have strengthened co-operation in some areas, such as developing common policies on personnel and allocation of human resources across the schools involved. There seems to be informal co-operation with other school levels, such as primary schools and special education, and there is still scope for co-operation in the future. However, co-operation could be stronger in some areas such as rationalising education supply and infrastructures across schools and in providing effective guidance for students. In addition, while some school communities organise working groups with union participation on a broad range of topics, in general, teaching unions complain that school boards and school leaders always want to push through their own proposals rather than work for the school communities (Department of Education, 2005b).

Overall, from the available evaluation of primary school communities (Box 6.2) and secondary education as well as from our observations and interviews, it became evident that the very existence of co-operation between schools was considered as an intrinsically positive development by all stakeholders (even if some remained sceptical whether the concept of school communities was the best way to achieve it).

Perceived benefits of co-operation through communities of schools are:

- the creation of an internal market which has reduced competition between individual schools;

- the possibilities of creating better student orientation and guidance systems;

- the possibilities of creating community-wide curricula which cater for students with special educational needs;

- the creation of an internal labour market for teachers;

- the creation of areas of community based discretionary judgement relating to the distribution of (marginal) resources, HR policy and care;

- reduced bureaucratic workload for principals and new possibilities for pedagogical leadership;

On the other hand, perceived constraints on co-operation are:

- communities cannot offer training or do not have capacity and resources;

- communities do not have significant budgetary control;

- several boards within one community can create tensions and may disagree as to vision, direction and strategy;

- the decision making power of communities is problematic because of their relationships with pre-innovation management structures which persist;

- separate communities of secondary and primary schools, and communities based on network membership, may not be conducive to the development of coherent localised systems of effective schooling.

The intention of creating a more efficient local/regional entity for policy implementation was only partly realised. Government representatives had hoped that the creation of communities of schools would induce mergers of school boards so that eventually all schools in one community would belong to the same board. The rationale behind this was to avoid inefficiencies and duplications of structures. While some mergers have taken place, this process of rationalisation seems to be slow and uneven.

Government representatives had hoped that the creation of communities of schools would lead eventually to all schools in one community belonging to the same board.

As to the third objective of improving school quality, tangible benefits for schools from this innovation seem from the outside to be small. So far, communities of schools do not seem to have any impact on students, who are generally not even aware of the existence of communities of schools. Though from the inside the innovation has been described as a "small revolution", opening up dialogue and new possibilities for learning and pedagogical leadership, there is as yet little evidence of the effect on teaching, learning and the equity gap.

6.7 Food for thought

It is important to note that the Flemish communities of schools fit well with this OECD activity's focus on school leadership for system improvement. The theoretical construct is that principals will work together across schools and act as leaders of schools as learning organisations which can contribute to positive learning environments and communities. The OECD team agreed that these communities have the potential to raise equity and quality of education outcomes and to improve co-operation in an environment of heavy competition. This can lead to improved learning outcomes in Flanders.

However, the way these communities of schools have been launched and implemented could be revised. Overall, the OECD review team felt that the government did not provide strategic leadership, educational vision, or a theory of action to guide the development of the communities of schools. The Flemish authorities initiated the development of communities of schools, but they did not further influence the development process or outputs. This hands-off policy has resulted in a lack of clarity about the purpose of communities in terms of school leadership and organisational culture. There are many different understandings of the nature and purpose of school communities at the levels of the schooling networks, school boards, communities, and individual schools. As a consequence, there is a diverse landscape of various types of school communities with different degrees of co-operation. Some issues and key tensions may need to be resolved if communities of schools are to be successful.

Leadership or management: Sustaining communities of schools

The evidence from many innovation practices around the world is that innovation is a process rather than an event. The process, therefore, needs to be managed in terms of resource allocation and infrastructure – for example, "in time" training and development programmes. However, while people need to feel involved and to have a sense of ownership through participation, the process also needs to be led. To achieve this requires leadership in, for example, the development of a collective and distinctive vision, sense of direction, collegiality and achievement. This is especially the case where new systems are developed while previous systems remain. At present, there is no evidence of a view of what communities of schools might become. It is a top down innovation for which, viewed from below, the government's vision seems unclear. Maybe that is one of the reasons why we could identify only incremental and very small changes.

It is a top down innovation for which, viewed from below, the government's vision seems unclear.

Improving school quality and equity

From our meetings it became clear that communities of schools did not as yet have any tangible impact on teaching and learning, and they did not seem to reduce the equity gap. However, we observed that communities of schools can provide a framework to improving equity, as they allow for improved student guidance. Teachers and principals affirmed that thanks to the communities of schools they are more aware of all available study options in the community. This knowledge allows them to better orient students according to their interests and abilities.

There is some evidence of changes in systems of student orientation and educational trajectory, of a focus on students with special educational and language needs, and on care and well being. As yet there seems to be no discernible change in teaching and learning strategies – at least, this did not feature in our conversations with the different stakeholders in the communities of schools. Communities of schools could become important tools to improve equity and quality of education if this was better spelled out and clear teaching and learning strategies were adopted for them.

Choice and co-operation: A dilemma of democracy

As funding follows the student, schools in Flanders have traditionally competed for students and resources. One aim of communities of schools seems to be to make schools work together rather than competing. As schools are allocated resources collectively, school leaders are compelled to get together regularly and consult on the use of these resources. We heard that in some cases co-operation is limited to this single aspect. In many schools, however, the externally imposed co-operation on resource matters has had a spill-over effect: communities of schools provided a structure and platform for knowledge sharing and collective action among school leaders and teachers from all types of secondary schools (technical, vocational and academic).

In order to cooperate it is necessary to give away a measure of individual voice and to accept the will of the majority. Where individual schools on the one hand and school boards and networks on the other are not willing to concede power over decision making it is unlikely that democracy in communities of schools will flourish.

Overall, the nature of collaboration-competition balance as it emerges from the interactions of principals within and across the communities of schools remains unclear. It is an irony that the government introduces collaboration but is in practice also strongly committed to competition as a means to increase effectiveness and school quality, as reflected in Section 6.2.

Identities and change: Bridging the old and new structures

Most communities of schools continue to locate their identity in the traditional networks, and the network managers encourage this. The strong power of the networks has not been significantly altered, as communities of schools remain affiliated to their respective networks. The new structure of communities of schools seems to have had a marginal impact on the institutional landscape of secondary schools. In a way, the creation of communities of schools has added an additional layer of bureaucracy without abolishing any of the old layers. At the same time, however, the intervention has induced a degree of localisation / regionalisation of responsibility from the networks and boards to the school community level.

If communities of schools are to continue to develop as means for improved education for all their students, they need to develop a strong orientation towards that community. So long as networks and school groups continue to absorb and control significant resources, it is unlikely that community oriented identities will develop.

In Flanders the diffuse borderline between political and professional power and responsibility seems to represent a major problem. Unless both the co-ordinating directors and the principals get better training, the communities of schools are unlikely to gain greater influence because the boards are so strong in some places. The ministry has the power to make leadership programmes mandatory, but so far, in accordance with tradition, it has been reluctant to intervene at the local level. If the intention is to give more power and responsibility to the communities of schools, both a unified board and better opportunities for robust leadership development are required.

Leadership training and support

There is no evidence that the Flemish authorities provide support to strengthen system leadership at the community level. There are no centrally organised support structures for principals, no monitoring and evaluation of leadership, and no dissemination of effective practices. However, we observed that in successful communities system leadership had evolved locally: school leaders had made use of the community structure to establish mechanisms for peer support, school leaders of successful schools had shared effective practices with more disadvantaged schools, and the co-ordinating director of the community had taken on a coaching and mentoring function to provide guidance for principals. We heard about communities of schools in Limburg and Antwerp where shared leadership evolved as each principal of the community specialised in a certain field such as personnel, pedagogy, or infrastructure. The quality of shared leadership at the community level seems to depend on local factors, especially on the involvement of committed individuals at the school, community, or board levels.

While networks have earmarked funding for in-service training for principals and staff, this is not always spent in meeting the needs which communities identify. This lack of training for leadership and management of these new communities of schools is a key reason for their uneven development and a hindrance to the establishment of strong community identities.

It is reasonable to assume that the less preparation co-ordinating directors and principals have, the more likely they are to fall back on their lay theories of leadership – often premised on a very narrow experiential base of prior experience as a teacher. Also, due to rapid changes in society, lay theories are likely to maintain outdated concepts of heroic leadership rather than a concept of sustainable leadership (Møller and Schratz, 2008). Leadership programmes have the potential to influence the principals' learning trajectories and their emerging leadership identities, to develop the form of leadership appropriate to the particular stage in the life cycle of a school (Sugrue, 2005).

Sharing practice: discussion and dissemination

At present there is no mechanism for identifying and disseminating the work of individual communities of schools. This is a responsibility of those who initiate innovation and needs to be addressed with urgency. To engage in this would mean the ministry and school boards representing communities working together in order to understand and define examples of good practice.

The ministry and school boards representing communities can work together to understand and define examples of good practice.

Box 6.3 Summary conclusions and recommendations

Flemish communities of schools fit well with our focus on school leadership for system improvement. The theoretical construct is directed to ensuring that principals work together across schools and can act as leaders of schools as learning organisations which in addition can contribute to positive learning environments and communities. The OECD team agreed that these communities have the potential to raise equity and quality of education outcomes and to improve co-operation in an environment of heavy competition. This can lead to improved learning outcomes in Flanders.

This chapter has revealed some obstacles for these objectives to be fully achieved and it has advanced a number of policy recommendations to address these:

- **Sustaining communities of schools:** Innovation practices like communities of schools need to be managed and led. For stakeholders to develop a sense of ownership through participation, it is important to develop a collective and distinctive vision, as well as a sense of direction, collegiality and achievement.

- **Improving school quality and equity:** School communities could have a stronger impact on quality and equity if this aim was spelled out more explicitly and if clear teaching and learning strategies were adopted.

- **Moving towards co-operation:** As currently the government seems to support both competition and co-operation between schools, there is a need to clarify a broader framework and vision for the communities in relation to an educational system traditionally based on choice and competition.

- **Bridging the old and the new structures:** There is a need to better define the roles and responsibilities of school communities vis-à-vis the networks, boards and individual school leaders. These stakeholders all need to give away some power over decision making to allow for community-oriented identities to develop.

- **Providing leadership training and support:** As communities of schools rely for their success on school principals, it is of utmost importance to provide training and support for them to develop their capacities.

- **Sharing practice:** An evidence-based approach geared towards monitoring and evaluating the development of school communities would allow for continuous learning and development of communities of schools to fit the evolving needs of schools and students. It is therefore essential to define, share and disseminate good practices.

Annex 6.A1
Case study visit programme
22-24 May 2007

Tuesday 22 May 2007, Department for Education, Koning Albert II-laan 15, 1210 Brussels

Time / Subject	Name	Post
09.00 – 10.30 Focus on context for policy making	Mr. Gaby Hostens	Director-General Member OECD Education Committee
10.30 – 11.30 Focus on roles and responsibilities of communities of schools in secondary education	Mrs Hilde Lesage	Head of Division for teaching staff policies
11.30 – 12.30 Focus on roles and responsibilities of communities of schools in secondary education	Mr. Michel Van Uytfanghe	Chairman of the Christian Teaching Union (COC)
12.30 – 14.00	Lunch	
14.00 – 15.00 Implementation of groups of schools and communities of schools Distributed school leadership	Mr. Jacky Goris	General Director group of community schools in Brussels (= former state school)
	Mr. Luc Debacquer	Director Coordinator of community of secondary schools (community schools)
15.00 – 16.00 Focus on roles and responsibilities in communities of schools in primary education	Mrs Sonja Van Craeymeersch	Head of Division policymaking in primary education
16.00 – 17.00 Implementation of communities of schools Distributed school leadership Preparation and development of school leaders	Mr. Luc Tesseur	Head of the Antwerp City School System

Wednesday 23 May 2007, Sacred Heart Institute Heverlee and Paridaens Institute Louvain with Mrs Hilde Lesage

Time / Subject	Name	Post
09.00 – 10.30	School visit Sacred Heart Meeting with school leaders, teachers and students	
11.00 – 12.30	School visit Paridaens Institute Meeting with students and teachers.	
12.30 – 13.00	Lunch Paridaens Institute	
13.00 – 13.30 Focus on distributed leadership within Community of schools Implementation of community of schools.	Mrs A. Claeys	Director of Community of Catholic Secondary Schools in Louvain
13.30 – 15.30 Focus on school leadership Effective school leadership	Mr. Debontridder	School leader technical school VTI
Distributed leadership in the Sacred Heart Institute (a diversity of schools with one board)	Mr Schoenaerts	Headmaster Sacred Heart Secondary Institute
School boards and their search for effective school leaders	Mr Haest	Chairman board of community of catholic schools Louvain and chairman board of the Sacred Heart Institute
15.45 – 17.00 Focus on improving school leadership through networking within community of schools	Mrs Claeys and Mrs Verhavert and Mrs Van Ael	Teachers

Thursday 24 May 2007, Morning: Willebroek Rivierenland Group of Schools

Time / Subject	Name	Post
09.30 – 12.30 Focus on distributed school Leadership and on development of school leaders	Mr. Luc Van Gasse	General director of regional group of community schools (= former state schools)
	Mr. R. Schoofs	Director, CLB (Guidance and Counselling centre)
	Mrs. M. Heynick	Director, primary school
	Mr. J. De Clercq	Senior primary school teacher
12.30	Lunch at school	
14.00	Brussels	
15.00 – 16.00 Focus on assessment and evaluation of communities of schools in the catholic school system	Mr. Geert Schelstraete	Deputy Chief of Cabinet Minister of Work, Education and Training
16.00 – 17.00 Focus on Communities of schools Distributed school leadership	Mr. Paul Yperman	Co-ordination of Flemish Jesuit Schools
17.00 – 18.00	Debriefing with Mr Gaby Hostens	

References

Department of Education (2005a), *Evaluatie Scholengemeenschappen Basisonderwijs*, Flemish Ministry of Work, Education and Training.

Department of Education (2005b), *De Scholengemeenschap in het Gewoon Secundair Onderwijs: Een Evaluatie*, Flemish Ministry of Work, Education and Training.

De Meyer, I., J. Pauly and L. Van de Poele (2005), *Learning for Tomorrow's Problems, First Results from PISA 2003*, Ministry of the Flemish Community, Education Department and Universiteit Gent, Department of Education, Ghent.

Devos, G. and M. Tuytens (2006), "Improving School Leadership - OECD Review, Background Report for Flanders", a report prepared for the Flemish Ministry of Education and Training, Belgium, available at *www.oecd.org/edu/schoolleadership*.

Hargreaves, A. (1994), *Changing Teachers, Changing Times: Teachers' Work and Culture in the Postmodern Age*, Teachers College Press, New York.

Hoyle, E. and M. Wallace, M. (2005), *Educational Leadership: Ambiguity, Professionals and Managerialism*, Sage Publications, London.

Karlsen, G. (2000), "Decentralised Centralism: Framework for a Better Understanding of Governance in the Field of Education", *Journal of Education Policy*, 15(5), 525-538.

Lundgren, U. (1990), "Educational Policymaking, Decentralisation and Evaluation" in Granheim, M., M. Kogan and U. Lundgren (eds.), *Evaluation as Policymaking. Introducing Evaluation into a National Decentralised Educational System*, Jessica Kingsley Publishers, London.

McKenzie, P., H. Emery, P. Santiago and A. Sliwka (2004), *Attracting, Developing and Retaining Effective Teachers, Country Note: The Flemish Community of Belgium*, OECD, Paris.

Møller, J. and M. Schratz (2008), "Leadership Development in Europe" in Crow, G., J. Lumby and P. Pashiardis (eds.) (forthcoming) *UCEA/BELMAS/CCEAM International Handbook on the Preparation and Development of School Leaders*, Erlbaum Publishing Company, Mahwah, NJ.

Opdenakker, M-C and J. Van Damme (2007), "Do School Context, Student Composition and School Leadership Affect School Practice and Outcomes in Secondary Education?", *British Educational Research Journal*, Vol. 33, No. 2, April, 2007, pp. 179-206.

OECD (2001), *What Works in Education: New School Management Approaches*, OECD, Paris.

OECD (2004), *Learning for Tomorrow's World: First Results from PISA 2003*, OECD, Paris.

Sugrue, C., (2005), "Principalship: Beyond Pleasure, Pain and Passion", in Sugrue, C. (ed.), *Passionate Principalship: Learning from Life Histories of School Leaders*, Routledge Falmer, London, (pp. 161-184).

Van Petegem, P., G. Devos, P. Mahieu, T.K. Dang, V. Warmoes (2005), Het Beleidsvoerend Vermogen in Basis- en Secundaire Scholen. OBPWO-project 03.07.

Weiler, H.N. (1990), "Decentralisation in Educational Governance: An Exercise in Contradiction?" in Granheim, M., M. Kogan and U. Lundgren (eds.), *Evaluation as Policymaking: Introducing Evaluation into a National Decentralised Educational System*, Jessica Kingsley Publishers, London.

Chapter 7

Building leadership capacity for system improvement in Victoria, Australia
by
Peter Matthews, Hunter Moorman and Deborah Nusche

This chapter provides information and analysis on the strategic approach to school leadership development in the Federal State of Victoria in Australia. The Victorian approach was selected by the OECD Improving School Leadership activity as an innovative example of school leadership development because of the state's remarkable drive to improve school effectiveness, in which leadership development plays a central part. The Victorian school improvement and leadership development strategies are thoroughly informed by national and international research. Implementation of the leadership development strategy reflects a close relationship between the Victorian education administration and school principals, in which the ministerial department provides consistent system leadership.

This chapter is based on a study visit to Victoria, Australia, organised by the Office for Government School Education (OGSE) of the Department of Education and Early Childhood Development (DEECD), at the request of the OECD in August 2007. It aims to illustrate state-wide developments in educational leadership, showing the interface between the central leadership and the framework of leadership development with which schools are becoming engaged.

The chapter begins with an overview of the systemic, state-wide approach to building leadership capacity and a shared school improvement culture within a highly devolved system. It shows how the model has been developed in the Victorian and Australian context, reviews the main features of the approach, and provides examples of leadership development in action. It concludes by analysing practice in terms of constructs and impact, highlighting features that may be of interest to other systems, and identifies matters that will be keys to the sustainability and impact of the strategy.

7.1 The OECD case study visit to Victoria, Australia

The OECD chose the Victorian model as an example of a state-wide approach to leadership preparation and development. From reading the literature and discussions with Australian representatives, it seemed that this approach matched the criteria defined for the selection of case studies and would represent a good model of education leadership capacity building at the levels of both the state and individual schools. Victorian government schools have a high degree of autonomy but vary widely in their effectiveness. The Victorian government has recognised the need to invest in leadership development at all levels in order to raise levels of educational achievement. This process has involved winning back the allegiance of schools to centrally driven policies and creating a system-wide vision of effective schools and culture of leadership development. The Victorian strategy for school improvement is being implemented in a range of parallel developments, central to which is a coherent approach to building an improvement culture and leadership capacity. Effective leadership, not only at school level but throughout the system, is seen as crucial to improving the effectiveness of schools and raising the achievements of students.

The study visit included meetings with a range of stakeholders in Melbourne and two site visits (Annex 7.A1). The study team met representatives from the Victorian Department of Education and Early Childhood Development and staff of the department's Office of Government School Education (OGSE) and its regional offices; officials from the Australian Government's Department of Education, Science and Training (DEST); a representative of the Australian Council on Educational Research (ACER); school principals, teachers and students; academics; leadership development providers; professional associations and other organisations. The site visits covered a primary and a secondary school. This study was also informed by a range of high quality documents published by the Victorian Department of Education and Early Childhood Development and draws from the draft country background report prepared for the OECD activity on improving school leadership (Anderson *et al.*, 2007). We take the opportunity to thank our Victorian hosts, particularly the deputy secretary for the OGSE and his staff, and all those we met, for their extensive preparation for the visit, their openness in discussions and their warm hospitality.

The study team comprised: Dr. Peter Matthews (rapporteur), Visiting Professor at the Institute of Education, University of London and educational consultant; Hunter Moorman, OECD consultant and expert in leadership, education reform, and organisation development; and Deborah Nusche from the OECD secretariat.

7.2 The Victorian context

Social and economic context

Victoria is one of the six states and two territories that comprise the Commonwealth of Australia. It is the smallest but most densely populated mainland state, containing only 3% of the Australian landmass but being home to over 5 million people (almost one quarter of the country's population). Victoria is highly urbanised, with nearly 90% of residents living in cities and towns. Its population is very diverse in terms of cultural and language backgrounds, and is becoming more so. Almost a quarter of the population speak a language other than English at home and 44% are either born overseas or have a parent who was born overseas. Schools and school leaders are expected to meet the needs of these increasingly diverse student populations.

Victoria's economy has done very well recently. In line with the national average, it has grown at an average annual rate of 3.6% over the past 10 years (1995/96 - 2005/06). Living standards in Australia have steadily improved since the beginning of the 1990s and now surpass all G7 countries except the United States. The Victorian society is experiencing a shift from an economy reliant on traditional manufacturing towards an increasingly knowledge and service based economy. The government emphasises the importance of gaining and retaining a competitive advantage through increasing the knowledge and skills of all Victorians. The education system is expected to provide students with the knowledge, skills and technological capacities required to participate effectively in a rapidly changing society and more broadly in the global economy.

Educational performance

The performance of Victorian students is continuously assessed through both national exams (in years 3, 5, 7, and 9) and international assessments such as PISA. According to Thomson *et al.* (2004), the 2000 and 2003 PISA studies showed good to excellent results for all Australian states and territories, in all subject areas. While there were performance differences between the states and territories in all domains, not many of the apparent score differences were statistically significant. Overall, Victorian students performed in line with the national average.

In terms of equity, the performance gap between the highest- and lowest-achieving students in Australia is smaller than the OECD average, and the "tail" of underachieving students was less than the average for the OECD. However, as in most countries, contextual factors such as location of school, language spoken at home and socioeconomic status had a significant effect on student performance in Australia:

- Students in metropolitan areas performed at significantly higher levels than students in provincial cities, who in turn performed at significantly higher levels than students in rural areas.

- Students who mainly spoke English at home performed significantly better than those whose main home language was other than English.

- While the relationship between socioeconomic background and performance was less strong in Australia than for the OECD average, there still exists a distinct advantage for those students with higher socioeconomic backgrounds, many of whom attend independent or Catholic secondary schools.

- While some indigenous students performed well, this was a very small proportion of the overall sample and many more were performing at the lower end of the proficiency levels.

While the PISA results paint a good picture of Australian performance, several countries outperformed Australia in both average achievement and equity. A report by the Australian states and territories (Council for the Australian Federation, 2007) states that the challenge for Australia is to match the performance of countries like Finland, Canada, Japan and Korea whose results are both high quality and high equity. In order to sustain and further improve the performance of Australian students, Australian schools are expected to continuously improve their practice and at the same time address the performance gaps and inequities outlined above.

Relationship between state and country

Australia does not have a unitary school system. Under the federal political structure, education is the responsibility of the individual states and territories, although the Commonwealth government significantly contributes to school funding and policy development. While schooling across the country has many commonalities, a number of differences affect school operations. In recent years there have been significant steps towards achieving greater national consistency across the eight states and territories. Nevertheless, caution is needed in generalising across the diversity of Australian schooling.

The ministers of the states, territories and commonwealth meet regularly in the Ministerial Council for Education, Employment, Training and Youth Affairs (MCEETYA), which provides a formal mechanism for agreeing broad directions and strategies for schools across the country. The major elements of federal policies for schools may be summarised as follows:

- a set of agreed, common, national goals which are kept under review and are reference points for strategies; benchmarks; and standards for particular subject areas and other aspects of schooling;

- continuing efforts to establish national measurement and reporting of student outcomes (including through national sample assessments in some key areas);

- national taskforces, working parties, committees, studies and reports addressing particular topics and reporting on progress in implementing the goals and attendant strategies.

The MCEETYA has launched the national co-operative project through its Improving Teacher and School Leadership Capacity Working Group, with one of its aims being to consider the development of an agreed, common framework for teacher quality and standards. This builds on moves already underway in the profession and at government level. It presages a considerable strengthening in the future of teacher professionalism at all stages, from recruitment through pre-service education to lifelong professional learning.

Schools in Victoria

In February 2007, there were 1 594 government and 701 non-government schools, providing for approximately 539 000 and 298 000 students respectively. Pre-schooling is voluntary, and availability and participation are highly variable. About two-thirds (67%) of students attend government schools; the remainder are in Catholic or independent schools, which at the secondary stage gain over 6 000 pupils who have attended government primary schools. Over 38 600 teachers work in the government sector. In-school expenditure per student was lower in Victoria than in other states and territories. Student-teacher ratios in 2006 were close to the national average in primary schools but slightly below in secondary schools. Enrolment numbers vary greatly between schools. At present, there are approximately 270 small schools (defined as those with 70 or fewer students) with an average enrolment of 37 students.

School governance and leadership

Although school governance and policy have traditionally been highly centralised, decentralisation has progressed further in Victoria than elsewhere in Australia owing to the very large measure of devolved decision making to the principals and school councils of government schools, which gives them considerable operational autonomy. The principals of government schools are required to work with their staff and community to develop strategic plans with clearly articulated outcome targets and improvement strategies. While principals are vested with overall operational authority, school leadership tends increasingly to be shared or distributed, school principals are expected to facilitate and work effectively with others with significant leadership roles. School networks are also becoming increasingly important and are broadening the scope of school leaders' work.

Leadership in Victorian government schools is recognised structurally by posts of assistant principals and principals, who together form the so-called "principal class". Distributed leadership is strongly encouraged, however, and the spreading leadership culture recognises that leadership qualities and opportunities apply across the education workforce. The demography of teachers shows an aging group (Figure 7.1) in which the subset of principals is likely to be older, complicated by the opportunity of retirement at age 55. This has implications for preparing more future leaders, and for the appointment, induction and mentoring of new principals, all of which are embedded elements of government policy.

Figure 7.1 Age profile of Victorian teachers and leaders (2006)

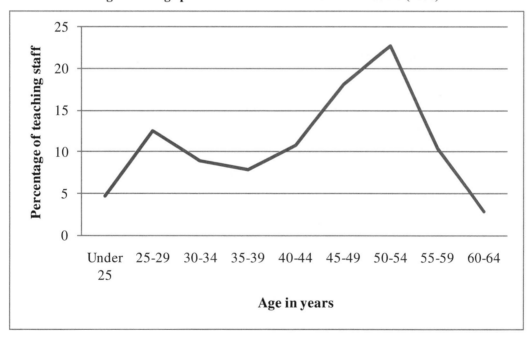

Source: Data provided by the Government of Victoria.

7.3 School improvement policy: *Blueprint for Government Schools*

The Victorian leadership development strategy (*Learning To Lead Effective Schools, 2006*) has been aligned with a reform agenda (*Blueprint for Government Schools, 2003*) comprising a consistent sequence of reform initiatives aimed at improving practice, enhancing performance and reducing achievement gaps in the government school system. The leadership development strategy is an essential part of this comprehensive framework for system-wide improvement. Before we turn to the Victorian strategy for building leadership capacity, this section will describe the genesis and implementation of the system-wide school improvement agenda.

In 2003, the Labour Government of Victoria identified a need to take action to improve educational outcomes for all students. Research evidence showed that three key features of the government school system needed to be addressed:

- a high concentration of poor outcomes in some schools and some regions;

- frequent high variations in outcomes between classes within a given school, which point to the centrality of the teaching-learning relationship;

- variations in outcomes between schools with similar student populations.

On the basis of extensive research into patterns of student outcomes, the factors that influence them and the performance of schools in delivering them, the government has provided its *Blueprint* for continuing improvement in progress in the quality of the government school system. There was wide consultation in the development of *Blueprint*, which was published in March 2003.

The government set out three priorities for reform, based on a broad consensus of what should be done to lift student outcomes. The priorities are:

- recognising and responding to diverse student needs;

- building the skills of the education workforce to enhance the teaching-learning relationship;

- continuously improving schools.

Although there have been a number of ministerial and departmental changes since *Blueprint* became government policy, the current minister recognises that exceptional leadership is necessary in such a highly devolved system. It appointed an experienced principal and outstanding leader to head the Office for Government School Education as deputy secretary. Our evidence supports the Minister's view that there has been common ownership of the *Blueprint* agenda.

Agenda for action: the seven "Flagship strategies"

The *Blueprint for Government Schools* identifies seven flagship strategies for addressing the three priorities. Each strategy includes an ambitious series of actions, shown in Box 7.1. The *Blueprint* provided a powerful and comprehensive agenda for educational reform, backed by political will and resources. It also introduced the operational challenge of implementing the raft of measures in a coherent and effective way so that they had the desired impact across the state.

The *Blueprint* could have evolved either as a collection of disparate initiatives or as a cohesive strategy. The threats to the cohesive approach were considerable. Relationships between the schools and department had been fragile before the reform. Many schools had regarded their high degree of autonomy as the signal for detachment from the department and its policies. Others had not used their devolved power to best effect: outcomes were too low, and public perceptions led to a drift away from government schools and into the Catholic or independent sectors, especially at secondary stage. Faced with falling enrolments, inter-school competition for pupils became more intense and the department and regional offices were not seen to provide effective solutions. Morale in parts of the system was low. The successful implementation of the *Blueprint* as a coherent system of reform initiatives is due in large part to the thoughtful strategy of school improvement the department adopted.

The department recognised the need for a culture shift. They considered that the best way of achieving this and delivering the range of reforms was to invest in school leadership, particularly by developing and, in effect, reprofessionalising the principals and assistant principals. This was an ambitious and risky project, but having conceived it, the leaders of the department set out to be leaders of the system by modelling their expectations for school leadership. Their recognition of the influence of leadership, second only to the quality of teaching and learning, was deliberately informed and supported by research (*e.g.* Leithwood *et al.*, 2004).

Box 7.1 Outline of the *Blueprint for Government Schools* commitments	
Recognising and responding to diverse student needs	
Flagship Strategy 1. Student learning	1a. Identify a framework of "essential learnings" for all students
	1b. Develop the principals of learning and teaching from prep to year 12
	1c. Improve reporting on student achievement
	1d. Develop a broad assessment processes against which defined standards of learning at key points of schooling can be measured
	1e. Develop a knowledge bank that documents exemplary practices in schools
Flagship Strategy 2. Developing a new resource allocation model	2a. Replace the school global budget with a new resource allocation model
Building the skills of the education workforce to enhance the teaching-learning relationship	
Flagship Strategy 3. Building leadership capacity	3a. Improved principal selection process
	3b. Mentoring programme for First time principals and a coaching support programme for experienced principals
	3c. A balanced scorecard approach to principal performance management
	3d. An accelerated development programme for high potential leaders
	3e. A development programme for high performing principals
	3f. Local administrative bureaux for networks of small schools

Box 7.1 Outline of the *Blueprint for Government Schools* commitments *(cont'd)*	
Flagship Strategy 4. Creating and supporting a performance and development culture	4a. Accreditation scheme for performance and development culture schools
Flagship Strategy 5. Teacher professional development	5a. 60 teachers to undertake 4–6 week teacher professional leave
	5b. Induction programme for beginning teachers, complemented by
	5c. Mentoring programmes for beginning teachers
Continuously improving schools	
Flagship Strategy 6. School improvement	6a. A differential model of school review
	6b. Schools with student performance outcomes above expected levels to: indicate plans to expand horizons; propose alternative models of review; act as mentor schools and share good practice
	6c. Support for schools where student performance is satisfactory but where indicators suggest there is scope for improvement
	6d. Improvement strategy for schools where student performance outcomes are below the expected levels
	6e. A range of interventions and support strategies
	6f. Schools to prepare single planning and accountability document
	6g. Schools to be provided with parent, teacher and student opinion data
	6h. Performance and development culture
Flagship Strategy 7. Leading schools fund	Provision of a leading schools fund

Source: DEECD (2003), *Blueprint for Government Schools: Future Directions for Education in the Victorian School System*, Department of Education and Early Childhood Development: State of Victoria.

The Departmental Office for Government School Education (the OGSE – formerly OSE) bases its approach to school improvement on the three core beliefs: all children can learn; work hard and get smart; and failure is not an option (Fraser and Petch, 2007). These are applied through a focus on creating the right conditions for improvement; developing the capacity of leaders to promote high quality instruction; increasing teacher effectiveness; building high-quality relationships with the educational workforce; and understanding the relationship between educational theory, research and practice.

The OGSE's approach to implementing the improvement strategy has been to "draw on the best evidence from international research, 'socialise' this evidence and then use the data available in the system to assist all schools to determine the most appropriate improvement strategy for their stage of performance and development. This includes "strategic interventions in schools that do not have internal capacity to respond effectively to the challenges they face" (Fraser and Petch, 2007).

A research-based approach to system-wide improvement

The OGSE recognised that a precondition for implementing the school improvement strategy was for teachers, principals, and staff of the education office to "understand and engage in the core work of school improvement" (Fraser and Petch, 2007). The DEECD has developed a common understanding of the principles and models for implementing key parts of the reform, with a shared language with which to discuss it. The common framework and vocabulary ensure that all stakeholders may engage in meaningful communication. High quality relationships are being built with the school leadership workforce and great emphasis is put on exposing them to educational theory and research. The process is supported by substantial capital and recurrent funding and validated through an intelligent accountability framework which is increasingly embedded in a system-wide performance and development culture.

The DEECD has drawn from international research to identify the most important characteristics of effective schools, effective leaders and effective professional learning. Three evidence based models were used as a basis for building shared understanding of how the education workforce relates and impacts on student outcomes: the effective schools model, and, further elaborating key provisions of this model, the effective leaders model and the professional learning model. At the outset, the OGSE adopted a model of school effectiveness (Figure 7.2) based on the review of school effectiveness research conducted by Sammons, Hillman and Mortimore (1995). Priorities within the eight characteristics indicated by the model were professional leadership, a focus on teaching and learning, and purposeful teaching.

Figure 7.2 The effective schools model (schematic)

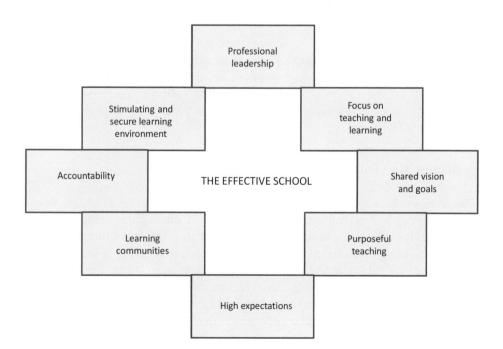

The effective schools model provides an organising framework for the range of strategies and initiatives which stem from the *Blueprint.*

Professional leadership is reflected in an emphasis on building leadership capacity. Adoption of the effective leaders model, based on Segiovanni's domains (1984), has provided a shared model for leadership development and the foundation for principal preparation, selection, performance and development. The effective leaders model is further elaborated in a system-wide model for leadership learning, the developmental learning framework (Office of Government School Education, 2007).

The *focus on teaching and learning* and *purposeful teaching* are reflected in a model for effective professional learning (Office of Government School Education, 2005). This puts student learning at the centre of a range of development programmes, such as leading for student learning and leading professional learning, which enable teachers to engage with school improvement, together with the development and practice of skills such as coaching and mentoring, which contribute to greater teacher effectiveness.

Shared vision and goals are clearly promoted system-wide through the *Blueprint* and the documents issued subsequently by OGSE, the regular and sophisticated communications with principals and others, the grouping of all schools into networks, and the alignment of all the development programmes and opportunities.

High expectations of the profession are applied through the leadership development framework, which raises the sights for leadership performance and also through the performance and development culture which forms the basis for accountability along with differential school reviews.

The department has promoted a wealth of *learning communities* intended to strengthen the professional culture and values. All schools, for example, belong to local clusters and wider school networks, supplemented by collegiates of principals. The networks all have links with the department through the nine regional offices; the regional directors are strongly committed to the delivery of the *Blueprint* school improvement policies.

Lastly, the provision of a *stimulating and secure environment* is reflected both in a major government commitment to rebuild or refurbish all schools by 2017 (50% of schools by 2011) and the provision of a "leading schools fund", which provides a programme of school development and enhancement including a large capital sum for investing in new facilities.

7.4 Strategy for building leadership capacity

The state-wide approach to building leadership capacity in Victorian schools (Flagship Strategy 3) has many parallel programmes. Coherence is achieved in a number of ways. First, the glue that provides cohesion is the inspired effort to create a leadership culture across the system, based on professional discourse using a common language. Second, the conversation about school improvement and leadership development is promoted across the system through all sections of the education infrastructure. This infrastructure, supports and transmits system-wide leadership. Third, a clear vision of the characteristics of effective leadership and developmental learning is understood throughout the system.

This vision has been expounded, not through a set of leadership standards or benchmarks, but through the more sophisticated "developmental learning framework for leadership" mentioned above, in which the different components of leadership are described as progressive levels of competence or performance. We discuss these cohesive strands in turn before illustrating the leadership development provision in Sections 7.5 and 7.6.

Creating a culture of reflective leadership and developmental learning

Ingenious strategies are used to raise the level of discourse and understanding about school leadership among the principal class in Victoria. These stem from the leadership of the Office of Government Schools Education, where the deputy secretary steers learning through the system. One initiative which provides an indicator of the changing relationship between the centre and schools is Big Day Out, an annual convention for all the principals in the state. Characteristically the minister and senior department staff take a lead in presenting policy issues and the expected role of principals. The event always includes an inspirational visiting speaker of international repute who provides the agenda for round-table workshop activities. Recent scholars at state-wide forums have included Richard Elmore and David Perkins (Harvard), Michael Fullan (Ontario) and Ken Leithwood (Toronto).

Other strategies for communicating in a common language and building a leadership culture having a shared vision and goals include:

- A fortnightly newsletter for all principals from the deputy secretary, detailing his work and developments in the system, and drawing attention of principals to some educational publications which are worth reading.

- Regional workshops for principals led by the deputy secretary and a colleague.

- Regular meetings of principals who are organised in 64 networks across the nine administrative regions, with the department meeting network chairs periodically.

- Short secondments of principals to the department.

- Standing consultation meetings with two principals from each region; the Principals Common.

- State-wide structured reading activities, encouraged by the occasional free issue of a key book to each of the 1 600 principals in Victoria. The first example was Leadership on the Line (Heifetz and Linsky, 2002). Individual chapters of the book were discussed in successive newsletters, and principals were invited to share their critiques in the newsletter (see illustrative comment in Box 7.2).

Box 7.2 Comment by school leaders on Chapter 2 of *Leadership on the Line* by Ron Heifetz and Marty Linsky (issued to all principals by the OGSE) – circulated in the fortnightly newsletter

A comment by Victorian school leaders: "Heifetz and Linsky's contention that 'to lead is to live dangerously' is explored in a most pragmatic and realistic fashion in chapter 2 – 'The faces of danger'. The four faces of leader-danger they expound upon are the risks of being marginalised, diverted, attacked or seduced by those who seek to retain the status quo in an organisation. All can result in leadership being shut down, and all are characterised by the element of surprise. The discussion of these and the examples given will, I am sure, strike a chord with many of us. Change is such a challenge for many people within a school, and many try to resist, using whatever tactics they can muster. It is difficult always to know the provocation source of the next attack and even more, at times, to realise that it is coming from those who generally seem to be supporters…. The distinction between the adaptive and the technical aspects of any issue can assist us in managing those whose primary concern is the preservation of self and position. Heifetz and Linsky show us how to identify the ways in which leadership may be undermined. A useful tool we think."

Source: OGSE (2007a).

Key books such as *Leadership on the Line* (Heifetz and Linsky 2002) are given free to each of the 1 600 principals in Victoria, and discussed in a series of newsletters.

Multi-layered system-wide leadership

The coherence and impact of the different school improvement programmes are due largely to the conversation which has been sustained across schools, regional offices and the central office to develop a collective understanding of the challenges confronting the government school system. System-wide leadership of the implementation of reforms in government schools, which stems from the deputy secretary and his OGSE senior team, is focused, analytical, challenging and visible. The vision and objectives are clear; development strategies are evidence based and designed to meet priorities for improvement; communication is continuous and consultation embedded. High expectations, individual and collective responsibility, and the principles of professional learning apply across the system to those working in education administration as well as in schools. The result is that the whole system is being encouraged to sing from the same song sheet.

The key agents of change are the deputy secretary and his colleagues in the Office for Government School Education, the nine regional directors and their colleagues, and the 1 800 or so members of the principal class, whose schools are grouped in 64 networks, each chaired by a principal. Local groups of schools also belong to other partnerships such as clusters, and the collegiates which work on shared interests. The layers of organisation are shown in Figure 7.3 together with links and a feedback loop through, for example, the Principals Common which meets the deputy secretary and in which every network is represented.

The regional offices have an important role in the school accountability and improvement framework by monitoring and reporting on the achievement of each school's progress towards its identified priorities. The offices also support the networks, foster the cluster arrangements and have a key role in assessing applications for leadership development programmes.

Figure 7.3 Some layers and groupings in the government school system

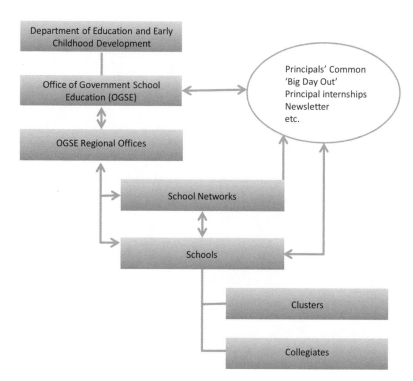

Regional structures and networks enable system leaders such as high performing principals to support their peer schools. In 2006 the department identified the need to harness the capacity of the networks to assume greater responsibility and accountability for the performance of their schools and to focus more on work in the classroom. Network meetings are increasingly concerned with the professional challenges involved in delivering school improvement imperatives stemming from the *Blueprint* and the three educational models discussed earlier. Much of the coaching and mentoring resource which is such a strong feature of leadership development programmes is applied within networks. Some principals have also spoken of the stronger collegiality with other principals: focusing on leadership issues of common interest is of particular value.

Conceptualising leadership

In all these groupings, common language about leadership and school improvement is becoming increasingly prevalent. In an initiative which typifies the research based approach to professional development, the Office of Government School Education constructed and delivered to every principal a *Developmental learning framework for school leaders* (OGSE, 2007b), which defines what effective leadership looks like in practice at different stages of development and growth. This taxonomy of leadership capabilities uses Sergiovanni's model of transformational leadership (Sergiovanni, 1984, 2005) as the basis of the framework (Box 7.3).

Box 7.3 Developmental learning framework for school leaders: Domains and capabilities

Leadership domains	Leadership capabilities
Technical An effective leader demonstrates the capacity to optimise the school's financial, human and physical resources through sound management practices and organisational systems that contribute to the achievement of the school's vision and goals	Thinks and plans strategically Aligns resources with desired outcomes Holds self and others to account
Human An effective leader demonstrates the ability to foster a safe, purposeful and inclusive learning environment, and a capacity to develop constructive and respectful relationships with staff, students, parents and other stakeholders	Advocates for all students Develops relationships Develops individual and collective capacity
Educational An effective leader demonstrates the capacity to lead, manage and monitor the school improvement process through a current and critical understanding of the learning process and Its implications for enhancing high quality teaching and learning in every classroom in the school	Shapes pedagogy Focuses on achievement Promotes enquiry and reflection
Symbolic An effective leader demonstrates the capacity to model important values and behaviour to the school and community, including a commitment to creating and sustaining effective professional learning communities within the school, and across all levels of the system	Develops and manages self Aligns actions with shared values Creates and shares knowledge with them
Cultural An effective leader demonstrates an understanding of the characteristics of effective schools and a capacity to lead the school community in promoting a vision of the future, underpinned by common purposes and values that will secure the commitment and alignment of stakeholders to realise the potential of all students	Shapes future Develops a unique school culture Sustains partnerships and networks

Source: OGSE (2007b), *The Developmental Learning Framework for School Leaders*, Office of Government School Education, Department of Education and Early Childhood Development, State of Victoria.

Box 7.4 Developmental leadership profiles in the *Educational Leadership* domain

Educational leadership	Capabilities
An effective leader demonstrates the capacity to lead, manage and monitor the school improvement process through a current and critical understanding of the learning process and its implications for enhancing high quality teaching and learning in every classroom in the school.	Shapes pedagogy Focuses on achievement Promotes enquiry and reflection

Level	Profile
Level 1	Leaders engage staff in professional discussions about effective learning and teaching. They implement processes that support the alignment of the curriculum, pedagogy, assessment and reporting and ensure the curriculum reflects system goals and requirements. The role feedback plays in supporting learning and teaching is articulated. They promote the use of multiple forms of data to determine starting points and goals of the learning. They create opportunities for people to use their expertise and assist them to enhance their practice by identifying strengths and areas for improvement. To promote intellectual exploration, they reference research material and source relevant data to determine priorities for school improvement.
Level 2	Leaders consider the nature of the student cohort when designing the school's curriculum. They establish processes in order to support the use of a range of feedback sources to inform teaching and learning. They help others to develop their capacity by creating opportunities for staff to learn from each other. Leaders develop a shared understanding of the implications of data for planning improvements. They support staff to experiment with a range of strategies to improve their practice
Level 3	Leaders design learning, teaching and management interactions based on how people learn and support the application of learning theories in classroom practice. School practices are monitored to ensure alignment of the curriculum, pedagogy, assessment and reporting with goals for student learning. They design a curriculum that is responsive to system changes and to changes in the student cohort. Leaders manage staff performance and development to improve student outcomes and monitor the extent to which feedback informs professional learning. Opportunities for reflection are incorporated in a range of forums
Level 4	Leaders challenge others to continually improve their performance. Classroom practice is evaluated to determine professional learning needs. They ensure that teacher performance and development processes are linked to teacher practice, programme effectiveness and professional learning. Resources are allocated in order to support the school community to engage in an ongoing process of enquiry and reflection. Leaders design improvement strategies based on empirical evidence.
Level 5	Leaders ensure models of learning and teaching underpin all classroom practice. They ensure that the principles of developmental learning inform the alignment of the curriculum, pedagogy, assessment and reporting. To improve learning outcomes, they verify that students and staff self-evaluate against goals and targets. Leaders promote further improvement by systematically collecting evidence of how reflective practices contribute to improvement in teacher practice. They influence curriculum practices in other schools and design initiatives that build the capacity of people across the system.

Source: OGSE (2007b), *The Developmental Learning Framework for School Leaders*, Office of Government School Education, Department of Education and Early Childhood Development, State of Victoria.

The leadership framework is intended to underpin all discourse and development related to school leadership. Sergiovanni's domains ("five forces of leadership") are already referred to widely in discussions with and between leaders and about leadership. Its power lies in the refinement of each of Sergiovanni's domains into developmental profiles (see example in Box 7.3). These are being used as a basis for self-assessment and 360° assessments, enabling teachers and school leaders to set direction for their professional learning. The body of content within each of the leadership domains compares with other, more empirical leadership taxonomies, such as the National Standards for Headteachers (DfES 2004) in the UK. The framework is also being used by leadership development providers, the education department and its regional directors and their staff. The leadership framework has become fundamental to the selection of new principals. School councils are required to advertise principal positions using five mandatory criteria based on the Sergiovanni leadership domains. A sixth community criterion reflects local needs and priorities.

Victoria, with the help of the University of Melbourne, has expanded the leadership domains into hierarchical levels at which performance can be demonstrated (Box 7.4). This ensures that the classification can be used developmentally, and there is evidence that principals and providers are doing so. Parallels exist in the rather more restricted contexts of urban leadership in the UK (NCSL 2003), which uses four rather than five development levels, and a range of school evaluation and inspection criteria used in different national accountability systems. The Victorian leadership framework breaks new ground in being applicable to leadership throughout the school at all levels in the school, showing where a teacher or school leader is located on a continuum and what they need to know and be able to do in order to improve.

Building leadership at all levels

The department recognised that effective leadership at all levels in the system was a pre-condition for implementing the school improvement aspirations reflected in the *Blueprint*. The increased investment in leadership development was based on a "comprehensive and deliberate suite of strategies aimed at improving the quality and performance of our leaders". These strategies include leadership development opportunities for aspirant leaders and principals, including a Master in School Leadership qualification for teachers who demonstrate high leadership potential; mentoring for new principals and coaching for experienced principals; and a programme for high performing principals that develops those who can contribute to system development.

7.5 Features of the leadership development programmes

The opportunities for professional learning for current and aspirant leaders are set out in *Learning to Lead Effective Schools* (Office of School Education, 2006) which provides a diverse range of 19 programmes for aspirant leaders, assistant principals and principals (Box 7.5). Some 3 000 people had participated in the suite of programmes between 2004 and 2007. In 2007 alone, most programmes have had between 50 and 100 participants per programme, and Leaders in the Making had more than 200 participants.

All 19 leadership development programmes aim to build the capacity of teachers and leaders to meet the *Blueprint* expectations for continuous improvement in the quality of learning and teaching (Box 7.5). Each programme is rooted in research evidence and best practice. The principles identified by the department in 2004 (OGSE, 2005) characterise effective professional learning as:

- focused on student outcomes (not just individual teacher needs);

- embedded in teacher practice and informed by the best available research on effective learning and teaching;

- collaborative, involving reflection and feedback ;

- evidence based and data driven to guide improvement and to measure impact;

- ongoing, supported and fully integrated into the culture and operations of the system – schools, networks, regions and the centre;

- an individual and collective responsibility at all levels of the system, and not optional.

As with other dimensions of the new professionalism expected of teachers and leaders in the Victorian system, individual development must contribute to the greater good – system-wide improvement. Professional development is seen as investment in capacity for which there needs to be some payback in terms of bringing knowledge into the system. The programmes use professional learning models, either singly or more often in combination. These include: action research, examination of students' work, study groups, case discussions, peer observation, lesson study, study visits and academic study. All professional development providers are required to have regard for the *Blueprint* principles and professional learning models. Leadership programmes are underpinned by the department's effective schools model (Figure 7.2). They include four key elements:

- the **knowledge and skills** that leaders need to develop the capability to influence how schools function and what students learn;

- the **experiences** to support the development of these skills;

- the **structures** that best support delivery of these experiences;

- the **resources** necessary for these programmes.

All programmes are structured so that participants can apply their learning in a practical context. "The programmes are designed to build on prior learning experiences and enable current and aspirant leaders to access learning opportunities at different stages of their careers." (OGSE, 2006)

These programmes put a responsibility on the participant to be an effective, self-motivated learner. The emphasis of much of the leadership development is on self-determined, practice-orientated experience. Mentoring and coaching play prominent parts in both policy and practice, as well as in supporting candidates' development, and other schools and their principals are important resources for professional learning.

In line with the new professionalism expected of teachers and leaders in the Victorian system, individual development must contribute to the greater good – system-wide improvement.

Box 7.5 Professional learning programmes for current and aspirant leaders

Name of programme	Open to:	Description	Aspirant leaders	Assistant principals	Principals
Master in School Leadership	All after 5 years teaching	Taught modules, in-school elements and mentoring or shadowing; 2 years	√	√	√
Building capacity for improvement	Teams of teachers	Briefing, residential and day workshops, coaching support and feedback; 1 year	√	√	√
Building the capacity of school leadership teams	School leadership teams	Three-day residential, action research in school, 3 coaching sessions, follow-up workshop; 1 year	√	√	√
Leading across effective small schools	Small school teams	Three 1-day forums, action learning project, web based support, mentor with small school experience; 1 year	√	√	√
Leading in effective schools (strategic planning)	High potential leaders	Briefing, preparatory activities and 360° feedback, two workshops, 4 coaching sessions and ongoing email contact; 1 year	√	√	
Preparing for leadership	Experienced teachers	Two-day conference, four day workshops, background reading pre- & post-programme 360o, school based project, shadowing; 1 year	√		
Leading for student learning	Expert teachers	Five days workshops, reading & data collection, 360o, peer learning groups; 1 year	√		
Leading professional learning	PD coordinators	One year part time programme ˙	√	√	
Scholarships at postgraduate study	Postgrad teachers	Range of postgraduate courses	√	√	
Eleanor Davies school leadership programme	Female leading teachers / APs	Five months including mentoring, reading, seminars, school based project	√	√	
Leaders in the making	Assistant principals	One year with workshops and strategic planning project.	√	√	
Stepping up to the principalship	Assistant principals	One year, including data-collection, workshop, shadowing, reviews		√	
Educational leadership: shaping pedagogy	APs and principals	One year, including preparation, intensive workshop, review, feedback, action planning		√	√
Human leadership: developing people	APs and principals	One year, development and implementation of a professional learning plan		√	√
Technical leadership: thinking and planning strategically	APs and principals	One year, including strategic planning project		√	√
Mentoring for first time principals	First time principals	One year			√
Coaching to enhance the capabilities of experienced principals	Experienced principals	One year with assigned coach			√
Development programme for high performing principals	Principals	Over a two-year period including contribution to system development and individual professional development			√
Building the capacity of the principals of small schools	Principals of small schools	One year			√
Teachers professional leave	All teachers	30 days	√		

Source: OGSE (2006), *Learning to Lead Effective Schools: professional learning for current and aspirant leaders*, Office of Government School Education, Department of Education and Early Childhood Development, State of Victoria.

Practice-based and tailored programmes

The high performing principals' programme allows principals the time and encouragement to travel, study worldwide leading edge practice, and reflect on applications to their own work (Box 7.6). Participants we spoke with were stimulated, informed, enthused and professionally rejuvenated by their experiences. They returned to Victoria with greater expertise in the topic they had studied, eager to apply their learning through the leadership of their school. They now saw themselves as high performing learners. Other themes for study included addressing disadvantage, personalised learning, learning management and ICT, and instructional learning. Many agreed that the biggest change was that they are more reflective about their practice. The programme demonstrated that the system values and trusts principals and believes in their importance in bringing about changes in schools and for students. High performing principals are actively used in mentoring and coaching roles, but engagement with the programme has enhanced their value. The department is seeking ways of disseminating their experience more widely, for this programme has given school leaders knowledge, skills and dispositions needed to meet new roles and responsibilities in the school and larger system. Another effect of the programme is to give outstanding leaders a greater incentive to remain within a system that cannot afford to lose them.

Participants we met told us that they used their horizon-broadening experience to reflect on the Victorian system (Box 7.6). They considered that one of the biggest challenges facing the system stems from increasing inequities: between the wealthy and the poor, between different schools and between the government and other school sectors. They recognised a need for education that would build the capacity of the workforce, but perceived many inequitable barriers to achieving this. Many were motivated to make a greater contribution to schools beyond their own, disseminating their accumulated experience and newfound expertise to help other schools to succeed.

Box 7.6 High performing principals: Experiences and impact

One participant had taken the Data-wise course at Harvard, examined the London Leadership Strategy and visited the Institute of Education, and paid a visit to Finland, returning with clear strategies for achieving improved student learning. This participant now perceived that "most of the copious data available to schools in Victoria is too aggregated to be of use in helping to improve student learning".

Another participant went to Harvard, Canada and the UK to study school networks. She described the experience as overwhelming and felt "reborn". Her network is now involved in professional learning. The opportunity came at the right time, for she did not know what to do next in her coasting school. She focused on instructional learning, which has led to the development of individual learning plans for every student. She is now "in classrooms a lot more" and has coached leaders and formed small collegiate groups within her network.

In contrast to the high performing principals' programme, teachers' professional leave (TPL) enables teachers within or across schools to undertake projects known as "challenges". The resource is between 20 and 50 days of paid leave, which can be used as a block of time or spread out. The programme has engaged 2 400 teachers (out of 40 000) to date (6%). In common with the high performing principals, participants in the TPL programme who met with the OECD team were enthusiastic about the opportunities it offered and the contribution that such development could make to schools and clusters (Box 7.7).

Box 7.7 Teachers' professional leave: Experiences and impact

In one example, a team of three primary school teachers (middle leaders) in a cluster of schools used the TPL programme to undertake development in peer coaching, focusing on coaching for the improvement of learning and teaching. The project fitted the schools' aspiration of sharing good practice. As one said: "my challenge is to challenge and energise the teachers I work with." The three participants were allowed 20 days each to develop coaching skills with the support of a practised coach, undertaking observation and coaching in each others' schools and feeding back to colleagues in their own school. They encountered barriers in disseminating their expertise, since even in effective and well led schools many teachers are reluctant to engage in peer evaluation of classroom work. Thus the translation of the new skills into improved classroom practice is not automatic or given, and demonstrates the necessity for additional support through the principal and other systemic interventions.

In both these examples, it was evident that strategies were needed for effective application and dissemination of the knowledge and skills developed by participants in order to maximise their value to the school system. Many of the structures are in place to achieve this – for example, regional leadership, networks and clusters of schools, and a thoughtful "principal class". One of the challenges for senior leaders may be their readiness (or reluctance) to model the roles and behaviours they wish to be reflected across the work of the school, leading by example in the classroom as well as the school.

The philosophy of learning in a practical context was reflected in the responses of educators who had participated in leadership development programmes. Many spoke warmly of the quality of mentoring or coaching they had experienced and the value of visiting other schools. Evidence was presented, for example, of the value of the Eleanor Davis school leadership programme (Box 7.5), which aimed to encourage more women into principalship through being mentored by a principal in another school, and the range of programmes aimed either at preparing leaders for the next step or building leadership capacity within schools and teams.

Academic and other provider-led programmes

The range of programmes commissioned by Victoria from higher education institutions and other suppliers of professional development, together with nationally funded programmes, fits well with the Victorian *Blueprint* priorities and leadership development strategy. Indeed, providers are required to reflect Victorian policies in their proposals. The Master in School Leadership (MSL) programme offered by both Melbourne and Monash Universities complements other postgraduate qualifications in education, and the graduates of these competing Masters programmes we interviewed were positive about the quality of their provision. Both universities have been closely involved in supporting the development of the research based strategies. Academic leadership programmes therefore reflect the recently published Developmental Learning Framework for School Leaders (OGSE, 2007b).

Members of the first cohort of the MSL programme told us they valued the challenges presented by the programme and its implications for them in their schools. Foremost is the shift from management thinking to leadership. Changing teachers' attitudes to seeing themselves as leaders was seen as a difficult issue, tackled by capacity-building strategies such as developing data-led shared ownership and responsibility for children's progress.

Changing community perceptions about what schools do was even harder. There was a recognition of the need to communicate with and educate parents more effectively.

The structure of leadership programmes, like those in the UK, facilitates progressive development opportunities. For example, one principal – now in her second principalship – recounted how she had been a mentee on the Eleanor Davis programme and was subsequently a mentor, as a principal. She undertook a Masters degree in change management in 2000 and is working towards a Doctorate. She is a trained and experienced coach and the chair of a schools network, and has undertaken study visits to Indonesia, Japan, New Guinea and elsewhere. For the capable and ambitious leader, it appears, there is a world of development opportunity.

Programmes funded by central government

In addition to the *Blueprint* programmes, there are other leadership programmes at a national level. Since 2006, Teaching Australia (the Australian Institute for Teaching and School Leadership, an independent national body for the teaching profession) has developed and delivered, in collaboration with the University of Melbourne and the Hay Group, a national professional leadership development programme, Leading Australia's Schools. This programme trains two cohorts per year of 40 principals from all Australian states and sectors. During the three months they spend in the programme, participants identify a major challenge, refine it, set goals for themselves and assess themselves against those goals, with peer group support, coaching and tutorial inputs and guidance. Challenges have ranged from overcoming the barriers to the amalgamation of two secondary schools to bringing change into an established primary school culture; motivating staff to continually reflect on their teaching and learning programmes; and introducing a performance and development culture. Participants' case studies showed that they benefited a great deal from the programme, gaining new skills and affirming their own moral purpose as prospective system leaders.

7.6 Programme effectiveness and continuous programme improvement

All those we met appreciated that the department had taken seriously the need to develop leadership, had made real investment in the programmes and had become much closer to schools. Principals endorsed the value of the shared readings promulgated in newsletters from the deputy secretary, and it appeared to principals that the OGSE was practising what it preached.

Independently evaluation of the leadership programmes has been very positive. For example a 2006 report (Roy Morgan Research, 2007) considered the Masters, mentoring, coaching and high performing principals programmes. Using multiple research methods, the evaluation concluded that the aim of the *Blueprint* Flagship Strategy 3, "building leadership capacity" was being achieved. Pre- and post-tests showed a positive change in the mean rating for each capability with every domain of leadership. Programmes targeted at less experienced and aspiring principals achieved greatest improvement, as expected. Participants in the development programme for high performing principals gave it exceptionally high ratings. Participants felt this was extremely worthwhile and commented that it gave them a renewed passion for their role. After three years, 10% of Victorian school principals have undertaken this programme, emerging as refreshed and invigorated potential system leaders.

In the leadership development programmes, there is evidence that positive gains continue after participants have completed the programme: an increasing proportion of graduates gain promotion after completing the Masters programme. The report also states: "What is also evident is that many participants are reporting personal outcomes which are outside building leadership skills, for example clarity and sense of purpose, feeling energised and motivated, and coping better and having more resilience, which are particularly beneficial and in addition to the specific leadership skills which were expected" (Roy Morgan Research, p. 56). Suggestions for incorporation into the programmes include more opportunities for shadowing and networking.

There are some frustrations, which we also heard from high performing principals, to the effect that insufficient use is made of their new knowledge and expertise in the role of system leaders. It may be the case that system leadership capacity is being generated at a faster rate than it is being absorbed.

Participants in these programmes identified the hierarchical nature of existing leadership and promotion frameworks as being a major barrier to change. The current approach to the recognition of performance, for example, "was regarded by some as rewarding length of service rather than encouraging leadership". There was a feeling that large scale changes are required to properly support aspiring and current school leaders. The report concludes that "changes in leadership behaviour are preceding the cultural changes required to actively encourage transformational leadership". This finding supports the emphasis placed on leading the whole system and on changing the culture so as to reprofessionalise leadership.

Little is said in the evaluation about instructional leadership – the focus on learning and teaching. This connection is essential if the investment in leadership development is to have an impact on what happens in the classroom. So far, there is little evidence of impact on students' learning and achievement.

The development opportunities provided to Victorian teachers and school leaders through the Australian Government Teacher Development Programme (AGQTP) – which directly contribute to the *Blueprint*'s flagship strategies – are also subject to commissioned external evaluation. The 2006 report[5] gauges evidence of impact from the perceptions of participants and third parties, such as observers or coaches. In most cases, around 60% of participants reported the activities as having a great or large impact, with up to 90% saying the impact was great, large or fair. These perceptions were validated by observers who assessed the impact of programmes on the skills of participants and generally rated the benefits higher than participants. Five to ten percent of the participants found little or no value in the experience.

One of the *Blueprint* activities which the AGQTP has evaluated is the Building the Capacity of Small Schools programme, which provides individual onsite coaching and support for principals of small schools. From May to November 2006, this programme involved 39 leaders of small schools, selected through a regionally based process, and used 16 trained coaches. Participants worked to develop a strategic improvement plan that they would implement during the year with the support of their coach and study groups. Despite having full teaching loads, the participants reported a significant increase in their

---

5.   The 2006 report of the AGQTP Longitudinal Evaluation (I & J Management Services, 2007) monitors and reviews AGQTP activities including the leadership development programmes "Building the Capacity of School Leadership Teams", "Leading for Student Learning" and "Building the Capacity of Principals of Small Schools".

capacity to develop and support a whole school culture orientated to school improvement. By early December 2006, participants were on average 74% along the way to implementing their plan and expectations were that most school improvement plans would be completed by early 2007.

The evaluation report (I & J Management Services, 2007) again shows that coaches assess the impact higher than the participants themselves, "seeing something in the participants that the participants are not seeing in themselves". Qualitative feedback on the impact of a coach and a network of peers was very strong

> A coach stated: "(Participants have valued)…. that they are not alone. They have a non-judgemental person to bounce ideas off, and can try new things with someone to support them to move their thinking from the day to day to the bigger picture."
>
> A principal stated: "I valued the collegiate discussions and sharing of good practice strategies that other schools use and that can be adapted to my school's needs."

Quality assurance of Victorian leadership development programmes rests not only with the commissioned evaluations but in the attachment of departmental staff to every programme. Close monitoring contributes to continuous improvement, as does the selection of providers through competitive tendering. To be successful, providers must be thoroughly familiar with the department's strategies and policies.

Quality assurance of Victorian leadership development programmes rests not only with the commissioned evaluations but in the attachment of departmental staff to every programme.

7.7 Policy conditions, implementation and impact

A number of policy conditions seem to have facilitated the implementation of the Victorian school leadership strategy. These are summarised below.

Continuing political support

The Department of Education and Early Childhood Development's initiatives have played a crucial part in the drive to build leadership capacity across the government school system. The *Blueprint for Government Schools* provides the aspiration for high-quality school education for all government school students. The flagship strategies have been designed to enable the system to respond to that aspiration. It is important that successive ministers have continued to support the *Blueprint*, protecting the system from distracting changes of course and contributing to its sustainability.

Strategic alignment

A significant feature of the Victorian approach to school and system improvement is the high degree of alignment of all its strategies. The language and culture of school improvement and professional development extend across the department and the principal class of the state and are penetrating to other levels of leadership in many schools. The strategy and its research foundations also extend to the partners of the school system, particularly the providers of leadership development programmes, and to the Catholic and independent schools which provide for a third of Victorian students.

This alignment is shown in the way leadership development programmes are embedded in the wider development context. Each of the formal programmes contains field based experience, and aspiring and incumbent leaders also apply and develop leadership competences in the context of their daily school practice, in which they seek to exercise the skills identified in the state's leadership model. In addition, there is extensive provision for the coaching and mentoring of leaders and aspirant leaders. This on-the-job learning and practice are aligned with the department's leadership strategy, which also includes an improved principal selection process, based around the Sergiovanni leadership model. Candidates move through the selection process aware of the model and its implications for effective leadership.

Performance evaluation is also aligned with the development programmes. Following a balanced scorecard approach to performance management, targeted coaching, mentoring, and performance feedback from a range of sources evaluate critical elements of effective leadership. Among the performance objectives for all principals is achieving accreditation through the Performance and Development Culture Process designed to encourage and support leaders in introducing high quality performance management and continuous improvement into their schools. A differentiated model of school performance measurement, reporting, review, and accountability concentrates principals' efforts on performance outcomes and continuous improvement. Such processes integrate and reinforce professional practice and professional development.

An intelligent accountability framework

Victoria has one of the most devolved school management approaches among OECD countries. Schools are self-governing bodies controlling 90% of their budget. This creates the need for an intelligent accountability framework that allows the education system to respond appropriately to the evidence that student outcomes and trend data provides.

A strength of the *Blueprint* is its context of a transparent and rigorous accountability framework. Plans for school improvement comprise a four-year school strategic plan and an annual implementation plan. The framework evaluates progress towards meeting improvement goals and targets using school self evaluation and external reviews; reports to the school community on progress in core performance indicators; and assures compliance with legislation. Independent as well as internal evaluation shows strong support for and effective use of the School Accountability and Improvement Framework.

The differing requirements of schools are accommodated by a flexible accountability arrangement. Rather than using accountability as a mechanism to distribute sanctions and rewards, the Victorian government uses performance data as a basis for decisions on intervention and support strategies for schools and school leaders. These strategies include:

- coaching;
- mentoring;
- expert administrators;
- expert consultants;
- partnership arrangements with tertiary providers to work on improvement projects;
- co-operative arrangements between schools;

- secondment of high performing principals to low-performing schools.

Timing and resourcing

Recognising that culture change in education will take time, no timelines were fixed for attainment of the reform objectives. There is an implicit appreciation of the need for ongoing constant funding and support efforts over a time frame that is longer than short term political interests.

The Department of Education and Early Childhood Development (DEECD) has provided the capital and recurrent funding to support the overall reform programme. The department has focused in particular on schools most in need and those with a strong argument for further investment. The support and resources available for radical change projects, urgent regeneration and improvement plans create a context conducive to innovation.

There is an implicit appreciation of the need for ongoing constant funding and support efforts over a time frame that is longer than short term political interests.

The DEECD has defined ambitious expectations about school improvement and it is ready to invest heavily in human capital development in order to achieve them. In 2006-07, the budget for *Blueprint* projects was over AUD 17 million. *Blueprint* allocations represent 0.44% of the total School Resource Package for government schools. By way of illustration, funding for teacher professional leave was over AUD 4.4m, compared with funding for high performing principals of AUD 0.75m. Individual participants rely on a variety of resources, from central coverage of the full cost to part school or self funded costs. The exact balance varies between programmes.

Evidence of impact

Evidence published in Fraser and Petch (2007) shows differential improvement of schools in the last three years, in a number of performance indicators, against a background of improvement in small incremental steps over the last eight years. The more marked three year improvement trends include measures of school climate, using teachers' perceptions of school morale and students' perceptions of their own motivation to learn; learning environment; student decision making; professional interaction; learning environment and a range of other measures. There is evidence that the quality of instruction in years 5–7 has improved, though this tapers off in later years. There are longer term small but positive trends in educational outcomes such as literacy, although little evidence to show a clear association with recent policy initiatives. The DEECD is monitoring performance trends systematically, and has the tools to track the impact of *Blueprint for Government Schools* on the quality of teaching and leadership, and outcomes for learners.

7.8 Food for thought

A world class approach?

Since the Victorian government published the *Blueprint* in 2003, the quality of the systemic approach to school improvement in Victoria has been excellent. Clarity of focus has led to a clear and persuasive research based school improvement, professional learning and leadership development culture, articulated through a common language. The programmes are well designed and comprehensive. Momentum has been sustained through highly effective communications and diligent consultation with all the major stakeholders. Most compelling is the way in which evidence based theory is aligned with school based provision of leadership development opportunities, reflecting a high degree of coherence in the Victorian school improvement strategy. The "theory of action" which underpins these developments is clear and rational, and can be commended to other education administrations.

Most compelling is the way in which evidence based theory is aligned with school based provision of leadership development opportunities.

The improvement strategy has also found ways of reconciling accountability and development. At the individual level, the performance and development culture framework (DEECD, 2007) provides for the accreditation of schools based on self assessment. This should reduce the need for the diagnostic reviews which are currently part of the external accountability arrangements.

Within this school improvement strategy, the Victorian leadership programme is an outstanding example of effective large scale reform. Its rigorous, systematic process is projected over several years in a carefully calibrated sequence with ample political support. The programme offers no promise of a quick fix, but deep belief in the chosen course and its ultimate success. The programme builds the capacity for the "steady work" of school reform (Elmore and McLaughlin, 1988). It fosters common understanding among policymakers and practitioners, builds practitioner capacity for reform and focuses that capacity on the development of feasible solutions rather than predetermined policy fixes. It provides for variable forms of practice suiting diverse conditions.

Much is demanded from the improving system, but the government makes an investment in building human and system capacity proportional to its expectations, thus satisfying Elmore's law of reciprocity (Chapter 3). In fact, the driving strategy is not accountability, or implementation of models, two otherwise popular approaches to reform, but investment in human capital. This is investment not in the acquisition of fixed knowledge and ability, but in the ability to learn, to lead others to learn, and to nourish systems of continuous improvement. Thus change is cast not as a process of technical engineering, though some of that is needed, but rather as adaptive work (Heifetz, 1994), a process of learning that leads to development of new ways of acting and solutions to commonly perceived but ambiguous, complex problems. Finally, the government is providing targeted resources and leverage at the critical trouble spots where it is most needed, ensuring that leaders have the wherewithal to support the changes that emerge through their adaptive work.

The driving strategy is not accountability, or implementation of models, two otherwise popular approaches to reform, but investment in human capital … the ability to learn, to lead others to learn, and to nourish systems of continuous improvement.

In international terms, the Victorian model of leadership development is at the cutting edge. The department has created professional learning opportunities for leaders at all levels in the system to seize, and the increasing numbers that have done so inject further knowledge and vitality into the system. This results in building human as well as knowledge capital on a large scale. The span of operation is large, probably approaching the limit for a strategy which is driven with a particular leadership structure and style, and supported by thorough consultative procedures, frequent communications and comprehensive networking. The Victorian model is exceptionally well documented; the high quality publications from the Office for Government School Education provide a clear rationale for the thoughtful approaches adopted.

Further strengths of the Victorian leadership development strategy

A coherent reform process: The department has adopted and propagated three educational models, reflecting current research evidence on effective schools, effective leaders, and effective professional learning. The models are interlinked and provide reference points for new policy initiatives, ensuring that the entire process is logically aligned. The DEECD continues to deepen the reform process; the recent introduction of a framework for purposeful teaching is linked to the existing models and the overall reform process.

Intellectual engagement of the education workforce: Despite the complexity of the Victorian reform agenda, the Victorian Department of Education and Early Childhood Development has focused on developing a few clear and simple messages to engage all members of the educational community. The DEECD has constructed a common framework and language to ensure that all stakeholders can engage in meaningful communication. High quality relationships are being built with the school leadership workforce and emphasis is put on exposing them to educational theory and research. The department draws on evidence from international research and shares this evidence as well as the data available in the school system to help schools in developing appropriate improvement plans.

Clear expectations for school leadership: The Victorian Department of Education and Early Childhood Development has chosen, refined and disseminated a specific model of effective leadership – Sergiovanni's model of transformational leadership – which provides an explicit statement of what is expected of school leaders. This model articulates the kind of knowledge, skills and behaviours leaders should continuously demonstrate in order to lead schools effectively. The model has been embedded in all leadership policies and initiatives; in particular, it underpins a developmental learning framework that guides school leaders' professional development, their recruitment, training and appraisal.

A focus on performance development: The performance review of school leaders is geared to support their professional development and improve practice, rather than as a mechanism for top-down control. School leaders use the developmental learning framework as a tool to define their learning needs as part of their annual performance and development cycle. Based on the framework, they identify leadership skills they need to successfully implement the school improvement plan. They provide details of the leadership capabilities they intend to develop, indicate professional learning actions to build their capacity, and choose evidence they will use to monitor their growth and development. In many cases, the performance and development plans are developed and monitored collaboratively with the leadership team or across the school.

Continuous learning linked to school based plans and challenges: All leadership preparation and development programmes have a school based component that matches the participants' performance plans as well as their school's strategic plan. Nineteen different programmes are available to school leaders in Victoria; their variety aims to address the specific needs of leaders at different stages of their career with different aspirations, experiences, needs and proficiency levels. Leadership development is recognised as a strategic issue; the capacities of current and future leaders have to be identified and continuously developed.

An emphasis on peer learning: The Victorian leadership strategy is built on the recognition that in order to develop professionally, school leaders need to be aware of themselves as learners. It highlights the importance of coaching, mentoring and peer observation processes. It encourages networking, collegial exchanges, and the involvement of "critical friends" within the educational community. School leaders are encouraged to seek multiple sources of feedback to develop a better understanding of and reflection on their own practice. They are expected to model such behaviours to their teachers in order to develop their schools as learning organisations. Professional learning is based on the principles of the professional learning model in evidence across the range of programmes.

Challenges

We identified some elements in the system that will require particular attention for large scale and sustainable school improvement to occur in Victoria.

Reducing the achievement gap: The key objective of the *Blueprint* reform is to improve learning outcomes regardless of students' socioeconomic background or geographic location. However, the available data on student performance is not as yet strategically used for that purpose. Performance data are not disaggregated by socioeconomic background to target disadvantaged students more specifically. None of the leadership development initiatives is specifically geared to building capacity to address equity challenges.

Involving parents and community more: The leadership development strategy aims to include leaders at different levels of the system, including the school, regional and central levels. Given the comprehensiveness of the approach, it is surprising that the school council, which has a formal role in school leadership, has so far been left out of the process. Addressing the leadership capabilities of the school council could also be a way of reaching out to the parents and community and addressing socioeconomic inequities more. In the UK, for example, government has initiated training focused on the leadership of school governing boards (DfES, 2005).

Integrating small, rural and isolated schools: The outreach to schools is still uneven and there are some schools where no member of the staff has undertaken training. Small, isolated, and rural schools have often not been sufficiently connected to the process. In small schools, teaching obligations make it difficult for principals to attend training programmes, network meetings or conferences.

Bringing transformation into the classroom: The Victorian approach recognises school leaders as leaders of transformational change in their schools. However, as in any education system, experienced teachers in Victoria may be reluctant to revise teaching practice which seems to have worked over the past and to accept new ideas that may not seem relevant to their local experience. School leaders will have to play a crucial role as mentors, role models and facilitators engaging teachers to reflect on and improve their practice using current research and evidence of effective teaching and learning. The success of the leadership reform will ultimately depend on school leaders' capacity to engage teachers with the reform process.

Avoiding over-complication: The publication of *School Improvement: A Theory of Action* (Fraser and Petch, 2007) provides a timely review of the many different strands of the school performance improvement strategy, spinning them into a cohesive thread. Seen in isolation, the different initiatives that contribute to the reforms are complicated components of a sophisticated machine. Taken together, they reinforce each other and provide coherence and direction in the drive for improved school performance. All the essential ingredients appear to be in place. It will be a challenge to embed, sustain and further develop them, and to ensure that current and new school leaders understand the principles on which effective school improvement rests.

Sustainability

The system-wide improvement and leadership development has undoubted momentum and will have an increasing impact as the system leaders among the principals engage more in work with other schools. The question of whether the strategy has passed a point of no return is not simply rhetorical; it would have real meaning if one of the key drivers of the strategy, a system-wide leader, was no longer on the scene. Other risks would include diminished government commitment to or funding for leadership development; failure to focus effectively on the development and quality assurance of learning and teaching; and any hesitation in generating and employing pupil-level performance data to inform their learning and enhance their rate of progress. Views expressed to us vary: the most capable principals are optimistic and enthusiastic; the OGSE is cautious; academics are reserved. The leadership framework has not yet penetrated much below the principal class. While the professional culture of this group has been invigorated, stimulated and in individual cases transformed, there is evidence that teaching is considered by many educators to be an activity conducted by an adult with acquiescent students in private. We were impressed with those teachers who have seen the power of peer coaching and are eager to open windows into lessons. This will be an ongoing challenge which may be accelerated if the members of the principal class emulate the leaders of the system and open their practice as educators to others in their school. Role modelling is central to what Sergiovanni terms "symbolic leadership".

We feel that the system is close to critical mass or tipping point, which the minister described as "the point where the majority is going down a different path and the minority becomes uncomfortable in not moving" (Bronwyn Pike, Victorian Minister for Education).

Victoria provides a working model of system-wide school leadership development from which other systems can learn.

In conclusion, we largely share the view expressed by Richard Elmore, who knows the Victorian system well:

> *"The good news is that Victoria, because of the thoughtful design of its improvement strategy, is on the leading edge of policy and practice in the world. There are few improvement strategies close to or as well developed, and probably none that are focused with such depth and complexity on the basic human capital problems associated with school improvement at scale. Unfortunately, this is also the bad news. What it means is that there are relatively few places Victoria can look to find the answers to the kinds of problems that will surface through the middle and later stages of the strategy. The special affliction of the precursor is to have to make the mistakes that others will learn from". (Elmore, 2007)*

As we have suggested, challenges remain in terms of embedding, sustaining and further developing the Victorian school improvement strategy, but mistakes were in conspicuously short supply. Victoria provides a working model of system-wide school leadership development from which other systems can learn.

Annex 7.A1
Case study visit programme,
20-23 August 2007

Day 1: Monday 20 August 2007

Time	Event	Participants	Location
09.00 - 10.00	The Victorian Context	Darrell FraserJudy Petch	OGSE
	The Education Reform Agenda	Dale Cooper	
10.00 - 11.00	Learning to Lead in Victoria	Darrell Fraser	OGSE
	The Leadership Agenda	Judy Petch	
11.30 - 12.30	Evaluations of Leadership programmes currently being run in Victoria	Judy Petch Dina Guest Raylene Dodds Dale Cooper	OGSE
13.15 - 14.15	Meeting with Leadership & Teacher Development Team to include a briefing on the Developmental Framework for School Leaders	Judy Petch Raylene Dodds Chris Thomson Jane Hendry Chris McKenzie Dale Cooper	OGSE
15.00 - 16.30	Meeting with the Representatives of the Department of Education, Science and Training (DEST). The purpose of this meeting is to provide the national context. This will include a briefing on the current work of Teaching Australia.	DEST reps (Ewen McDonald, Shelagh Whittleston) Teaching Australia reps (Helen O'Sullivan, Nicolas Jackson, Kathy Lacey) Darrell Fraser Judy Petch Dale Cooper	OGSE
16.30 - 17.10	Meeting with the Victorian Minister for Education, Bronwyn Pike	Minister Pike Professor Peter Dawkins	Minister's room
17.10 - 17.30	Meeting with the Secretary, Department of Education Victoria, Professor Peter Dawkins	Peter Dawkins	
19.00 – 21.50	Darrell Fraser	Deputy Secretary Government School Education	Level 46 Collins Tower
	Judy Petch	General Manager Govt School Education	
	Dale Cooper	Senior Policy Officer Govt School Education	
	Dina Guest	General Manager Govt School Education	
	John Allman	General Manager Govt School Education	
	Dianne Peck	General Manager Govt School Education	
	Katherine Henderson	Deputy Secretary Policy and Evaluation	
	Dahle Suggett	Deputy Secretary Policy and Innovation	
	Jeff Rosewarne	Deputy Secretary Resources and Infrastructure	
	Tony Bugden	Genereal Manager Human Resources DEECD	
	Glenda Strong	Regional Director Barwon Region	
	Vicki Forbes	Principal Brentwood Secondary College	
	Gabrielle Leigh	Principal Carolyn Springs Secondary College	
	Chris Chant	Principal Mentone Primary School	
	Michael Bell	Principal Euroa Secondary College	
	Julie Podbury	Principal Brighton Secondary College	
	Gordon Pratt	Principal Brighton Primary School	
	Professor Field Rickard	Dean of Education University of Melbourne	
	Professor Patrick Griffin	Deputy Dean of Education University of Melbourne	
	Professor Jack Keating	Faculty of Education University of Melbourne	
	Tony Mackay	Director, Centre for Strategic Education	
	Professor Peter Dawkins	Secretary DEECD	
	Louise McDonald	Amrita Chandra, Larry Kammener, Drew Arthurson	
	Sue Buckley	Tony Bell, Chris Bennett	

Day 2: Tuesday 21 August 2007

Time	Event	Participants
08.30 – 10.45	Murrumbeena Primary School Discussion with Principal about the Victorian Leadership development strategy High Performing Principals Coaching & Mentoring Programme Teacher Professional Leave Principals Common The Ultranet Tour of school	**Heather Hill** Principal and colleagues
11.15 – 14.00	Balwyn High School Discussion with Principal about the Victorian Leadership Development Strategy High Performing Principals Coaching & Mentoring Programme Teacher Professional Leave Development Learning Framework for School Leaders The Ultranet Include a discussion with a group of students in the Xplore centre. Tour of school	**Bruce Armstrong,** Principal Senior Leadership Team, Staff and students
14.30 – 16.00	Meeting with the nine Regional Directors Presentation on the role of Regions and Regional Directors. Discussion with Regional Directors about Impact of Leadership Strategy and their work Two Case Studies Bendigo Regeneration Project Targeted School Improvement initiative, two examples to illustrate approach to school improvement and the role of the school leadership team.	Nine Regional Directors

Day 3: Wednesday 22 August 2007

Time	Event	Participants
09.00 – 10.30	Discussion with 8 Principals who have participated in the High Performing Principals initiative.	Eight High Performing Principals
11.00 - 12.15	Meeting with eight participants in the Masters of School Leadership Programme	Eight Masters of School Leadership participants
12.15 – 13.15	Meeting with 8 participants from the other leadership development programmes	Eight programme participants
14.00 – 15.00	Meeting with the Presidents of the three associations that represent Victorian principals to examine the complimentary set of leadership development programmes their organisations deliver. Brian Burgess President - Victorian Association of State Secondary Principals Fred Ackerman President Victorian Principals Association Jeff Walters & Bob Parr Organisers Principal Class Association Australian Education Union.	
15.00 – 16.00	Meeting with Tony Bugden, General Manager of Human Resources Workforce Corporate Leadership Strategy Enterprise Bargaining Agreement	Tony Bugden and colleagues
16.00 – 17.00	Meeting with Programme Providers from Victorian Universities and private providers: Prof Len Cairns Monash University Prof Field Rickards Melbourne University Prof Sally Walker Deakin University Prof Jack Keating Melbourne University Steve Atkinson Sharon Butler Ross Dean Karen Starr	

Day 4: Thursday 23 August 2007

Time	Event	Participants
09.00	Meeting with the other deputy secretaries in the department of education to discuss policy agenda and how resources are used to deliver the government agenda.	Dahle Suggett Katherine Henderson Jeff Rosewarne
10.00	Meeting with Professor Peter Dawkins to examine the work of the Victorian Department of Education in the national context.	Peter Dawkins Tony Mackay
11.00	OECD team meeting	
14.30	Plenary session for OECD team to feed back, raise questions and to test their first impressions.	Darrell Fraser Judy Petch John Allman Dina Guest Dianne Peck

References

Anderson, M., P. Gronn, L. Ingvarson, E.K. Jackson, P. McKenzie, B. Mulford and N. Thornton (2007), *OECD Improving School Leadership Activity. Australia: Country Background Report*, a report prepared for the Australian Government Department of Education, Science and Training (DEST) by Australian Council for Educational Research (ACER), *www.oecd.org/edu/schoolleadership*.

Bolam, R., G. Dunning and P. Karstanje (eds) (2000), *New Heads in the New Europe,* Waxmann, Munster.

Council for the Australian Federation (2007), *Federalist Paper 2. The Future of Schooling in Australia: a report by the States and Territories*, Department of Premier and Cabinet, Melbourne, *www.dpc.vic.gov.au*.

DEECD (2003), *Blueprint for Government Schools: Future Directions for Education in the Victorian School System*, Department of Education and Early Childhood Development: State of Victoria.

DEECD (2007), *Blueprint for Government Schools: Flagship Strategy 4 – Creating and Supporting a Performance and Development Culture*, Department of Education and Early Childhood Development: State of Victoria.

DfES (2004), *National Standards for Headteachers,* Department for Education and Skills, London.

DfES (2005), *Taking the Chair: A development programme for Chairs, Vice-Chairs and Chairs of Committees of School Governing Bodies*, Department for Education and Skills, London.

Elmore, R., (2007) *Educational Improvement in Victoria,* Unpublished internal communication.

Elmore, R.F. and M.W. McLaughlin (1988), *Steady Work: Policy, Practice, and the Reform of American Education*, The RAND Corporation, Santa Monica, California.

Fraser D. and J. Petch (2007), *School Improvement: a Theory of Action,* Office of School Education, Department of Education and Early Childhood Development, State of Victoria.

Heifetz, R.A. (1994), *Leadership Without Easy Answers*, Harvard University Press, Cambridge, MA.

Heifetz R.A. and Linsky M. (2002), *Leadership on the Line,* Harvard Business School Press, Boston, MA.

I & J Management Services (2007), *AGQTP Longitudinal Evaluation,2006 Report,* Department for Education and Training, Victoria.

Leithwood, K., K.S. Louis, S. Anderson and K. Wahlstrom (2004), *How Leadership Influences Student Learning,* Learning from Leading Project, New York.

OGSE (2005), *Professional Learning in Effective Schools: The Seven Principles of Highly Effective Professional Learning,* Office of Government School Education, Department of Education and Early Childhood Development, State of Victoria.

OGSE (2006), *Learning to Lead Effective Schools: Professional Learning for Current and Aspirant Leaders,* Office of Government School Education, Department of Education and Early Childhood Development, State of Victoria.

OGSE (2007a), *Letters from the Deputy Secretary OGSE, 2004-2007,* Office for Government School Education, Department of Education and Early Childhood Development, State of Victoria.

OGSE (2007b), *The Developmental Learning Framework for School Leaders,* Office of Government School Education, Department of Education and Early Childhood Development, State of Victoria.

NCSL (2003), *A Model of School Leadership in Challenging Urban Environments*, National College of School Leadership, Nottingham.

Roy Morgan Research (2007), *Evaluation of the Blueprint Leadership Initiatives: 2006 Annual Report,* Department of Education, Victoria. (Also the 2006 Annual Report)

Sammons P., J. Hillman and P. Mortimore (1995) *Key Characteristics of Effective Schools: A Review of School Effectiveness Research,* Office for Standards in Education and Institute of Education, London.

Sergiovanni, T.J., (1984), *Handbook for Effective Department Leadership: Concepts and Practices in Today's Secondary Schools*, Allyn and Bacon, Boston.

Sergiovanni, T.J., (2005), *The Principalship: A Reflective Practice Perspective,* 5th Edition, Allyn and Bacon, Boston.

Thomson, S., Cresswell, J., De Bortoli, L. (2004), *Facing the Future: A Focus on Mathematical Literacy Among Australian 15-year-old Students in PISA 2003*, Australian Council for Educational Research, Victoria.

Chapter 8

Building leadership capacity for system improvement in Austria
by
Louise Stoll, Hunter Moorman and Sibylle Rahm

This chapter provides information and analysis on Austria's Leadership Academy. The Leadership Academy (LEA) is an initiative of the Ministry of Education, Science and Culture (now Education, Arts, and Culture) launched in 2004 to equip leaders in Austria's education system with the capacity to lead an emerging body of reform initiatives and help establish a new culture of proactive, entrepreneurial school leadership.

The Leadership Academy was selected by the OECD Improving School Leadership activity as an innovative case study because of its system-wide approach to leadership development, its emphasis on leadership for improved schooling outcomes, its innovative programme contents and design, and its demonstrated potential to achieve effective outcomes.

This chapter is based on a study visit to Alpbach and Vienna, Austria, in April 2007 organised by the Ministry for Education, Arts and Culture at the request of the OECD. The visit included review of documentation, meetings with stakeholders, and some site visits at both locations. The chapter provides the rationale for exploring this programme, sets the Austrian national and provincial context within which LEA operates, describes the programme design and content, analyses the practice in terms of constructs and impact, and ends with some reflections. The list of documents consulted and the visit itinerary, showing respondents contacted during the visit, are included in the annex.

8.1 The OECD case study visit to Austria

Austria faces challenges from global economic competition, technological change, and demographic shifts experienced by many other countries in Europe and the rest of the world. To address these challenges, Austria is adopting more flexible, inventive forms of public policy decision making, favouring devolution to local levels and market-based choice. The government is also committed to developing a more flexible, responsive education system that will achieve higher quality outcomes for all pupils. This commitment implies, and necessitates, change in the established manner of doing business in schools, provincial and national government, and in the larger culture. Austria's social and political traditions and the organisation of its government and education system are not always well suited to support such change. Powerful central, hierarchical, and consultative traditions must be modified in ways that both maintain continuity with the past and adapt to the needs of the future. Policymakers, the education system at large, and school leaders themselves – at all levels – need to feel responsible for developing more effective leadership, in greater quantity and distributed among a larger share of the education enterprise, needed to meet the current challenge.

It is the mission of the Leadership Academy to prepare the new order of leadership. More ambitiously, it aims to:

- change the culture of the education system so that it can embrace change;
- adopt new values and practices;
- serve well a diverse pupil population and their communities;
- continue to improve according to the requirements of a changing society and a changing world.

The study team comprised the rapporteur, Louise Stoll, visiting professor at the London Centre for Leadership in Learning, University of London; Hunter Moorman, OECD consultant and expert in leadership, education reform, and organisation development; and Sibylle Rahm, Professor at the Otto-Friedrich University in Bamberg, Germany.

Following this introductory section, the chapter moves to a description in Section 8.2 of the context, highlighting key conditions in Austria that explain or influence the Leadership Academy, including its policy rationale. In Section 8.3 we examine the Leadership Academy programme, outlining its purpose, goals and key features and considering its conceptualisation of leadership, school improvement and leadership learning. Programme effectiveness and ensuring continuous improvement are the focus of Section 8.4, while Section 8.5 addresses the necessary policy conditions and implications. We conclude the chapter, in Section 8.6, with some areas for reflection and recommendations for other countries considering such a programme.

8.2 Background to the Leadership Academy: the Austrian context[6]

Austria's historical and social context

Austria is a parliamentary democracy organised as a federal state comprising nine provinces (Länder). The official language is German, but the country is home to diverse ethnic groups who come largely from Eastern European countries, the former Yugoslavia and Turkey, among other countries.

Austria has a well developed market economy. The country is prosperous, but the economy has slowed down recently and unemployment has risen (although the unemployment rate is still substantially lower than the EU average). Globalisation and the expansion of Europe pose long term challenges, bringing more competition and the need to develop knowledge based and value added sectors. The previous government sought to introduce a more liberal, market oriented economic agenda and to revamp the role of the state, emphasising deregulation and privatisation, reform of public administration, and narrower targeting of social benefits.

Two-thirds of Austria's population of just over 8 million inhabitants (2001 census) live in urban areas, but the country has a substantial rural tradition. The population is ageing and population growth is low. Austria's social context is also changing. Single parent households and working parents have become more common. Immigrants comprise a growing share of the population, with 12.5% of the population foreign born (OECD, 2006). An older and increasingly immigrant population puts pressure on the national treasury and the country's generous health and pension systems. Schools are under increasing pressure to meet diverse student needs, satisfy roles formerly played by the family, and maintain public confidence.

Yet some long standing social conditions persist. Austrians tend to live and work close to their places of birth and to identify closely with their local and regional areas. Geographic and job mobility are low, and teachers and school leaders customarily remain in one school over a career, occasionally hampering recruitment of teachers and school heads. Values and traditions emphasising social cohesion, trust, and stability strongly influence social and governmental processes. Decision making in schools and school systems is a highly consultative process encouraging participation and negotiation among diverse interests. Decisions carry the weight of social commitment but come slowly and tend not to reach too far.

Austria's changing education system

The Austrian educational system is highly structured and differentiated. It offers pupils and parents many choices and avenues, alternatives and second chances.

---

6.   This section draws heavily on the Austrian country background report prepared for the Improving School Leadership activity, "Improving School Leadership Country Note: Austria", by Michael Schratz with the support of Katalin Petzold, December 2007, available at *www.oecd.org/edu/schoolleadership*; on background information provided in "Attracting, Developing, and Retaining Teachers, Country Note: Austria", by Françoise Delannoy, Phillip McKenzie, Stefan Wolter and Ben van der Ree, April 2004, available at *www.oecd.org/edu/teacherpolicy*; and on the Eurydice Database on Education (2006).

Schools are organised into general and academic secondary schools, with upper and lower secondary education levels and an elementary level. In upper secondary education the school system is divided into a general education branch and a vocational branch. Both, however, lead pupils towards higher education entrance qualifications.

The Austrian school system is selective, tracking pupils after only four years in primary school into either general or academic secondary schools according to their marks. There is pressure on students and parents to compete for more prestigious schools, on teachers to prepare students well, and on schools to compete for students.

In the early years of this century, there have been on average approximately 853 000 pupils and students per year in elementary, general secondary and academic secondary level schools combined (based on 2004/05 data for primary and Hauptschule pupils and 2002/03 data for academic secondary school students, found in Eurydice Database on Education, 2006). The number of primary school pupils has been declining, a trend that is forecast to continue until 2008 and further. The number of secondary school students has also begun to decline. Austrian schools are becoming more multicultural and classrooms increasingly marked by heterogeneity of language, religion, ethnicity and national origin.

Responsibilities for education legislation and implementation are divided between the federal government and the Länder. Decision making authority for financial, personnel, and other policy decisions is divided within the ministry (and in some cases the chancellery), between federal and the provincial school authorities, and between the different layers of the school system and school leaders.

Consultation plays an important role in the system. Stakeholders – teachers, parents, students and the community – are afforded formal participation in decision making, and teacher unions, organisations, and groups have a strong influence on decisions.

Education has always been heavily contested among political decision makers. The extensive distribution of responsibilities between different bodies and entities can be seen both as a product of and a brake on political interests. Prior membership in the teacher union or support for a political party seems to exert a strong if informal influence in the selection of school heads.

The differentiated system, divided governance, extensive consultation, and partisanship contribute to the strengths and quality of the education system. At the same time, they can complicate governance, slow decision making and impede change.

Reform context

The Austrian school system is by tradition compliance oriented, bureaucratic, and cumbersome. In solving educational problems schools and other parts of the system have tended to look up the hierarchy for guidance and to respond reactively, rather than proactively to take the initiative. Much of the policy debate and dialogue about improvement has focused on inputs rather than outputs. The discussion tends to be on how to operate the system, instead of questioning whether the system is producing the most appropriate results for society. Diffuse decision making limits and slows the pace of change.

Membership in the European Union and the shock of PISA results have underscored these shortcomings. PISA findings indicate that many students are not developing the skills necessary to participate in lifelong learning. They also reveal substantial disparities in the performance of students and allocation of entitlements in different classes, schools and regions (Haider *et al.*, 2003, in OECD, 2007).

The results of PISA and other large-scale assessments like TIMSS and IGLU have generated heated political and public discussions about the quality of schooling, and triggered a major educational "culture change". A growing system of standards, assessments, and transparency measures has introduced greater school accountability and heightened pressure to perform. Devolution has increased local autonomy – and conflict. Numerous individual reforms and efforts to streamline the education governance and delivery system are shifting power and responsibility, opening new opportunities, and creating tension where duties and privileges are added or lost.

In 2005 the Austrian Ministry of Education's *Zukunftskommission* (Future Commission) proposed a framework for education reform and numerous specific proposals for improvement. The principles included systematic quality management, greater autonomy and more responsibility, improvement of the teacher profession, and more research and development and better support systems (cf. Haider *et al.*, 2003, cited in Schratz and Petzold, for the OECD, 2007). Among the panoply of specific initiatives which are starting to be implemented, some of the most far-reaching are:

- The adoption of national standards (Bildungsstandards) and assessments in year 4 (primary school) and year 8 (general secondary school and academic secondary school). The emphasis on outcomes, monitoring, and accountability represents a major change for Austrian schools.

- A measure to improve teaching and enhance learning centred leadership by limiting class size to 25 pupils per class. An initiative for individualised teaching and learning (including quality assurance) will complement this measure.

- Authorisation (and in some cases funding) for some schools to provide extended day supervision for pupils.

Austria's long tradition of school inspection is also changing. School inspectors, organised by province, district, and subject and by school type, regularly examine the quality of teaching and the implementation of leadership and management tasks in a school, and identify areas in need of improvement. Two quality assurance programmes are adding a broader dimension to schools' and inspectorates' interaction, strengthening schools' own quality assurance roles and emphasising inspectors' leadership and enabling roles.

The changing role and conditions of school leadership

Heads of school in Austria are civil servants either of the federal government (the heads of academic secondary schools and secondary vocational schools) or of the province (the heads of primary, general secondary schools, special schools, pre-vocational schools and vocational schools).

The traditional duties of the school head have been to implement laws and directives from above, administer the budget and school resources, monitor curriculum and teaching and learning, and work with teachers to modify them as needed. Heads also maintain communication with the school authorities, parents, and community and manage the process of school partnership consultation. In smaller schools, they also teach classes.

Both the duties of school heads and the way they carry out their duties are changing. Deregulation and somewhat expanded local autonomy have added broader pedagogical leadership duties to their traditional administrative and fiscal responsibilities. The impending introduction of national standards with result-based assessments and national tests also intensifies heads' responsibilities to provide pedagogical leadership. A large list of specific reform initiatives means that school heads must now lead successful change processes, support teachers in their new duties, manage the collaboration of school partners and increased levels of conflict and stress in schools, and ensure the success of the large variety of school reforms for which they are responsible.

Austrian school heads must now lead successful change processes, support teachers in their new duties, manage the collaboration of school partners and increased levels of conflict and stress in schools, and ensure the success of the large variety of school reforms for which they are responsible.

Although school heads' autonomy in budgetary, staffing, and curricular decision making has been increased by recent government policy, their discretion is still limited. Schools do not have authority for employing or dismissing staff. The complex distribution of responsibilities and extensive consultative processes constrain the autonomy of school leaders. Strong traditions of teacher autonomy and responsibility for interpretation of curricular guidelines further dilute decisive leadership and change.

As new laws and functions redefine the role of the school head, the relationship between school head and teachers is becoming more complex. While the head is the teachers' supervisor, teachers have a substantial degree of independence, resulting both from the tradition of classroom autonomy and from provisions requiring teacher and parent (and sometimes pupil) participation in important school decisions. Heads are responsible for monitoring and mentoring teachers, but most do not go deeply into teacher evaluation and coaching, because of collegial relationships or the lack of time due to pressure of administrative tasks. School heads have little direct authority to reward or sanction teachers. They do not, as noted above, have authority to hire and fire teachers, although they may advise on the choice of new teaching candidates. They have no say in setting teacher pay, which is uniform across the country, or in offering extra pay or bonuses, although they can recommend them to higher authorities. School heads are supposed to build teacher commitment to professional development, and as leaders of teaching and learning need to be able to direct teachers' continuing growth, but they have little authority or leverage for doing so.

School heads do not have authority to hire and fire teachers. They have no say in setting teacher pay, which is uniform across the country, or in offering extra pay or bonuses.

Leadership learning in Austria

The most significant opportunities for leadership learning consist of a compulsory management training, individual courses offered by the teacher training institutions on a variety of topics, and the Leadership Academy.

New school heads are required to complete a compulsory management training programme within the first four years of their provisional appointment for their contract to be extended. The programme is offered as a part time course by the individual provincial in-service training institutes. Broadly, the training includes a set of modules and a phase of self-study. Modules cover communication and leadership, conflict management, lesson supervision, school development, and educational, vocational, and household legal rights, regarded as core competencies for new school leaders (Fischer and Schratz, 1993, in Schratz and Petzold, 2007). Participants use self-study to explore pertinent literature, conduct projects combining theory and practice, and take further training to their needs.

There is no required pre-service preparation for aspiring heads. Aspirants can take modules of the compulsory management training, but they are still required to take the full programme upon being named head of a school. Apart from the compulsory management training, no induction programmes are required. The different provinces however offer new heads a variety of special support programmes on topics such as coaching, supervision and other regular meetings to exchange experiences of novices and experts. Further participation in professional development programmes is expected but not compulsory. Nor is it a condition of continued employment as a school leader, or for promotion or increased compensation. There are no systematic professional development programmes on the regional level; only short term options. Thematically focused training supports the introduction of new reform initiatives and keeps school leaders abreast of innovation on the regional and national levels. In addition, a pilot project has been conducted in different provinces to explore innovative practices of blended learning through e-learning components in different content areas.

Policy rationale for the Leadership Academy

National policymakers in Austria identified the need to prepare school leaders to lead and sustain systemic change. In 2004, the Minister of Education, Science and Culture founded the Leadership Academy (LEA).

School heads have newly acquired autonomy but little experience of operating outside a hierarchical, bureaucratic structure. The original intent of the LEA was to develop in heads the capacities to act more independently, to take greater initiative, and to manage their schools through the changes entailed by a stream of government reforms. As the benefits to systemic change of involving a wider participant group became apparent, inspectors, staff of in-service training institutes, and executives from the Ministry of Education and provincial education authorities were added as participants. The LEA's brief in its first phase became to train 3 000 school leaders and other executives in education leadership positions in a very short period of time on the basis of the latest scientific findings on innovation and change.

8.3 The Leadership Academy programme

Ambitious objectives

The Leadership Academy provides leadership development for school heads, inspectors, government officials, and staff from university, in particular from university colleges of education. It aims to enable them to manage the introduction of national reforms and to lead processes of school improvement. Individual learning and development, project leadership, and network relationships are the key elements of the programme. Each year, a cohort (called a "generation") of 250 to 300 participants progresses through four "forums", three-day learning experiences consisting of keynote presentations with group processing and of work in learning partnerships (pairs of participants) and in collegial team coaching (CTC) groups, each comprising three sets of partnerships. With support and critique from these learning partners and CTCs, each participant develops and implements a project in his or her own institution over the course of the year. Learning partners and CTCs meet regionally in the interim between forums and also come together with other participants in regional networks. Generation IV was completed in October 2007, with generation V scheduled to start December 2007.

With support and critique from learning partners and collegial team coaching groups, each participant develops and implements a project in his or her own institution over the course of the year.

The formal goal of the Leadership Academy is "sustainably improving the preconditions and processes of young people's learning in all educational institutions" (LEA, 2007a). The purpose more simply stated but equally ambitious is to prepare leaders at all levels and in all types of schools to *work in and on the system* (LEA, 2007b).

The programme has in its sights two levels of change. At one level, leaders are prepared to implement the government's ambitious reform agenda effectively and to enable schools to function with greater local autonomy and initiative. Thus, LEA builds participants' capacity to play their roles more intentionally and proactively, to take more responsibility, to motivate their staff teams and develop their organisation. In this way they will be seen to be working effectively within a system where autonomy has been increased. They will be using new skills, systems understanding, and relationships to focus on the core task of education for the future. This involves building vision, developing team spirit, clarifying roles and values and emphasising pedagogy. Public law cannot be easily changed and, therefore, effective school leadership and management in this context means achieving as much as possible within the existing system.

But the introduction of several recent reforms under the impetus of the Future Commission also underscores the need for school leaders skilled at managing change.

At another level, LEA is creating the critical mass needed to fuel systems change. Leaders emerge from LEA with new values and attitudes in place of the traditional compliance-oriented stance, with new relationships across a traditionally segmented education system, and with a systems understanding that puts their practice in a far larger context. A critical mass of such leaders should begin to "reculture" the system, to introduce new understandings and norms of professional practice. As stated in the project documentation (LEA, 2007a, p. 1): "The programme for the professionalism in leadership works along a new understanding of theory and practice which transforms the educational system by taking the quality of leadership as the starting point for systemic innovation." In the end, the system should be more open, flexible, and inclusive, inclined to balance stability with innovation, and committed to and accountable for high quality outcomes.

In the end, the system should be more open, flexible, and inclusive, inclined to balance stability with innovation, and committed to and accountable for high quality outcomes.

Well considered theories of action

Programmes are more likely to reach their goals when they are guided by a theory that effectively links action to outcome. Theories of action in relation to school leadership, as Elmore (Chapter 3) interprets them, are "a set of logically connected statements that…connect the actions of leaders with their consequences for quality and performance". Ideally the theory of action will provide a logical, powerful, and actionable relationship of action to change, and leaders' (or programmes') actual practice will correspond to their espoused theories (Argyris, 1993; Argyris and Schon, 1978).

The LEA programme is based on theories of action about effective learning-centred leadership, about effective learning of leadership learning, and, implicitly, about effective systems change. These are described below.

Leadership

The leadership theory of action links a set of outcomes through intervening conditions to a set of leadership skills, attitudes, and dispositions. The outcomes are implementation of national reforms and creation of more independent, solution-oriented schools. Intermediate variables are conditions shown by research to lead to effective schools, like motivated and high quality teachers and engaged parents, and those conditions shown by experience to diminish school effectiveness, like compliance orientation and classroom isolation. The programme provides the third ingredient in the equation, a repertoire of attitudes, skills, and dispositions equipping leaders to work with these conditions.

The programme sums up its approach with the dictum *Handlung schafft Wirklichkeit*, or "action creates reality". The LEA attempts to instil a bias toward the effective action needed to implement reforms and to solve problems and succeed locally. The several elements of this approach are:

- building self-knowledge needed to marshal personal resources for emotionally and intellectually stressful challenges of leadership;

- instilling an orientation toward proactive behaviour and initiative;

- replacing the "heroic problem-solver" stance with a future-oriented solution-creating disposition;

- creating an understanding of the complex nature of learning;

- building a systems orientation, awareness of the larger context of schooling and reform, and openness to relationships needed for strategic leadership;

- opening participants up to the habit of changing their mental models and assumptions of "the way it is";

- developing new skills like giving and receiving feedback, working collaboratively, delegating and sharing work.

Leadership learning and development

The LEA programme approaches leadership learning as a complex task that takes place over time and as a result of several interactions. Presentations draw on general and adult learning theory by, for example, grounding new knowledge in participants' current knowledge and combining academic and experiential processes to construct new knowledge. New material and exercises are sequenced logically and coherently to establish the emotional and intellectual conditions necessary for effective learning. The key theoretical construct is that training and experience pursued according to the principles embedded in the programme design will produce learning that can be effectively applied in the participant's home organisation. Core elements of the learning model are:

- sequenced introduction of new ideas (usually in familiar contexts);

- engagement of participants' own base of knowledge and experience;

- demonstration and modelling;

- frequent opportunity for discussion and development of applications;

- basing learning around problems and projects in the participants' own organisation;

- using diverse approaches to fit diverse learning styles;

- providing emotional and intellectual support, feedback and correction in a safe, trusting atmosphere;

- establishing a comprehensive professional learning community practice to sustain application of learning and change.

Systems change

Also underlying the LEA programme is an implicit theory of systems change with two key elements: programme graduates who have new attitudes, skills, and dispositions will change their own schools through their behaviour and the impact of their projects; and a critical mass of graduates will lead over time to a broadly changing education culture.

Carefully blended programme design, content, and operation

The Leadership Academy programme consists of a seamless mix of leadership focus, principles of learning, structure, and curriculum content. To an exceptional degree, "the medium is the message", as all the elements of the programme are designed with the participant's learning in mind. In the following sections, what is in actuality a composite blend is described as a set of discrete elements for the purposes of presentation.

Focus on leadership

The programme is premised on the idea that leadership quality is the starting point for systemic innovation (Schratz and Petzold, 2007). The central design feature of the programme is its concentration on leadership in several dimensions.

Learning-centred leadership

The leadership competence model (Figure 8.1), based on the work of Riemann (1977) and Ulrich *et al.* (1999), underpins the theoretical approach to the programme. The model shows how leaders balance their work between promoting change and leading for the future on the one hand and recognising the need for continuity on the other. At the same time they balance the orientation towards results against the importance of communicating with people and the capacity to build up relationships through working together. The model suggests that leaders need to give direction, show strength of character and mobilise individual commitment as well as creating an atmosphere of achievement within organisations.

Figure 8.1 Leadership competence model

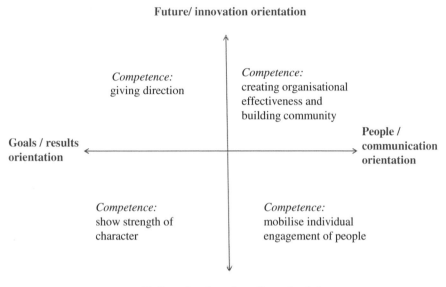

Future/ innovation orientation

Competence: giving direction

Competence: creating organisational effectiveness and building community

Goals / results orientation

People / communication orientation

Competence: show strength of character

Competence: mobilise individual engagement of people

Daily action / continuation orientation

This is not straightforward in a system with many stakeholders. As a union leader we interviewed described it, the effective leader has to work with pupils, parents, peers and teachers "in a complex network".

Our visit to a school led by one of the first Leadership Academy alumni highlighted these competences at work. The head felt very much in charge of the school's future and possibilities, and was described by her school inspector as having clear aims, being confident, feeling responsible to follow national educational policy but comfortable to inform the inspector of specific doubts about ministry policy: "She takes responsibility for the details which she forms according to her beliefs and has the capacity to shape policy to the school's needs." Colleagues, parents and a student we spoke to felt that there was a sense of democracy and that decisions were not taken without a consultation process. This included students, the representative of whom described a good leader as one who "listens to students and respects their ideas". Teachers in this school wanted to be involved in school development and, somewhat unusually within the Austrian context, admired leadership that: "leaves space for the energy teachers bring by themselves".

Leadership for learning

Leadership for learning through leaders' influence on learning has been identified as a critical element of successful school leadership (Leithwood and Riehl, 2003) and is central to the LEA approach. Schratz (2006) explains how, in Austria, "leading" and "learning" have traditionally been considered as separate domains of thought associated with different people. School leaders lead (also sometimes teaching), teachers teach and learners learn. The LEA, however, systematically co-ordinates leadership and learning, by emphasising the learning of both pupils and school leaders.

The LEA programme aims to bridge the gap between leadership and learning by drawing on a model of five dimensions of leading and learning developed at the University of Innsbruck (Schratz and Weiser, 2002): knowledge; understanding (meaning); ability (application); individual (personal) and group (social). It is seen as applicable to leadership and learning for the future. The pedagogical focus on learning has grown since the programme's first generation. During our visit to a Leadership Academy forum, we attended an engagingly presented session introduced by an LEA director with the questions: "What are we doing in leadership for learning? What is the focus? What is the impact on pupils?" The five dimensions were then introduced through "leadership theatre". Participants were invited to consider them in relation to the school's role, teaching methods, a particular subject, assessment and people's personal biographies. Interviews with several participants suggested that this was new thinking for them. This session followed up one at the previous forum which had focused on how pupils, staff and leaders learn.

Leaders' learning is also critical, as described in a "chain of effects" model (Schley and Schratz, 2004), developed for and used with generation 1 participants. This chain of effects is described as a mental web of meaningful relationships pointing the way from leading to learning and back again (Schratz, with Petzold, 2007). It shows, "in theory how leadership impacts on people, planning, culture and structures and how, through interaction, it produces action and results related to the school's goals".

Leading school development and change

Focusing on school development is a key feature of improving schools, enabling leaders and teachers to monitor and evaluate practice in order to improve the practice of teaching and learning (Elmore, Chapter 3). Austrian quality initiatives (*e.g.* QIS; QIBB) sustain the maintenance and enhancement of quality in the educational sector, focusing on teaching and learning in a changing society. Quality development includes a changed view on school management and leadership. Teachers must become learners and school heads have to cope with the tasks of school development and school improvement. As outlined in an OECD report on teacher policy in Austria (Delannoy *et al.*, 2004), the increase of schools' autonomy makes it more difficult to become an effective head. Furthermore, with the inspectorate's changing role, we heard several times about the importance of a positive working relationship and of how school leaders inform their inspectors of their plans and discuss with them their aims, grades and development. One head reflected that positive relations with her inspector provide a good basis for what she wants to do.

The shift to greater school-level autonomy has meant that schools now need to be learning organisations, finding solutions to everyday problems and challenges such as personalisation, the increase in information, social changes and global thinking and acting (Austrian Federal Ministry for Education, Science and Culture, undated).

Heads have to be aware of their strategic role and to take responsibility for leadership of learning. Heads have to implement external reform strategies and activate reform energies in their staff. Leaders must not only care for resources and outcomes but also for the development of the school's vision and educational offerings. They must inspire, motivate and create an atmosphere that will lead to staff commitment and students who are highly motivated to learn: in short, they need to build the capacity for continuous and sustainable learning (Stoll *et al.*, 2003). Leadership in autonomous schools is a challenging task that includes having the personal capacity to bring about positive change and paying greater attention to the emotional side of leadership.

Leading learning organisations, professional learning communities and networks

Increasingly, leadership and improvement literature are pointing towards the benefits of collaborative working in what are variously described as learning organisations (Mulford, 2003) and professional learning communities (Stoll and Seashore Louis, 2007). This is a challenge in a culture where many teachers have been used to working independently. Leaders have to aim at enhancing the practice of individual teachers, developing collaborative capacities of all professionals working at school, and making connections with other schools through learning networks (OECD, 2003) and other partnerships. The intention is that schools in Austria will increasingly become professional learning communities. The Leadership Academy promotes this approach by creating a professional learning community among its participants and introducing learning strategies that can be adapted for use back in schools.

Systemic and distributed leadership

Systemic thinking as the basis of change management involves thinking about the system as a whole. From a systemic point of view, the interrelationship and interdependence between different levels of the system is critical. This requires a multi-level approach to influence the system and leadership at all levels throughout the system.

Promoting system leadership is a key intention of the Leadership Academy; a commitment to collaborating with colleagues at all levels for the benefit of all children and young people, not just those for whom they have the closest connection, described both in this programme and elsewhere as "system thinkers in action" (Fullan, 2005). This has been a major consideration for involving large numbers of leaders at different levels of the system – schools, districts, training colleges, and the ministry – working together in partnerships, teams and networks.

Hopkins (2006) argues for "a systemic approach that integrates the classroom, school and system levels in the pursuit of enhancing student achievement". Our experience suggests that while the intention is to promote the development of professional learning communities within schools, issues relating to teacher professionalism need to be addressed (see final section) before greater distribution of leadership will occur throughout Austrian schools.

Schools themselves are complex organisations, with several intersecting domains: curriculum and teaching and learning, organisational structure and processes, school culture, professional development, and pupil and classroom management, as well as budget, personnel, and facilities matters. The addition of school autonomy, school improvement and development processes, and quality initiatives creates a complex, challenging learning process for those in it. It is not enough to be skilled in managing the individual parts, though that is important; the competent leader must also understand and be able to guide the system as a whole.

School heads also operate in a larger system environment beyond their schools. This necessitates a pattern change in individual leaders' thinking, as most have been accustomed to acting in passive compliance toward that outside system. School autonomy, quality programmes, accountability, and extensive reforms now require leaders to have a broad network of contacts in the system, to understand and anticipate the reaction to their actions of other parts of the system, and to be effective in creating strategic collaborations and negotiating for support and resources from the system.

Project planning, management and costs

The LEA is a project in which the Ministry of Education, Arts and Science, *Kulturkontakt Austria*, the University of Innsbruck, the University of Zürich and the *Institut für Organisationsentwicklung und Systemberatung (IOS)* Hamburg closely cooperate. The two project directors collaborate, one providing the greater share of personal professional development know-how, the other the greater share of education and host country expertise. The project directors manage a scientific team, of which they are a key part, and are linked to an organisational team managed by the project manager in the ministry who is responsible for the overall organisation of LEA and the co-ordination among stakeholders. The teams have clearly assigned responsibilities, and regular meetings are scheduled in which planning can take place for the forums, research and evaluation and ongoing activities with participants and alumni. The scientific core team is small, consisting of the two directors with two assistants (one oversees the design of the LEA's training didactics, the other co-ordinates research activities) and a project manager who looks at how the LEA's aims and goals can be put into practice. They are supported by the wider team, who include the regional network coordinators. The ministry partner also oversees the policy aspects, checks qualifications of potential participants and is responsible for communication with participants in between the forums.

The ministry's contract with the universities has funded the full start-up and operating costs of the programme. The cost for supporting the programme each generation (programme cohort) has been a little over 500 000 Euros, or, after the initial year in which overall costs were slightly higher, just under 2 000 Euro per participant. The cost per participant covers all programme planning and management, costs to put on each forum (including presenters, conference site rental, media, lodging and food for all participants), services and support for such items as the website and learning materials, and miscellaneous costs. Participants' organisations are responsible for transport to and from the conference site for each forum.

A high degree of substantive and training expertise is required of the expert team providing the programme. At least at present, it is not intended that the programme will be institutionalised or incorporated into existing routines or organisations; rather, needed resources will continue to be procured from external sources.

Powerful learning principles

A set of principles of learning underlie the Leadership Academy curriculum.

Creating a trusting environment and relationships

Establishing trust between the professional members of the Leadership Academy is the starting point of the training. The forums start with an emotional "invitation", as one of the directors described it. A regional coordinator explained how "LEA offers an emotional access to people, therefore it becomes easier to work on the cognitive level", and a primary head said "trust helps us to expose ideas we may not expose in other situations". The result, as one secondary head commented, is "I can't describe my feeling. I feel very close to colleagues I didn't even meet before October".

The forums start with an emotional "invitation": a primary head said "trust helps us to expose ideas"; the result, said one secondary head, is: "I feel very close to colleagues I didn't even meet before October."

Providing self-directed and constructivist learning opportunities

In many senses, the learning is self-directed (Hallinger, 2003). Learning opportunities give participants the freedom to make their own choices. They are responsible for their decisions, but they reflect on alternative ways of acting in the pedagogical arena. Networking and learning partnerships provide opportunities to experience leadership. In addition, plenary meetings focus on school life issues and collaborative team coaching group members work together on tasks related to the presentations. This means that learning is considered as one's own activity, as a constructive activity, and not as a simple consequence of training.

The starting point for leadership learning is developing the personal capacity of individuals. School leaders need to understand themselves as leaders as well as in relationship to others and the system. It is a fundamental programme assumption that leadership, and growth as a leader, begins with knowledge of self. A leader has to know about his/her "inner team" (LEA, 2007b) – the different facets of personality that shape any person's action – and be able to balance those inner voices to become authentic. Clarifying one's own position before communicating with colleagues is essential. Knowledge about the team members in the school community and the ability to communicate with them and to motivate them follows this self-knowledge.

Experiential learning and varied learning strategies

The participants' everyday problems play a central role in the design. Each person brings their own development "situation" – generally some problem in their home organisation – to the Academy as a learning project case. Participants develop and implement their projects using new learning gained from the LEA. CTCs serve as "critical friends" (Costa and Kallick, 1993) or coaches to project owners over the course of the year, helping them gain new insight, confidence, and competence in their roles as school leaders.

Learning is structured in ways that appeal to a variety of learning styles. Forum trainers employ a mix of approaches including large-group lectures, case studies, scenarios and stories. Serious content is leavened with self-deprecation and ample humour. Great care is taken in "scaffolding" new knowledge with existing knowledge, and participants are frequently invited to reflect on, discuss, and speak to the plenary audience about their emerging understanding. Formal learning sessions are mixed with informal learning conducted in social settings. In the course of their learning participants listen, watch, write, create, and act out (in drama, dance, or other kinaesthetic methods). Through their learning partnerships and CTCs, participants are often in the role of learning facilitators. The scientific team members themselves model the importance of different learning and teaching styles through their different personalities and experiences.

The LEA training equips participants with skills, techniques, and tools they can use as school leaders. While these can change from year to year, depending on the particular programme emphasis, the training usually includes skill development in communication and feedback, mentoring and coaching, project management, working strategically, and leadership competence.

The LEA training equips participants with skills, techniques, and tools they can use as school leaders, including skill development in communication and feedback, mentoring and coaching, project management, working strategically, and leadership competence.

The training also emphasises the importance of understanding the different dimensions of learning. These are identified as learning to: know, understand, do, live together, and be. These underscore the cognitive, constructive, practical, social, and existential dimensions of learning. The programme seems to say that all dimensions are present in any learning situation, but learners will have different preferences for or strengths in the different dimensions. Learners can be more effective when they understand these dimensions and their preferences, and teachers and leaders of learning can be more effective in supporting others when they too appreciate the implications of these learning dimensions. Participants report that after identifying their own learning preferences and understanding the preferences of others, they began to feel more responsible for and competent at managing system change.

Learning as part of a community of learners

The LEA functions as a community of learners that enriches the individual growth of participants and models principles of learning communities that participants can introduce in their home organisations.

A learning community or learning organisation is reported to perform more effectively and to improve its performance on the basis of experience (Senge, 1990a, 1990b; Marquardt, 1996; Mulford, 2003). Typically such organisations incorporate values, structure, and processes that enhance the capacity of workers to perform at high levels, to adapt to change in the organisation's environment, and to make ongoing improvements in the quality of their work and output. Key elements are reflection and openness to learning, collective responsibility and shared goals, collegial and transparent work habits, explicit and common definition of effective practice, quality systems, flexible allocation of resources, and maximum use of internal expertise. The community is carefully developed, building from the pairs of learning partners, to CTC groups, to regional networks (see details below). Conditions for learning and professional development are introduced and extended at each level.

The LEA's commitment to operating as a learning organisation reflects the assumption that personal development and school development to improve pupils´ learning are interrelated. Personal change of leaders who help each other in learning communities makes possible the improvement of their learning outcomes. Social bonds and norms inspire trust, a sense of safety, and confidence. Transforming the educational system needs a multi-level approach. Starting with individuals, helping them to reflect on their own attitudes, making them communicate in networks and then changing learning communities in the larger system are the crucial points in the Academy's change process.

Taking a holistic approach

Reflecting the belief that learning is a complex process involving all dimensions of the human being, the LEA also provides the opportunity to develop and nourish other skills and talents. It invites participants to walk in the Alpine surroundings of the residential forums, to dance, to practise gymnastics, and to experience survival camp techniques. LEA participants initially show a rather reserved attitude towards this extended learning approach, but such reservations vanish over time.

The LEA also invites participants to walk in the Alpine surroundings of the residential forums, to dance, to practise gymnastics, and to experience survival camp techniques.

Creating the LEA culture

The creation of a body of shared norms, concepts, and vocabulary is one distinctive feature of a reculturing effort. A few examples will illustrate the LEA's practice in this regard. In a break with custom, all participants and staff immediately adopt the familiar form of address *(duzen),* equivalent to connecting on a first-name basis but an even stronger indication of openness and trust. Terms like *Handlung schafft Wirklichkeit* and *Musterwechsel,* the notion of altering fixed patterns or mental models, serve as banners of the new attitudes and practices LEA introduces. Teaming and collaboration are the dominant modes of interaction and learning; habits of going it alone are quickly broken down. Responsibility for self and for learning is constantly underscored. When, for example, participants ask trainers questions or appeal to the trainers' expertise, the trainers often turn the matter back to the participant, putting the responsibility for thinking and learning on the participant's shoulders.

Connected programme structure and strategies

Forums

In the initial meeting, the first forum, participants are introduced to the philosophy, organisation and structure of the LEA. Learning partnerships and collegial team coaching groups are formed. The second forum is important for defining development projects and practising collegial team coaching. The scientific team provides tools for professional project management. The third forum invites participants to talk about their experiences while implementing their reform initiatives. Workshops provide communication skills, problem solving strategies and motivation. In the final certification forum, participants present their projects, deciding in their collegial team groups which project will be presented. For graduation each participant has to write up their work and document their personal and professional development processes.

Learning partnerships and collegial team coaching (CTC)

The LEA offers learning opportunities for school leaders by building learning partnerships and networks of learning leaders. The learning partnerships and the CTCs function as discussion groups in which members develop understanding of new learning and link new to existing knowledge. They also serve as critical friends supporting participants in their learning from project experience and seeing their situation from different perspectives. As one primary head commented: "The diversity of participants is very important to help me look beyond the four walls of my school." CTCs follow well defined rules for coaching that include giving and receiving feedback and helping participants take responsibility for their learning. The Leadership Academy's directors observe team interaction. Although they do not interfere in the group process, they take "time out" opportunities to raise questions or offer analysis about project substance and group process.

Teamwork is an important condition for successful schools, and interviewees described the contribution of learning partners and CTCs to their competence in teamwork. Motivating others to follow new pedagogical concepts was, from their point of view, a very difficult task. Knowledge about different ways of learning and tensions in the "inner team" (different inner voices or identities) of their colleagues and staff clarified for them the nature of resistance to change. This seems to be the starting point for collegial team coaching that opens up action possibilities. Team members together reflect on difficulties in the change process and seek solutions. The disposition to clarify one's own position, then to listen to others, to leave one's comfort zone and to motivate others to improve pupils' learning is at the heart of the LEA approach.

The disposition to clarify one's own position, listen to others, leave one's comfort zone and motivate others to improve pupils' learning is at the heart of the LEA approach.

Collegial team coaching is a structured micro-world in which participants find their way with the help of others. Field-based experiences are brought forward for systematic analysis. The working process of the CTC groups is characterised by a sequence of steps to discuss each person's case. After the presentation of one CTC member there follow questions from other participants, a coaching conference, the definition of the main subject, brainstorming ideas, a reflection on the process and feedback. The CTC work is a team reflection which leads not only to insights about the challenges of leadership but also to ideas about solutions.

Regional networking

CTCs are grouped into regional networks that meet periodically to explore substantive and administrative topics related to the LEA programme and to link graduates to the alumni network. The networks support leaders in many ways. Trust and co-operation among professional colleagues can activate innovative resources. In a safe environment, leaders can test out and receive feedback on their ideas and school practice. The networks foster school leaders' capacity for systemic thinking – establishing a connection between individuals and system structures. Transformation of the educational system needs a multi level approach. Helping leaders to reflect on their own attitudes, recognise interrelationships between different levels of the educational system, and discerning critical system variables that make system change possible are crucial elements in the change process.

Assessment, certification and membership

The assessment of the personal development of candidates in the Leadership Academy is based on their documented projects. Learning partnerships, CTC meetings and regional group meetings provide feedback for participants. The CTC provides two reviewers for each report and the participant has to defend her or his report to these two peers, one of whom is the learning partner. In addition to the formative evaluation there is also a summative assessment by the scientific team.

The Leadership Competence Scale defines indicators for assessment of leadership abilities. Participants complete this at the beginning and end of the experience and, since generation 2, some colleagues are also asked to complete the scale as part of a 360° feedback process.

A "micro article", in which participants write about a critical incident, was used in earlier generations but stopped because it did not help participants think about their project in a positive, forward-oriented manner. Project leaders hope to reintroduce it in a revised form. A "photo evaluation", whereby participants took pictures of how they envisaged leadership in schools, was also used with earlier generations, but the scientific team did not have the capacity to evaluate these.

Those successfully completing the assessment tasks become certified as members of the Leadership Academy. Others receive confirmation of participation but do not become members of the Leadership Academy network.

Participants who successfully complete the full training and assessment are certified and admitted into the graduate ranks of the Leadership Academy. The fourth and final forum concentrates on synthesising key learning, project presentations, planning continuation of the learning partnerships, CTCs, and regional networking, and award of certificates. The expectation of graduate members of the Academy is that they will continue the process of learning and they will contribute to the learning of others

LEA alumni have an important role to play in the personal development of leaders and in supporting the networking of groups. Alumni serve as mentors of subsequent candidates. They lead regional meetings and give advice to collegial teams. The network coordinators establish contacts between LEA generations (generation I-IV) and foster open communication in the system.

8.4 Programme effectiveness and continuous programme improvement

Quality assurance and ongoing quality improvement of leadership development programmes are critical to ensure programme goals and participants' needs are being addressed and the programmes are responding to contextual changes and updates in the knowledge bases. In this section we draw on and extend an evaluation framework used at the National College of School Leadership in the UK, based on a framework used to evaluate training programmes (Kirkpatrick and Kirkpatrick, 1998) to present information about programme effectiveness and continuous improvement.

More than one in six leaders have taken part

As noted, this is an ambitious programme, with the intention of reaching half of all Austrian school leaders in a relatively short period of time; hence the large size of each generation. From 2004 to autumn 2007, 1 015 school leaders (16.9%) have completed the LEA, and a further generation of 259 was due to start the programme in December 2007. Several of those we interviewed spoke positively of the experience of being with a large number of colleagues and also the access to colleagues from other generations.

High degree of engagement

Our observations and interviews suggested a high level of engagement with the programme, and considerable enthusiasm about both the content and processes of the Academy. The ideas were new to most participants and there seemed to be an excitement about being able to "see" different ways of communicating and resolving issues. Inevitably, in any externally guided professional learning experience, trainer quality is an important factor for a positive experience. The consensus was that the quality of inputs during the forums was very high, professionally stimulating and challenging, and greatly appreciated. For the most part, CTCs were equally engaged and self-sustaining, although some required more focusing and support during the forums, raising an issue for those considering this approach about how to ensure engagement and high quality partnership work between forum meetings. The extended nature of the programme and its demands in terms of having to carry out a project and write a report was also particularly helpful for some participants in sustaining commitment.

Follow-up after graduation appears to be a less successful dimension of the programme. Programme alumni are intended to constitute a virtual academy providing benefits and support for ongoing leadership practice and sustaining momentum for the new leadership culture. Regional networks are the vehicle for alumni participation. Participation rates and effectiveness of the regional networks are reported to be uneven. Lack of focus and direction in some networks elicited more negative comment than any other element of the LEA programme. Yet anecdotal evidence of successful ongoing interactions across learning partnerships, CTCs, and regional networks indicates the potential of the virtual academy to be an effective mechanism.

Positive impact on leadership practice

While this is a relatively young programme, it seems to have a powerful impact on individuals. A leadership competence scale (Pool, 2007) is used to assess the participants at the beginning and end of the programme. Originally, this was just completed by the participants, but since the start of generation 4, it has also been given to ten members of staff in participants' organisations, as a form of 360° feedback.

On one hand, our interviews highlighted many examples of personal leadership outcomes. While, in some cases, prior beliefs had been reinforced, we heard many stories about how patterns of thinking about problem solving and communication with colleagues had been changed. Creating a more supportive atmosphere through being more self aware, taking a sensitive approach towards others and encouraging mutual appreciation, building trust and involving others were important outcomes. Examples cited by colleagues of alumni showed the impact from their perspective. And inspectors spoke of school heads who had taken up their more autonomous role more quickly. They described evidence that these heads were more goal- oriented and their aims were clearer and better focused, they communicated better and more precisely and involved teaching staff more, they were freer in their decisions and were able to look at their problems from different points of view and compare results.

These heads were more goal oriented and their aims were clearer and better focused, they communicated better and more precisely and involved teaching staff more, they were freer in their decisions and were able to look at their problems from different points of view and compare results.

As a consequence of these changes, colleagues sometimes saw a chain reaction, with heads presenting an example for teachers and students who then began to act in a similar fashion. We also heard from an alumnus involved in research exploring the impact of the Leadership Academy on generation 1 that there was much greater self-reflection, leading to a noticeable change in communication: "You can feel the work of the LEA."

In addition, an important outcome of leadership learning is its application in practice and how this affects others with whom participants in leadership learning come into contact. Again, there were many stories of how what participants learnt through the Leadership Academy was influencing daily work outside. Apart from the project that all participants are expected to carry out in their organisation as part of the programme, other examples included: applying the patterns of thinking to a range of different problems; using the leadership competence survey with staff throughout schools or all school heads in districts; developing middle managers; and integrating CTC groups into a regional school management course. Participants and some alumni also use their learning partner or other members of the CTC as sounding boards if they have a problem, and it was clear that a number of personal friendships have developed between learning partners. We also heard from some colleagues of how the new culture of communication is having an impact on staff in participants' organisations.

An interesting example of change within an organisation is where the director general of one of the ministry directorates participated, and has applied the Leadership Academy approaches across the directorate. A colleague described how it is helping them clarify their vision and change their orientation to work and ways of communicating with each other.

This brings us to the question of system impact.

On the way to system-wide changes

Bringing about system-wide change is notoriously difficult. Later in the chapter, we consider this in more depth, but we were interested to consider what evidence there was of system-wide change. In a sense, the considerable change in attitudes and orientation to leadership that appears to be a result for many of the Leadership Academy participants produces a groundswell at various levels of the system where people have been involved – schools, districts, regions, teacher training institutes and parts of the ministry.

Two factors appear to be particularly significant, however, in whether a leadership academy such as this can achieve the change articulated in the phrase "working on the system".

The first is critical mass. The more people who participate, the stronger the impetus for change is likely to become. For example, we heard of a situation where almost a third of school inspectors from a particular region have now participated in the Leadership

Academy and are creating a new culture in their area. It appears, however, that at present the Leadership Academy is not at the point where critical mass has been reached.

The second factor is the involvement of ministry leaders at the most senior level. Our discussions suggested that those ministry officials who have participated have, for the most part, found the Leadership Academy experience as powerful as their peers. Many of these officials, however, are not at a high enough level within the ministry to be able to effect the kind of structural changes that might be needed to ensure the greatest system-wide impact. Certainly, some graduates of the Leadership Academy are moving into positions of influence throughout the system and this may have an effect, but it will depend on how many people are involved and the particular positions into which they move.

A minority of participants did not find benefit

The effects of the programme, of course, were not identical for all participants. It sometimes depended on where people came from and their prior experience. The project documentation states that participants must have had three years experience of being a school head. In more recent generations, this rule has been relaxed. It appeared, in a few cases, that those who were in the first few years as a school head sometimes found that dealing with management issues prevented them getting the most out of the LA processes.

More particularly, impact seemed to depend to some extent on whether people were open to the experience and in particular to reflecting on questions of their own leadership and their personal role. The general view was that the Leadership Academy was successful for the large majority of participants who took up the mindset and method of working. There appeared to be several reasons why there was a lack of change in a small minority (approximately 10-15%) of participants. Some were able to feel the need for leadership but unable to engage deeply because they were very content oriented. Others were unable to translate all their reflection back into the reality of life as a leader, especially if faced with resistance to change from teachers. For some others, the LEA experience was unable to address a lack of sensitivity in terms of communication or, occasionally, might have exacerbated it.

As far as the different roles of school heads, inspectors, teacher trainers or ministry leaders is concerned, there does not appear to be a noticeable difference in impact between the groups. Their spheres of influence are of course different, and some individuals in particular groups may have greater scope to bring about significant change in other people's daily work.

Sustained impact on participants

Inevitably, ensuring impact over time is important for the Leadership Academy and any similar ventures. From discussions with a number of alumni, it appears that the personal effects of the Leadership Academy do last over time. Changed patterns of thinking and ways of operating seem to be long lasting, and many alumni have continued applying ideas and approaches they have learnt, even if they engage less frequently or hardly at all with the Leadership Academy's offerings for alumni. The research currently being carried out in generation I schools will clarify what aspects of the Leadership Academy experience retain their effects over time and how it has infiltrated into the schools and other communities. We talk further about the challenge of sustainability in the final section.

Ongoing monitoring and evaluation

Each forum is evaluated by participants and they can also write their opinions on cards. The feedback is considerable. A team member has the brief to promote effective programme delivery by planning ahead, anticipating problems, taking feedback into account, analysing any problems, and liaising with the programme directors and other team members to ensure that adjustments are made. Team meetings are held to discuss quality improvement, and team members consider these meetings a critical part of their ability to make necessary changes. The team also has external critical friends with expertise in organisational development and school development. These people have attended forum sessions and provided their own feedback, which is incorporated into programme planning and revisions.

Every participant brings their "case" (project) to their CTC meetings. In the first generations, one member of the leadership team was responsible for three CTCs during the entire period and monitoring was not specifically scheduled. The leadership team felt that the coaching was not operating as well as it might, so each CTC is now observed at least once by a member of the leadership team during every forum to check for problems with the coaching process. A "time out" signal is used if the leadership team member wishes to make a point that will help the team's metacognitive perspective on their learning, and the leadership team member may also step in to model the kinds of questions to ask or highlight, for example, when the CTC is ignoring the human side of a problem.

In addition, each of the six cases is documented at every CTC meeting. Roles are assigned at the beginning of each session with one member of the team taking the role of writer who completes a form and checks back with other members of the CTC that she/he has accurately represented the situation, colleagues' responses and decisions. By looking at the forms for each case over time, it is possible to see whether and how participants are reframing problems or if they are just jumping straight in to dealing with them. This information is fed back into the programme design.

Furthermore, a national research project started in late 2006 to look at generations 1, 2 and 3, to follow the 10 schools involved over a 15 year period. Questionnaires were sent out to school leaders, teachers, pupils and parents, with follow up interviews. At the time of our visit the initial data were being analysed. Alumni are also involved as part of the research team.

8.5 Policy conditions

This section examines a broad set of policy conditions related to the LEA's quality and impact and to the ultimate achievement of the government's overall goals in education leadership.

Issues of implementation and co-ordination

The federal government's initiative and support have been critical to the launch and implementation of the Leadership Academy. It is unlikely that a programme of this sort –

addressing a national need, requiring considerable resources to support, and depending on large enrolments – could have been initiated by a provincial government, a university, or a private provider. The government is unusual in its recognition of the importance of leadership for learning and leadership for system change. It has launched a visionary and innovative initiative in the Leadership Academy.

The government is unusual in its recognition of the importance of leadership for learning and leadership for system change. The Leadership Academy is an innovative initiative.

There is, however, a legacy of issues arising from the manner of the programme's launch. LEA was begun as a personal initiative of the former minister and introduced into the bureaucracy, as it was described to us, "from the side". That is, the programme was not developed in accordance within the customary bureaucratic procedures. Advantages were speed of launch, dedicated resources, and attention as a ministerial priority. While this has led to a positive response from many school heads, there seem to have been several potentially adverse consequences.

Ministry support and connections with other related national initiatives

The ministry is in a position to provide symbolic and substantive support for the LEA by enrolling ministry officials, including those at the top levels in the programme. There is disagreement within the ministry whether ministry participation in LEA has been adequate so far. LEA participants have been recruited from seven directorates and 78 departments in the ministry. Programme advocates state that attendance by top officials has been strong: 21 of the 85 officials who are in the position of director general or department Head have participated, which is just under one quarter. Others disagree. "If you have a rigid system that doesn't want to change and then a LEA that stimulates change, you'd have to hope management would be the first to attend, but this is not what has happened," stated one official. It seemed to the visiting team that some conflict over "bureaucratic turf" could either limit participation or create impressions of lack of support for the programme in some quarters.

The programme also appears to lack the fully co-ordinated connections with other national initiatives on school leadership and school reform that might have resulted had it been developed within the main education policy framework.

Lack of complementary structural change

Some officials pointed out that the LEA's impact will be blunted because its drive to change culture through individuals has not been accompanied by a parallel effort to change the structure of the system. The LEA is a logical approach to changing school leadership, they say, but it clashes with the power structure. They feel it is important to know what the political context is in the country and bring together (make congruent) the logical and political structure. Programme graduates, they imply, will still end up working in a cumbersome system characterised by layers of government, separate school systems, extensive consultation processes, civil service based personnel systems, and other impediments; and existing holders of power will resist the new ways. It was no doubt easier to launch a culture change initiative than to take on the political interests behind the structure, and it may be that once critical mass is attained, there will be sufficient momentum to create structural change. But for the moment, almost the entire burden for systems change rests on the LEA, and this may be too much to ask of any one leadership development programme.

Almost the entire burden for systems change rests on the LEA, and this may be too much to ask of any one leadership development programme.

Coherence of national reform agenda

The LEA does not appear to be part of a coherent overall national agenda for education reform. There are certainly a large number of reforms underway. The team was impressed at the intent behind the work of the Future Commission and the commitment to create a responsive, world class education system evident in the many initiatives underway. But we did not see that there was a coherent agenda behind these initiatives, nor was it clear where the LEA fitted into an overall plan. Any success LEA enjoys, and there seems to be ample promise of success, would be greater within the context of a well aligned body of reforms supported by a coherent policy agenda targeting school leadership and school outcomes.

The Leadership Academy's "home"

Finally, the LEA has no permanent structure or organisational home. What once might have been an advantage, offering speed and flexibility, now seems to some observers within the system to be a potential liability. As a programme that is both outside the bureaucracy and "virtual", the LEA now seems vulnerable to bureaucratic whim and to lack the impact of a programme more centrally situated in the bureaucracy. Moreover, LEA relies on the unique talents and background of two individuals and their teams. The programme quality, direction, and continuity rely almost entirely on this capacity. The ministry does not have such capacity, nor are steps being taken that could somehow institutionalise it.

Assumptions about change impact

Since the LEA is designed as a change programme, it is appropriate to examine the assumptions of its change strategy. The theory of change can be stated as follows: a well designed programme, following established principles of change management, will produce effective individual leaders whose projects and subsequent behaviour will help change each individual's organisation. These leaders will eventually constitute the critical mass needed to change the overall system culture. We explored programme effectiveness in Section 8.4. Here we raise some points on the programme's assumptions about its change impact with policy implications.

Adaptive change

The LEA appears to exemplify principles of managed change. Viewed from the perspective of general systems change theory, the programme incorporates such requisite elements as a vision of the desired future, modelling appropriate behaviours, generating a constant stream of pertinent information, providing ongoing feedback and support, and celebrating success. The LEA also fits well with the elements of the more particular model of "adaptive change" (Heifetz, 1994; Heifetz and Linsky, 2002), with for example a safe "container", consistent modelling, and "turning up and down the heat". However, these change elements are confined to the LEA programme itself; they are less evident in the larger system. That is, with the exception of one directorate where the LEA programme was made a very high priority, and thus modelling commitment to change, we saw less indication that the ministry was acting as an effective change agent itself by adhering to these principles. The LEA thus bears a very large burden for effecting change in the overall system. This burden would certainly be better off shared.

The LEA's success as an agent of culture change will depend first on the quality and impact of each participant's project and behaviour in their organisation and, second, on the programme's capacity to create the needed critical mass of change agents within the system. It is hard to assess the impact, current or potential, of either of these conditions. Again, however, it does seem that their success would be greatly enhanced by parallel structural change and by more powerful change management efforts beyond LEA itself on the part of the ministry.

An early policy decision to expand participant eligibility has had profound and positive consequences for the programme. Originally intended for leaders of schools at all primary and secondary levels and with general, academic, and vocational focus, eligibility was opened up to include school inspectors, university programme providers, and regional and national government officials. Such diverse participation across all elements of the education governance, accountability, training, and delivery system has enhanced the programme emphasis on breaking down system boundaries and barriers and promoted the development of a deeper, more inclusive systems orientation among participants.

The decision to apply to the LEA is made by the applicant, although at times official encouragement or directives motivate applicants. The LEA accepts a balanced cohort that is representative of the diverse target population. It is not clear how well this voluntary approach works, given the LEA's aim to produce culture or systems change and create a critical mass of change agents. Some observers in Austria question whether the national government shouldn't put all or the majority of its middle or top level officials through the programme early on. In their view the ministry at present lacks the breadth of understanding, commitment, and coherence needed to fulfil the LEA vision. Similarly, where school inspectors play so potentially central a role in school quality and accountability, and in hastening or slowing school-level change, training the entire corps early on could create more powerful leverage for change.

Leverage points

Because most of the structural factors that make the education system complex and slow to change are also deeply embedded in the country's culture and traditions, it does not seem likely that these will be changed any time soon, either through policy decision or more indirect culture change. There are, however, a few leverage points where disproportionately large improvements in school leadership could be returned at relatively low levels of investment.

Changes to tenure of teaching staff

School heads identify a variety of conditions that would help them perform better. Cited more often than any condition was the authority to choose or change their school's teaching staff, something out of their reach at present. Using a football analogy, one head said that as long as he has a mediocre team over which he has no selection control, he cannot take full responsibility for his school.

Reducing administrative overload

Among a variety of conditions hindering the exercise of effective pedagogical leadership, school leaders – especially primary and general secondary school heads with little or no administrative support – report feeling overloaded with administrative tasks and heightened feelings of stress. As one school head phrased it: "The school head's duties are so manifold, diverse, and widespread, and we are not trained for them or able to find the time to manage them all." In fact, far from easing such burdens, the provision of legal autonomy has created new administrative and managerial duties. Assignment of personnel who could relieve some of the administrative burdens from school heads could pay large dividends.

Amending criteria for selection of school heads

There appears to be the need for greater rigour and objectivity in the selection of school heads for the job. Respondents with a variety of different positions in the system identified the tradition of political intervention, favouritism, and patronage as problematic. Requiring that selection be made according to explicit criteria related to the job requirements of pedagogical leadership would be one step toward the selection of principals on merit and fitness for the job.

8.6 Food for thought

The Austrian Leadership Academy is an ambitious and innovative programme, with an aim to reach many leaders throughout the system. It seeks to influence their individual professional practice and, as a consequence, bring about system-wide change to address the needs of a rapidly changing world. At this point, approximately 40% of the 3 000 school leaders for whom the programme was initially developed have received their certification; that is, approaching one fifth (16.9%) of the total number of Austrian school leaders. This is a considerable achievement in two-and-a-half years. It has impact in terms of coverage, as not only school leaders but a diverse range of participants benefit from the interaction. As a regional coordinator described, it regional inspectors "… have formed a new culture".

But there are other indicators of success. Most participants reflect on the powerful and sustained impact the Academy has had on their leadership practice. They are applying a new set of skills in their daily practice. Furthermore, engagement with the Academy remains high even after the training process is finalised: 60% of participants stay connected, valuing the networks they have developed.

In this section, we raise issues that countries would want to consider if developing a similar programme within their context, other than ensuring that the programme addressed their own important contextual issues. For us, the key challenge in relation to the Leadership Academy can be summed up as one of sustainability. Here, we consider sustainability from a number of perspectives: depth, length, breadth, capacity, integration, and system change (see Hargreaves and Fink, 2006).

Depth: the power of change through continued development

This is a demanding programme, seeking significant change in personal patterns of thinking, responding and communicating. From our limited experience, it is hard to tell whether the depth of change experienced by individuals through the LEA will enable them to promote the necessary innovation to deal with increasingly adaptive challenges. Our guess is that, with system support and continuous training, this is possible. However, the timing of participation in the LEA needs to be aligned to leadership training and development trajectories. If initial management training occurs after people become school heads, then it makes sense to recruit people to the Leadership Academy after 3 to 5 years as a school head. This is because our interviews suggest that some practical management issues tend to overwhelm new school heads, making it hard for them to focus on the Leadership Academy curricula. Bringing the compulsory management training forward so that it occurs before people take up their role as school head, as used to happen in Austria and happens in some other counties, would be another way to address this.

Length: ongoing involvement and support structure for alumni

Maintaining the spirit of the Leadership Academy is not always easy. Once out of the programme, the intention is that alumni will create collegial commitment through the alumni network. In reality, approximately 50% carry on with collegial links and approximately 60% with their partnership dialogue. A member of the programme team explained how alumni attend follow up events: "to feel the spirit/the power [but] they say it's hard to continue when so many people are looking at problems. So they are looking for a support structure and systems that will sustain it. It's not enough to meet. It's about having a connection."

From experience of other networks, we know that sustainability requires a common purpose and task, facilitation, infrastructure, face-to-face meetings and a small amount of money to cover these. A few people felt that the significance of membership in the Academy following graduation was diluted by the lack of active involvement among many graduates. They recommended that ongoing membership be granted only to alumni who stayed active in the network. It certainly makes sense that membership should be linked to active contribution to the Leadership Academy, whether through alumni events, support meetings, the website or learning partners and CTC colleagues. There was even a suggestion that alumni should be helped to start a new project. It seemed to be understood, therefore, that after all of the intense work to bring about change, continuation of commitment and use of ideas is essential.

Ongoing involvement appears to be a particular issue for ministry participants because offerings for alumni tend to be school focused and, as a ministry leader described it, "at the operative level", while ministry leaders focus more "at the abstract level". It seemed that an ongoing support network for ministry personnel would be valuable, although some ministry leaders particularly valued the CTC connections they had made with school and inspector colleagues

Breadth

Critical mass

At what point does the number of people who have been through the LA experience translate into a critical mass of education leaders who can exercise strategic, person-centred leadership for learning? We heard of one region where eight of the 26 school inspectors have participated in the LA and, as a regional coordinator described it, "have formed a new culture". Some interviewees wanted to see more school heads and inspectors participating because, in a ministry leader's words: "Whether we'll succeed in bringing about systemic change depends on how many we can penetrate…. It's only possible if the process continues and more take part." Another ministry leader commented: "If all 6 000 were in the Leadership Academy, there would be nobody left with responsibility in teaching in education who could say 'this is not possible, this doesn't concern me, I can't do this'." If the other points raised in this section are addressed and not too many alumni retire in the next few years, it may be a matter of only a few years before critical mass is reached.

Involvement of senior ministry leaders

A ministry leader was not alone in commenting: "it will only succeed if the people who take part are in leading positions". It appears that the involvement of senior ministry leaders can have a particularly powerful effect on the system when they follow up their own participation by replicating LEA processes with their staff, as has happened throughout one directorate. At present, from seven ministry directorates, one director general and three deputy directors general have participated. Indeed, while few senior ministry leaders had participated in the Leadership Academy, a number felt that the decision makers at ministry and provincial level should be involved: "Start at the top of the system" (ministry leader).

Spreading ideas across regions

Several school leaders and inspectors share their experiences with other non-involved colleagues in their own regions, but this seemed to depend on individuals and the number of the LEA's current participants and alumni in a district or region. Perhaps some independently offered regional seminars and regional leadership meetings might help to spread leadership ideas across the whole region. Some participants also felt that more regional meetings for people working at a particular level – "speciality meetings" – would help people to apply what they have learnt. A regional coordinator suggested that there would be more power if the Leadership Academy could be experienced by regional policy makers, "so LEA projects are seen by people at the policy level". Like any other voluntary initiative, however, this one faces the challenge of persuading uninvolved people (heads, inspectors and ministry personnel) to become involved. Some see it as a club, others feel "we don't need it – you just deal with your school" (primary school head), while some inspectors, in particular, appear to be afraid that they may lose power by attending given that in their current role, as one interviewee described it, "compulsory school sector inspectors tell schools what to do". Developing a regional strategy with regional partnerships may be beneficial. This has already been started in one region, where the regional coordinator is in close contact with local politicians.

Parallel development of increasing teachers' professionalism and distributing leadership

An issue highlighted many times throughout our visit was that of teacher autonomy and the need for greater teacher professionalism. We are aware that the Ministry of Education has invited one of the Leadership Academy directors to lead a group looking at increasing the teachers' "professionalisation", and has developed a model with five domains of professionalism: personal mastery of their craft (individual competence); capacity for reflection and discourse; considering and sharing their knowledge and skills; awareness of their professionalism (seeing themselves as experts); collegiality (understanding the benefits of co-operation); and capacity to deal with differences and diversity. This model seems to support the concept of a professional learning community, but the extent to which it is realised in teacher practice will depend in part on the extent to which it influences the curriculum of the new *Pädagogische Hochschulen.*

In addition to the need for a parallel approach to teacher development, there is the issue of increasing pressure on school leaders. This may need addressing through widening the client group for leadership development. School administrators already have their own development programmes but these are not focused on leadership for learning. It may be valuable to place a greater emphasis on development of senior leadership teams as well as promoting greater distribution of leadership through teacher leadership development. As one ministry official commented, "the definition of leadership is not just heads. It is teachers who have influence on a team. It's difficult. In a future oriented society, I see a strong role for the LEA." It would be ideal if there were a coherent stream of professional preparation and development programmes for administrators and teachers. Such a programme stream would align the current compulsory management training, the LEA programme, and other training for administrative leaders. It would also align with the content of teacher preparation, in order to promote coherent concepts of the school as a learning community.

Capacity for programme delivery

With such a large programme, it is impossible for the project directors and scientific and administrative project team to facilitate the entire programme. Ensuring that all CTCs are visited once during each forum is a demand on the project team's time, and providing facilitation support to CTCs between forums would certainly help those who experience difficulties with the process. The initiative requires high quality facilitation. It makes good sense that there is an extended project team with regional coordinators who facilitate network meetings but, inevitably, the success of regional networks depends on the quality and leadership of coordinators and their ability to draw out the leadership and ownership of members. Already, some generation 1 participants are playing support roles. Other alumni might also become more involved, but ministry involvement is needed to institutionalise this capacity.

Clearly, the planning required is extensive and having a co-ordinated team that meet regularly is valuable. With oversight of more than one generation at a time, this task becomes even more critical and depends on being able to plan ahead.

Integration into national leadership training frameworks and with other initiatives

For successful change initiatives to become institutionalised, they need to become integrated into the system; part of the normal way of life. One ministry official thought it is possible that because the original idea came from outside the system the ground for innovation was more open. It is important for the Leadership Academy to be connected to the system and its other initiatives. It does complement the mandatory management training, and it is helpful that it draws some regional network facilitators from those involved in school management courses. Regional network coordinators also reflect different roles in the system – heads of different kinds of schools, school inspectors and regional inspectors – which is likely to promote further integration. Furthermore, helping school leaders engage effectively with national quality development initiatives and making the best use of the new standards as they are introduced is a useful effect of the LEA. Additional links can be seen with the QIBB. Other important connections are being made by the LEA alumni who have become experts in quality assurance and standards, and who have been invited to act as role models and provide examples at sessions at the teacher training colleges.

More efforts are needed to co-ordinate the content of the compulsory management training and that of LEA. First, both programmes should share a common vision of leadership for learning and of its management and leadership aspects. It is especially important that the initial training for new school leaders contain not only straightforward managerial content, important as that is, but also material that links management functions with the overriding goals of leadership for learning. At the same time, there is room in the LEA programme for more explicit and fully developed focus on the content and operation of schools as learning communities. Second, our informants expressed a range of views about the quality of their compulsory management training. Given that the programmes are offered in a variety of institutions, it seems likely that quality and content vary by provider. The state should continue its efforts to monitor programme quality and take steps to ensure the uniform quality of the management training and its co-ordination with the LEA.

While increasing integration is desirable, the LEA needs to continue to have the flexibility to adapt as necessary and help lead innovation. This could be stifled if it is bureaucratised within a system of hierarchical structures. So far the Leadership Academy appears to have been able to achieve this fine balance. It may be time for closer integration, but if system change is not addressed, the challenge will be to retain its adaptive quality and sustain the energy of cultural change (see next section).

System change

Aligning cultural and structural change

The key question here is whether cultural change, in itself, is enough to achieve the impact desired for the Leadership Academy, or whether it needs to be accompanied by structural change. A ministry leader reflected, "How long do the flames exist? What happens if you come back to school and you are faced with the old structures?" The Leadership Academy was introduced fairly quickly into the system: this meant there was no preparation of the system and no accompanying structural changes. Given the cycle of political change, it may be necessary to change structures such as those for the hiring of teachers: "Otherwise it won't have the impact they expect/hope it to have" (ministry leader).

National change strategy

We have commented on issues related to overall national reform strategy and the Leadership Academy's place in it. The LEA is a bold and innovative initiative, but we are inclined to think that it is asked to do too much – that achieving the goals for which it was instituted requires a more comprehensive national message and strategy for school reform. (If these elements are in fact to be found in the Future Commission report or some other document or policy, we have not come across them.) In particular, the message would communicate a vision of the effective or high-performing school, of dynamic professional learning communities, and of powerful leadership for learning. The strategy would generate pervasive dialogue about this message and use key points in the system to apply the vision. We note, in this regard, the intent of the Austrian Federal Economic Chamber to promote a shared vision and understanding of school leadership and responsibility for school performance. Even the process of formulating such a vision and strategy could play a significant educative function as well as generating broad based support for the outcome. A more explicitly framed and comprehensive national reform message and strategy would advance the work of the Leadership Academy and achieve the results intended for it.

Summary

The Austrian Leadership Academy is a bold and creative initiative that, in three years, has already reached approximately 40% of the 3 000 leaders for whom it was designed. We conclude that its future can be viewed in terms of sustainability, essentially:

- whether it can promote the depth of change necessary for the changing educational landscape;

- whether its alumni will maintain an ongoing involvement with its ideals and practices and whether the support they need will be available;

- whether a critical mass of leaders, including key ministry leaders, will be reached and ideas spread across regions so that other leaders can become engaged;

- whether the programme leaders can involve enough high quality people to help build their capacity for delivery and facilitation of a very large and growing programme;

- whether the LEA is integrated into national leadership frameworks and other related initiatives;

- whether the necessary changes occur to system structures as part of a coherent national change strategy.

These are challenges that we believe any system considering such an innovative approach to leadership development will want to consider seriously.

Box 8.1 Summary conclusions on Austria's Leadership Academy

This chapter provided information and analysis on Austria's Leadership Academy (LEA), an initiative of the Ministry of Education, Science and Culture (now Education, Arts, and Culture). It was launched in 2004 to equip leaders in Austria's education system with the capacity to lead an emerging body of reform initiatives and help establish a new culture of proactive, entrepreneurial school leadership. The Leadership Academy was selected by the OECD *Improving School Leadership* activity as an innovative case study because of its system-wide approach to leadership development, emphasis on leadership for improved schooling outcomes, innovative programme contents and design, and demonstrated potential to achieve effective outcomes. This chapter is part of a larger OECD activity, *Improving School Leadership*, designed to help member countries improve policy and practice related to school leadership.

Austria is undergoing social, economic, and political change in response to global economic competition, membership in the EU, immigration and changing family structure, an ageing population and growing social programme costs, among other causes. The nation's strong, cohesive social structure and traditions provide stability but also hinder desirable change. Schools and the education system have been generally compliance oriented, bureaucratic, and cumbersome. The national government has introduced a large agenda of school reform, and school leaders with new skills and initiative are needed to implement these reforms. The Leadership Academy responds to this need.

The Austrian Leadership Academy is an innovative and carefully crafted response to a need to prepare a large number of school leaders over a short period of time to fulfil their role effectively in an increasingly autonomous system. Blending content and process, it focuses on developing learning centred leadership and an orientation to systems change through an approach that emphasises building personal capacity in a supportive learning community.

Positive outcomes of the LEA can already be seen. In three years, it has reached approximately 40% of the 3000 leaders for whom it was designed. A high proportion of leaders have participated voluntarily; there is generally a high degree of engagement; it has had a positive impact on leadership practice; and it has produced some changes in the wider school system. Sustained impact, while not entirely clear at this point, shows signs of promise. Further research and evaluation should help to assess this.

This study has identified some obstacles to the LEA reaching its full potential, and some conditions that could enhance the likelihood of achieving the overall goals for education reform for which the LEA is one strategy:

- *Ministry support and integration with other national initiatives:* High participation by senior ministry officials would strengthen the LEA's message and impact, and could also help improve co-ordination between the LEA and other ministry initiatives to improve education. Integrating the LEA and other national and provincial leadership and management training into a coherent framework (as well as co-ordinating with teacher training) would also pay dividends for all programmes.

- *Institutionalisation of the LEA programme:* Without compromising its current flexibility and innovative nature, consideration should be given to grounding the LEA on a firmer institutional base, so as to provide longer term capacity for sustainability and growth.

- *Structural change and national change management:* Changes in education structure and processes could reinforce and extend the changes the LEA achieves through individual and culture change, as would a more coherent government agenda and message for education reform.

- *Changes at key leverage points:* More rigorous principal selection procedures, greater principal authority or influence in selecting and dismissing (and rewarding) teachers, and reducing the principal's administrative workload would enable improvements in school leadership practice.

- *Programme sustainability:* the LEA's long term effectiveness can be enhanced by continuing the programme and graduating increasing numbers of leaders, strengthening ministry participation, improving the alumni and network follow up experience, and taking steps to make teachers more professional and distribute leadership more widely.

Annex 8.A1
Case study visit programme
15-19 April 2007

Sunday 15 April 2007 Site Visit and Interviews in Alpbach

19.30   Informal dinner with team members and guests of the Academy

Mrs Maria Gruber-Redl, Ministry for Education, Arts and Culture
Mr Wilfried Schley, IOS Hamburg
Mr Michael Schratz, University of Innsbruck
Mr Bernhard Weiser, University of Innsbruck
Mr Paul Resinger, University of Innsbruck
Mrs Katharina Barrios, IOS Hamburg
Mr Eike Messow, Breuninger Stiftung
Mr David Green, Director of the Centre for Evidence-Based Education (CEBE), Princeton, New Jersey
Mrs Eisele, Ministry of Education, Baden-Württemberg, Germany

Monday 16 April 2007, Site Visit and Interviews in Alpbach

08.30 – 10.30   Plenary meeting: "5 Dimensions of Leadership for Learning"

10.30 – 11.00   Interview with a LEA participant (target group school head/primary school)
Nora Hosp, school head, primary school, Innere Stadt, Innsbruck

11.00 – 12.30   Plenary meeting: Collegial Team Coaching (CTC) – Methods and Specification

12.30 – 14.00   Lunch

14.00 – 15.00   Collegial Team Coaching: observation of a selected coaching group
15.00 – 16.00   Interview with the ministry´s project manager
Mrs. Maria Gruber-Redl, Ministry for Education, Arts and Culture
(alternative: observation of a 2nd CTC-Group)

16.00 – 17.00   Walk in the Alpine surroundings (alternative: Interview with the ministry´s project manager)

17.00 – 18.00   Interview with the LEA participant and dean of the University College of Education in Klagenfurt (target group Teacher Training Institution)
Mrs. Marlies Krainz-Dürr, PH Klagenfurt

18.00 – 19.00   Interview with a LEA participant (target group school inspectorate)
Mr Wilhelm Prainsack, provincial school inspector, Klagenfurt Stadt

19.00 – 20.00   Dinner with the scientific deans of the academy

20.00 – 21.00   Interview with the scientific deans of the academy
Mr Wilfried Schley, IOS Hamburg
Mr Michael Schratz, Universitiy of Innsbruck

Tuesday 17 April 2007 Site Visit and Interviews in Alpbach / Journey to Vienna

08.30 – 09.30	Interview with representatives of the QIBB quality initiative in the Länder Mrs Judith Wessely, provincial school inspector for technical schools in Vienna, LEA alumna Mr Wilhelm König, provincial school inspector for technical schools in Lower Austria, LEA participant
09.30 - 10.30	Interview with scientific team members of LEA Mr Bernhard Weiser, University Innsbruck Mr. Paul Resinger, University Innsbruck
10.30 – 12.00	Interview with the regional coordinators of LEA in the Länder
12.00 – 13.00	Interview with officials of the Union of Public Services representing teachers/school heads *Mr. Walter Meixner, Chairman, Regional Directorate for teachers/school heads of general compulsory schools* *Mr. Wolfgang Muth, Chairman, Regional Directorate for teachers/school heads of academic secondary schools*
13.00 – 14.00	Lunch break
14:00 – 14.45	Interview with LEA alumnus (target group school head/VET schools) Mr. Jordan, school head, Vocational College
14:45 – 15.30	Interview with LEA alumnus (target group Teacher Training Institution; school management programmes) Mr. Happ, In-service training institution Innsbruck

Wednesday 18 April 2007, Vienna

08.30 – 11.30	School visit to the academic secondary school GRG 21 "Bertha von Suttner" Schulschiff Mrs Judith Kovacic, school head, LEA alumna who is realising an innovative school based project and takes part in the midterm research project on the effectiveness of LEA Interviews with school head and members of the teaching staff working on the LEA project parents representatives of the SGA the administrator
12.00 – 13.00	Interview with Mrs Silvia Wiesinger, In-service training institution Vienna Director, dep. of school management training and international co-operations
13.00 – 14.30	Lunch
14.45 – 15.30	Interview with LEA alumnus, representing the target group school head ofgeneral secondary school / special needs school / pre-vocational school
15.30 – 16.30	Interview with LEA alumnus representing the target group ministry and members of his staff Mr Friedrich Faulhammer, Ministry for Science and Research DG for higher education and University Teacher Training

Thursday 19 April 2007, Vienna

08.30 – 09.30	Visit to the Austrian Federal Economic Chamber and presentation of recent involvements in educational policies, project "Leadership Award - School Head of the Year", event "Entrepreneurship Education for Schools´ Innovations"

- Mr Michael Landertshammer, Director, dep. of educational policy

10.00 – 12.00   Round Table "School management and policy related to school improvement"

- Mr Anton Dobart (opening), Ministry for Education, Arts and Culture. DG responsible for broad education policy related to school improvement and reform in general schooling; project owner QIS
- Mr Josef Neumüller (moderation), Ministry for Education, Arts and Culture. Director, dep. for international relations
- Mr Edwin Radnitzky, Ministry for Education, Arts and Culture. Deputy Director, dep. research, planning, quality development; project manager QIS
- Mrs Anneliese Ecker, Ministry for Education, Arts and Culture. Deputy Director, dep. of vocational education and training and in-service teacher training

12.15 – 13.15   Interview with DG Theodor Siegl, Ministry for Education, Arts and Culture
DG responsible for broad education policy related to school improvement and reform in vocational schooling; project owner QIBB

14.00 – 17.00   OECD review team meeting

References

Argyris, C. (1993), *Knowledge for Action: A Guide to Overcoming Barriers to Organizational Change*, San Jossey-Bass, San Francisco, CA.

Argyris, C. and D. Schön (1978), *Organizational Learning: A Theory of Action Perspective*, Addison-Wesley, Reading, MA.

Austrian Federal Ministry for Education, Science and Culture (undated), *White Book: Quality Development and Quality Assurance in the Austrian System of Education*, BMBWK, Vienna.

Costa, A. L. and B. Kallick (1993), "Through the lens of a critical friend", *Educational Leadership*, 51 (2): 49-51.

Delannoy, F., P. McKenzie, S. Wolfer and B. van der Ree (2004), "Attracting, Developing and Retaining Effective Teachers - Country Note: Austria", OECD, Paris.

Fischer, W.A. and M. Schratz (1993), *Schule Leiten und Gestalten. Mit einer Neuen Führungskultur in die Zukunft,* Österreichischer Studienverlag, Innsbruck.

Fullan, M. (2005), *Leadership and Sustainability: System Thinkers in Action*, Corwin Press, Thousand Oaks, CA.

Hallinger, P. (2003), "School Leadership Preparation and Development in Global Perspective", in P. Hallinger (ed.) *Reshaping the Landscape of Leadership Development: A Global Perspective,* Swets & Zeitlinger, Lisse, the Netherlands.

Hargreaves, A. and D. Fink (2006), *Sustainable Leadership*, Wiley, San Francisco, CA.

Heifetz, R.A. (1994), *Leadership Without Easy Answers*, Harvard University Press, Cambridge, MA.

Heifetz, R. and M. Linsky (2002), *Leadership on the Line: Staying Alive Through the Dangers of Leading*, Harvard Business School Press, Boston, MA.

Kirkpatrick, D. and J. Kirkpatrick (1998), *Evaluating Training Programs: The Four Levels*, 2nd edition, John Wiley & Sons, New York.

LEA (2007a), *Leadership Academy: Generation I Executive Summary,* bm:ukk. *www.leadershipacademy.at/index.en.php.*

LEA (2007b), *Programm Generation IV/Forum 3*, April 15-18, 2007.

Leithwood, K.A. and C. Riehl, C. (2003), *What we Know About Successful School Leadership*, Report for Division A of AERA, Laboratory for Student Success, Temple University, Philadelphia, PA.

Marquardt, M. J. (1996), *Building the Learning Organization*, McGraw-Hill, NY.

Mulford, W. (2003), "School Leaders: Challenging Roles and Impact on Teacher and School Effectiveness", a paper prepared for the OECD *Improving School Leadership* activity, available at *www.oecd.org/edu/schoolleadership*.

OECD (2003), *Networks of Innovation: Towards New Models for Managing Schools and Systems*, OECD, Paris.

OECD (2006), *Where Immigrant Students Succeed – A Comparative Review of Engagement In PISA 2003*, OECD, Paris.

Pool, S. (2007), "Leadership auf dem Prüfstand, Mit der Leadership-Kompetenz-Skala Führungskompetenzen von Schulleitungspersonen auf der Spur", *Journal für Schulentwicklung*, 11 (1), 42-53.

Riemann, F. (1977), *Die Grundformen der Angst*, Reinhardt, Munich.

Schley, W. and M. Schratz (2004), Leadership Academy, Generation 1 – Abschlussbericht, Mimeo, Zurich & Innsbruck.

Schratz, M. (2006), "Leading and learning: 'odd couple' or 'powerful match'?" *Leading and Managing*, 12 (2), 40-53.

Schratz, M. and K. Petzold, (2007), "Improving School Leadership. Country Background Report for Austria", a report prepared for the Austrian Federal Ministry of Education, the Arts and Culture by the Department of Teacher Education and School Research, University of Innsbruck, Austria, available at *www.oecd.org/edu/schoolleadership*.

Schratz, M. and B. Weiser (2002), "Dimensionen für die Entwicklung der Qualität von Unterricht", *Journal für Schulentwicklung*, 6 (4), 36-47.

Senge, P. (1990a), *The Fifth Discipline: The Art and Practice of the Learning Organization*, Doubleday, New York.

Senge, P. (1990b), "The Leader's New Work: Building Learning Organizations", *Sloan Management Review*, Fall, 7-23.

Stoll, L., D. Fink and L. Earl (2003), *It's About Learning (and It's About Time)*, RoutledgeFalmer, London.

Stoll, L. and K. Seashore Louis (eds.) (2007), *Professional Learning Communities: Divergence, Depth and Dilemmas*, Open University Press, Maidenhead.

Ulrich, D., J. Zenger and N. Smallwood (1999), *Results-Based Leadership*, Harvard Business School Press, Cambridge, MA.

Chapter 9

Approaches to system leadership: lessons learned and policy pointers
by
Beatriz Pont and David Hopkins

The purpose of this concluding chapter is to provide a first international comparison and assessment of the state of the art of system leadership in OECD countries. The chapter summarises what the research is saying about system leadership, and examines the actual practices in which school leaders are collaborating and working together with other schools in five different countries. The analysis reveals the benefits: leadership capacity building, rationalisation of resources, improved co-operation, a greater distribution of leadership within schools and improving school outcomes. It also presents the challenges to sustainability of system leadership: the difficulty of marrying co-operation and competition; the need to recognise and support distributed leadership within the school; the need to identify, recruit, develop and reward system leaders; and the need to find the right institutional support for the practice. The authors propose that eventually, the collective sharing of skills, expertise and experience will create richer and more sustainable opportunities for school transformation than can be provided by isolated institutions. But attaining this future demands that we give school leaders more possibilities in taking the lead.

9.1 Introduction

System leadership is a new and emerging practice that embraces a variety of responsibilities that are developing either locally or within discrete national networks or programmes. When taken together they have the potential to contribute to system transformation. Because this is an emerging practice, there has been little attempt to date to document how system leadership is being enacted. The purpose of this concluding chapter is to provide a first international comparison and assessment of the state of the art of systemic leadership in OECD countries.

The chapter first summarises what the research and the specialists are saying about system leadership, then continues by examining the actual practices in which school leaders are collaborating and working together with other schools in five different countries. It then analyses the perceived benefits and the potential challenges, and ends with a summary of the key issues and recommendations of the implications of this system leadership role for policy makers and stakeholders.

9.2 System leadership: A new role for school leaders?

There has been little attempt to date to document how system leadership is being enacted. This section of the chapter elaborates the concept of system leadership and illustrates its potential power as a catalyst for systemic reform in two ways:

- providing an initial conceptualisation of system leadership based on the contemporary literature;

- building on the papers by Richard Elmore ("Leadership as the Practice of Improvement") and David Hopkins ("Realising the Potential of System Leadership") included as Chapters 2 and 3 of this book by giving a broader perspective on their work.

The concept of system leadership has recently caught the educational imagination. Take for example this quotation from a leading educational commentator whose work has a global reach:

"... a new kind of leadership is necessary to break through the status quo. Systematic forces, sometimes called inertia, have the upper hand in preventing system shifts. Therefore, it will take powerful, proactive forces to change the existing system (to change context). This can be done directly and indirectly through systems thinking in action. These new theoreticians are leaders who work intensely in their own schools, or national agencies, and at the same time connect with and participate in the bigger picture. To change organisations and systems will require leaders to get experience in linking other parts of the system. These leaders in turn must help develop other leaders within similar characteristics."(Fullan, 2004)

This quotation contains three implicit assumptions. The first is that if we are ever to achieve sustainable education change it must be led by those close to the school; the second is that this must have a systemic focus; and the third is that "system leadership" is an emerging practice. As a concept it has a rich theoretical and research context. The conceptual concerns of system theory for relationships, structures and interdependencies (Katz and Kahn, 1976; Senge, 1990; Campbell *et al.*, 1994) underpin the contemporary work of system leaders in practice. The key insight here has been well summarised by Kofman and Senge, (1993:27) when they state that the "… defining characteristic of a system is that it cannot be understood as a function of its isolated components. … the system doesn't depend on what each part is doing but on how each part is interacting with the rest".

This leads to the realisation that to maximise the value of system leadership one needs to view it within the context of a learning organisation. This in turn requires the assiduous development of the range of skills to transform not only the organisation but also the system as a whole.

An important perspective on this skill set, as seen in the chapter by Hopkins, is offered by Heifetz (1994) through the concept of "adaptive leadership". His argument is that leaders increasingly require skills that move beyond traditional management solutions for technical problems to provide adaptive responses to challenges "without easy answers". Technical problems, such as how to teach numeracy, and their solutions will of course remain vital. But system leaders will also need to work adaptively to lead people and organisations beyond restrictive boundaries, perceived wisdoms and entrenched cultures where they exist as obstacles to improvement.

This theme underpins Fullan's (2005) exposition of the role he believes school leaders will need to play as "system thinkers in action" if sustainable large scale reform is to be achieved. This, Fullan argues, will necessarily involve adaptive challenges that "require the deep participation of the people with the problem; [and] that is why it is more complex and why it requires more sophisticated leadership" (p. 53). For Fullan, examples of this new work include: leading and facilitating a revolution in pedagogy (p. 57); understanding and changing the culture of a school for the better (p. 57); relating to the broader community, in particular with parents, and integrating and co-ordinating the work of social service agencies into the school as a hub (p. 61). This will demand "… above all …powerful strategies that enable people to question and alter certain values and beliefs as they create new forms of learning within and between schools, and across levels of the system" (*ibid,* p. 60).

These demands are further illuminated in theory by Peter Senge (1990), who argues that for organisations to excel, they have to become "learning organisations", which he defines as "organisations where people continually expand their capacity to create the results they truly desire, where new and expansive patterns of thinking are nurtured, where collective aspiration is set free, and where people are continually learning to see the whole together" (p. 3).

To Senge, the key to becoming a learning organisation is for leaders to tap into people's commitment and capacity to learn at all levels, to clarify broader systemic interdependencies and how to make them more effective (*ibid,* p. 4).

System leaders need a shared, central skill set to be effective. There is however a real concern about the increasing tendency in the literature to distort the generic competences of leaders through celebrating singular aspects of the role. Leithwood and his colleagues (2004, p. 4) express this worry succinctly: "… we need to be skeptical about the 'leadership by adjective' literature. Sometimes these adjectives have real meaning, but sometimes they mask the more important themes common to successful leadership, regardless of the style being advocated."

However, the concept of system leadership is embracing rather than esoteric, for three reasons. First the concept of system leadership flows from the general literature on systems theory and thinking. Second system leadership is a theory of action that embraces a range of disciplines in order to exert its power (see for example Elmore 2004, Leithwood *et al.* 2006). And third, system leadership will only exert any influence to the extent that it focuses on teaching and learning (*i.e.* is instructional), shares its authority with others (*i.e.* is distributed) and so on.

The literature, the evidence and the practice are pointing to a set of school leadership roles that are key to improving teaching and learning, as the companion volume, *Improving School Leadership, Volume 1: Policy and Practice,* proposes based on a review of the literature. There is a set of core responsibilities which lead effective school leadership: *i)* supporting, evaluating and developing teacher quality, *ii)* goal setting, assessment and accountability; *iii)* strategic resource management; and *iv)* leadership beyond the school borders. It also proposes that school leadership needs to be distributed. Richard Elmore in his inspiring Chapter 3 on leadership as the practice of improvement proposes that leadership in the context of improvement is about *i)* managing the conditions under which people learn new practices; *ii)* creating organisations that are supportive coherent environments for successful practice; and *iii)* developing the leadership skills and practices of others. It is within this mandate that the systemic approach to school leadership appears.

Professor Elmore also proposes that there is a need to invest adequately in knowledge and skills needed for effective leadership and for the "practice of improvement" (Chapter 3). There is a failure to invest adequately in the human capital required for this practice. He suggests that policies need to create the institutional structures that support the development of the knowledge and skill to lead improvement, and the social capital that connects individuals' knowledge and skills. What is most interesting is that according to Elmore, the most effective way to do this is by investing close to the ground – through networks and institutional arrangements that connect people with the knowledge required to the classrooms and schools, and with other practitioners faced with similar problems of practice. From that base leadership development approaches can build knowledge and skills throughout the practice of leadership.

Richard Elmore pursues these ideas in more depth in his book *School Reform from the Inside Out*. Illustrative of this is his definition of the leadership purpose:

> *"Improvement, then, is change with direction, sustained over time, that moves entire systems, raising the average level of quality and performance while at the same time decreasing the variation among units, and engaging people in analysis and understanding of why some actions seem to work and others don't....Leadership is the guidance and direction of instructional improvement. This is a deliberately de-romanticised, focussed and instrumental definition."(Elmore 2004, P. 66)*

This definition of leadership underpins Elmore's (2004, p. 68) further contention that "the purpose of leadership is the improvement of instructional practice and performance" and its four dimensions:

- instructional improvement requires continuous learning;

- learning requires modelling;

- the roles and activities of leadership flow from the expertise required for learning and improvement, not from the formal dictates of the institution;

- the exercise of authority requires reciprocity of accountability and capacity.

David Hopkins in Chapter 2 proposes that "… if our goal is 'every school a great school' then policy and practice has to focus on system improvement. This means that a school head has to be almost as concerned about the success of other schools as he or she is about his or her own school. Sustained improvement of schools is not possible unless the whole system is moving forward."

To him, system leadership is a new role, and he bases his evidence on review of current practice in England. System leaders engage with the organisation of teaching and learning, curriculum and assessment to personalise learning for all students and reduce within-school variation and to support curriculum choice. To do this, these leaders develop their schools as personal and professional learning communities, with relationships built across and beyond each school to provide a range of learning experiences and professional development opportunities.

This leads Hopkins in his book *Every School a Great School* to claim that:

"There is a growing recognition that schools need to lead the next phase of reform. But if the hypothesis is correct, and this is much contested terrain, it must categorically not be a naïve return to the not so halcyon days of the 1970s when a thousand flowers bloomed and the educational life chances of too many of our children wilted.… The implication is that we need a transition from an era of Prescription to an era of Professionalism – in which the balance between national prescription and schools leading reform will change." (Hopkins 2007, p. 44)

However, achieving this shift is not straight forward. As Michael Fullan (2003, p. 7) has said, it takes capacity to build capacity, and if there is insufficient capacity to begin with it is folly to announce that a move to "professionalism" provides the basis of a new approach. The key question is "how do we get there?", because we cannot simply move from one era to the other without self consciously building professional capacity throughout the system. This progression is illustrated in Figure 9.1.

Figure 9.1 Towards system-wide sustainable reform

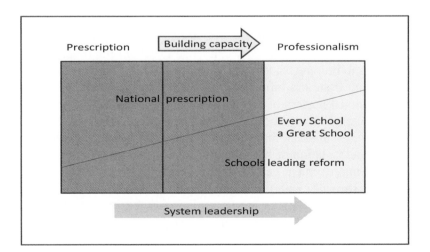

It is worth taking a little more time unpacking the thinking underlying the diagram. This is because it is fundamental to an understanding of the connection between "every school a great school", systemic reform and system leadership. There are three further points that underpin the argument.

The first is to emphasise that this not an argument against top down change. Neither top down nor bottom up change work by themselves, they have to be in balance – in creative tension. The balance between the two at any one time will of course depend on context.

Second it should be no surprise to realise that the right hand segment is relatively unknown territory. It implies horizontal and lateral ways of working with assumptions and governance arrangements very different from what we know now. The main difficulty in imagining this landscape is that the thinking of most people is constrained by their experiences within the power structure and norms of the left hand segment of the diagram. Glimpses of the new landscape envisioned by the right hand segment are scattered throughout the book.

Third, this is not to suggest that one always has to start form the left hand side of the diagram and move in some sort of uniform way to the right. Some systems may well start from the middle and move into the right hand segment, as could be the case in Finland. Others may initially believe that they are in the right hand segment. However on further reflection it may be realised that if they really want to raise the standards for all students, then as in the case of Ontario a clear direction of travel from left to right may be the best place to start. If this diagram has any value it is as a heuristic – its purpose is to help people think rather than tell them what to do.

The OECD report has termed this "leadership beyond the school borders" and proposes this as one of the key roles for improved school outcomes. These wider engagements focus leadership beyond the people in the school leaders' own buildings to the welfare of all young people in the area and to the improvement of the profession and its work as a whole, but in ways that also access learning and support from others to provide reciprocal benefits for leaders' own communities. Schools and their leaders are strengthening collaboration, forming networks, sharing resources and working together. The report actually presents evidence of much school and leadership collaboration approaches across OECD countries.

This concept of moving beyond the school borders is also proposed by Hargreaves and Fink (2006), who explain that the key challenge to school improvement today is for school administrators to become leaders who develop and raise high level achievement by working with, learning from and influencing the behaviour of others within and beyond their schools. Educational leaders of the future will be system leaders as well as school leaders. They summarise what Michael Fullan and David Hargreaves term "lateral leadership". They refer to this as a reaction to top down policy strategies and to increased school competition and isolation of schools, by which there has been a growth of school networks that create improvement gains by schools helping schools through sharing best or "next" practices, especially with the strong helping the weak. This is happening more and more, as principals and teachers are becoming engaged in more lateral networked leadership that promotes participation in networks for improved learning and achievement.

In summary, linking schools together can contribute to improving capacity of the education system with common purposes and improvement goals. At the heart of this role is the fact that schools and their leaders are not alone, and that working together they can reach higher levels of practice. Practitioners are trying to respond to the broadened roles and responsibilities that have not been reciprocated with appropriate development efforts for them to take on these tasks. It can also be something that is coming as a top down initiative to help improve performance of schools, develop capacity quickly and help rationalise resources.

9.3 How are school leaders collaborating and becoming system leaders in practice?

Throughout OECD countries, there is a great deal of school leadership co-operation and collaboration going on. Practitioners do not work alone, and many benefit from a variety of networks. Approaches to co-operation range from informal networking to new management structures, such as the Portuguese or the Dutch approaches, in which structures are created above the school level to share management issues (Pont, Nusche and Moorman, 2008). In Hungary "micro-regional partnerships" have been sponsored for economic and professional rationalisation. In Norway, some schools merge to form an administrative unit governed by one principal. In the Netherlands, the increase in scale following merged schools has led to educational innovations that have had a considerable effect on the duties of school leaders. In Portugal, this approach is the regular governance structure. In fact, in all countries participating in the OECD *Improving School Leadership* activity, there are some arrangements for co-operation between schools. School leaders are the key to these and are also strongly influenced by them.

Table 9.1 lists different types of approaches and some of the reasons for co-operation across OECD countries. There are school communities, school pools, networks, possibilities for sharing expertise by principals, actual merging of schools and shared management across schools. We are not able to gauge the extent of their success in most countries because we have not pursued this systematically, but we can say that most of these have explicit objectives which concentrate on the following: sharing and rationalising resources, improving coherence of educational provision, supporting well-being and improving educational opportunities and outcomes.

Instead, to explore the practice, we have chosen to focus on a set of innovative practices that we think can provide good examples of systemic approaches to school leadership. These are particular innovative approaches adopted or developed in England, Finland, Belgium, Austria and Victoria (Australia) which are showing emerging evidence of positive results. Annex 9.A1 provides a summary, description, some results and challenges. Each individual case is developed in detail in the relevant chapters of this book.

Comparing these approaches shows that different countries and different political, social and economic contexts may respond differently to similar challenges and pressures; alternatively, the system approach may be a response arising from different sets of needs. Each individual case has its specificities, as we describe in the following paragraphs, but there are also common patterns and features.

Table 9.1 Co-operation arrangements across OECD countries

Belgium	School communities have been created as voluntary collaborative partnerships between schools. They aim to have common staffing, ICT and welfare resources management.
Denmark	Co-operation in post-compulsory education has been promoted by the creation of administrative groups set up locally or regionally to optimise the joint resources of several self governing institutions.
Finland	2003 legislative reform has enhanced school co-operation aiming to ensure integrity of students' study paths.
France	"School basins" have been implemented to ensure collaborative partnerships between schools to work together in student orientation, educational coherence between different types of schools, common management of shared material and human resources.
Hungary	"Micro-regional partnerships" based on economic and professional rationalisation have resulted in the spreading of common school maintenance in almost all Hungarian micro regions. This network-type co-operation enables professional and organisational learning leading to new forms of education governance and efficient innovation.
Korea	Small schools cooperate to overcome problems of size in teacher exchange, curriculum organising, joint development activities, and integrated use of facilities.
Netherlands	In primary education, "upper management" takes management function responsibility for several schools. About 80% of primary school boards have an upper school management bureau for central management, policy staff and support staff.
New Zealand	School clusters are based around geographical communities and communities of interest.
Norway	Tendency is to merge several schools to form an administrative unit governed by a school principal. Three-level municipalities require networks between schools.
Portugal	Schools are commonly grouped together with a collective management structure; executive, pedagogical and administrative councils are responsible for their areas.
Scotland	Important political promotion of collaboration. "Heads together" is a nationwide online community for sharing leadership experience.
Sweden	Municipal directors of education steer principals. Most of them are members of director of education steering group where strategy, development and results are discussed.
UK (England)	There are different approaches to co-operation stimulated by the government – federations of schools, national leaders of education, school improvement partners…

Source: Pont, B. D. Nusche, H. Moorman (2008), *Improving School Leadership, Volume 1: Policy and Practice*, OECD, Paris.

The English practices of system leadership are some of the most developed in this field, and have been publicly developed and supported in recent years. There are a wide range of possibilities: schools can collaborate with each other formally with the possibility to "federate" since 2002. In addition, a specialised institution has even been created to such effect. The Specialist Schools and Academies Trust (SSAT) is an independent organisation that promotes school networks of different types. Its network approach to school improvement applies clearly defined tools for principals and its many programmes follow the philosophy "by schools, for schools". There are also special training courses to develop the capacity of leaders to become skilled in system leadership.

Individuals can work as "change agents" by acting as mentor leaders in networks or becoming school improvement partners. Also in England a group of National Leaders of Education has been created to take on a system leader role and their schools become national support schools (Matthews, 2008).

Two of the schools visited during the OECD study visit had successfully introduced a school improvement model that had managed to turn around some negative school results and in three years had significantly improved test results. This was done by a strong leader and a leadership team that focused on instructional leadership. They used an IT tool by which with individual students were followed up every six weeks, and they were able to measure school, classroom, individual teacher and individual student performance. Specific teams distributed the roles of detecting the key areas for improvement and intervention teams focused on quickly finding solutions to the key challenges. In one of the schools, after watching this success, and finding that a neighbouring school was going through rocky times, both schools voluntarily decided to join forces to improve performance overall. The more successful school's leader became school director of the other school and they jointly started working on applying the school improvement model in the second school site.

In Finland, the OECD team was able to find two approaches which seemed to be systemic. On the one hand, from the way in which Finnish education responsibilities are distributed and shared across the system, one could say that there is system leadership of an organic nature. It is embodied in Finland in the way policy making and collaboration play out. The national curriculum is the driving force, and in order to define it, there is a wide scope of consultation and co-operation from the national down to the school level. Once the curriculum is finalised at all levels, there is a high degree of consensus built around the professional body of teachers, principals and policy makers at local, regional and national level. At the same time, teachers are of extremely high quality and have a high degree of professionalism, teamed with a high degree of decentralisation and a national consensus on the value of learning. The whole system cooperates for school improvement. This shows in its excellent PISA results, which are not only consistently the best among all the countries studied but also highly equitable, so that any student is assured high quality education no matter what neighbourhood he or she lives in.

In addition, there is a new scenario in Finland due to declining school enrolments, declining resources in education, and an increasing workload for principals (who have been calling for strategies to deal with these issues). Municipalities are developing ways to transform school leadership to benefit the broader community. We found one of these municipal reforms which had redistributed leadership at different levels: five school principals were working as district principals, with a third of their time devoted to the district and the rest to their individual schools. This meant also the leadership was redistributed within the schools. Although when the OECD team visited it was too early to know about results, this looked promising and had created a new environment of co-operation and interdependence. Overall, it showed signs of: rationalising resources; integrating services; increasing transparency; improving problem solving; enhancing a culture of co-operation; and developing leadership capacity.

In Flemish Belgium, the development of communities of schools has tested the benefits and effectiveness of collaboration. The Flemish education department gave these school communities specific competences and additional resources by way of staff points (chapter 6). These competences are establishing agreements in the organisation of education provision, pupil orientation, the establishment of a common staffing policy, establishing teaching labour markets, or ICT co-ordination. They can eventually name a co-ordinating director to ensure that these communities operate smoothly.

This innovative approach has had some positive results (at least at secondary level, where it has been going for longer): at present, communities of schools cover more than 95% of secondary schools in Flanders, with an average of 6 to 12 schools belonging to a community. The immediate effects of the innovation were to establish internal markets which regulated competition for students between schools and increased opportunities for collective action on allocation of staffing and other resources, and for student guidance systems and curriculum. Yet, while these are important features, it must be acknowledged that the scope for collective decision-making was at the margins and did not affect the principals' autonomy.

An extremely interesting aspect of this approach is that it was possible to see how co-operation could be more or less successful, as each community of schools was left to themselves to develop their own strategies. Some schools did not make any changes while at the other extreme a school community has appointed a principal as a full-time co-ordinating director of the community. In this setting, the principals of this community have begun to meet monthly and are building trust and working together. They have established a clear agenda for improving guidance and counselling services, agreeing a common process for selection, and thus reducing competition within the community, and negotiating common working conditions for teachers, and creating curricula for students with special educational needs. They had recently agreed to provide targeted support (from the envelope of hours provided to the communities) for one of its schools having recruitment difficulties.

The Austrian and Australian innovations concentrate on leadership development, but both also have a systemic dimension to them that merit their inclusion with the rest of the approaches analysed in this report.

In Victoria, Australia, a state wide approach to leadership preparation and development (*Learning to Lead Effective Schools*, 2006) was developed as part of a broader strategy targeting school improvement (*Blueprint for Government Schools*, 2003) (chapter 7). The reform consisted of initiatives aimed at improving practice, enhancing performance and reducing achievement gaps. Leadership development was an essential part of this strategy. There is multi-layered system-wide leadership, which provides a common vision of leadership, promoting a common shared vision of high, evidence based expectations and collective responsibility. The conceptual framework for this vision of transformational leadership follows a specific model (Sergiovanni) which provides clear domains and descriptions of responsibilities for leadership. Nineteen different training programmes for different stages of leadership underpin this programme.

The Victorian vision of effective schools and culture of leadership development is leading to system leadership capacity with a common view. Through participation in these programmes and the creation of strong networks of common practices, school leaders are contributing to the improvement of Victorian schools as a whole; one of the courses is specifically on developing high performing system leaders. This results in strategic alignment, and the common language and culture of school improvement are permeating all levels of school leadership. The approach engages the workforce, provides clear expectations and emphasises peer learning.

Austria's approach to support leadership reform is built around the Austrian Leadership Academy, which was launched in 2004 to equip leaders with a new, more proactive and entrepreneurial vision of leadership that would focus on improving school outcomes. It aims to meet the challenges facing Austrian education, and "should have the skills to implement significant new educational reforms and constitute a critical mass of proactive, system-wide leaders capable of transforming the system". The Leadership Academy participants meet twice a year for two years and gain a combination of principles of learning, structure and curriculum, focused on developing leadership skills. They form partnerships, coaching teams, regional and virtual networks. At the outset, participants were school leaders, but as the Academy developed, it was clear that to develop capacity and system change it was also necessary to involve those working in leadership and management at regional and national departments of education. At present, around 20% of the total potential participants have graduated from the Academy, and there are plans to continue until around half of principals, or enough critical mass has been reached. The Academy follows a model of leadership for learning developed at the University of Innsbruck which draws on five dimensions of leading and learning.

The Academy has already begun to achieve a degree of culture and systems change, with a high degree of voluntary participation, engagement and enthusiasm and appears to have positive effects on individual development and improved practice over the long run. It is introducing system change by acting on the agents who are to introduce this change. However, to reach its full potential and to be sustainable it would need to have formal, structured support from the Ministry and be more embedded within the broader initiatives for reform. In addition, for system change to occur other variables in the system might need to be modified to adapt to this new reality.

These country innovations provide a range of examples of leadership for systemic school improvement. (The detailed case study reports describe these innovations, develop the theoretical underpinning, provide some evidence and analysis of effectiveness, and offer some recommendations for sustainability). The countries have worked or are working to strengthen leadership practice, through either development or creating co-operation networks that promote going beyond leaders' own schools. These practices have some common features: They are all focusing on preparing and developing leadership for system-wide school improvement through capacity building, sharing of resources and working together.

9.4 Benefits of system leadership

Most of these innovations have had some success because they had clearly defined objectives, and strategies to reach them. Yet the results are still tentative, mostly because these practices were just starting when the OECD teams visited the countries. Still we can say that they are slowly producing desired results. They are changing the perception and the practice of school leadership to focus on broader system outcomes, in different ways. The Belgian, the Finnish and the English examples are focusing their efforts on school improvement by strengthening shared leadership capacity and shared practice. The Austrian and Victorian approaches are directly acting upon developing system capacity through training and development.

There are some common patterns as well as differences in these practices. We have grouped the benefits, positive outcomes and challenges together. Overall, these innovations are responding to new education environments that are calling for changes in schools and school leadership practices. Some are focusing on improving school outcomes overall and some are rather managerial processes.

a) *Developing leadership capacity*

Strengthening leadership capacity implies creating opportunities for school leaders to work with each other, to share ideas, and to learn through the development of networks and by collaborating in their day to day practice. In the English example of a federation of schools, an underperforming school working with a neighbouring school develops its own capacity because the school team has the opportunity to train, to follow more successful patterns of school improvement and to learn. Both schools benefit: even a successful school can learn things from a struggling one. In Finland as well, the leaders who were working one third of their time with the municipality were also developing and strengthening their capacities as system leaders. The broader benefit was that they were all working together for the improvement of the municipality as a whole.

In Victoria and Austria, the leadership training programmes are directly influencing the development of leadership capacity at a larger scale. They are aiming at changing the perception and the practice of leadership to focus much more on school outcomes, and to develop clearly defined sets of leadership skills that seem to be missing in the system.

All these approaches can have the positive effect of systemic change in education if they manage to make long lasting sustainable impact on the people who participate in these training and co-operation actions.

b) *Rationalising resources*

Much of the school and school leadership co-operation across countries shows that there is a need to rationalise management processes, sharing appropriate tasks, which may involve financial and resource management. It can allow principals to concentrate on their key pedagogical leadership tasks. Rationalisation can also increase efficiency when budgets are limited. In Finland, for example, budget reductions were one of the reasons for sharing work between the municipality and individual schools. Similarly in Belgium part of the rationale behind the creation of communities of schools was rationalisation of resources.

Sharing resources and infrastructures can also broaden the supply of courses or services. The case of special needs provision in England was an example. In local authorities, special needs students were benefiting from the provision of different schools, working together to respond to this specific group. Working with other schools can attain economies of scale, reduce individual school costs and improve provision as a whole.

c) *Increased co-operation*

Working together has developed greater interdependence among leadership teams in Belgium, Finland and England. This also happened in Austria and Victoria, through participation in training. A principal in Belgium, comparing how schools used to compete against each other while now they are collaborating, described it as a small revolution. Over the long run collaboration generates better processes and outcomes. In Finland, this greater degree of co-operation was enhancing a shared culture of trust, co-operation and responsibility in the pursuit of increased effectiveness.

But co-operation for its own sake, which has been described as contrived "collegiality", may not produce the desired results; some may even see it as simply a burden. The Flemish example shows that some communities of schools have not evolved, and pushing co-operation on to agents who are not willing to take on this task may not work. In England, we were told that the federations or networks that worked were based on successful matching up of the partners. This may be crucial, and that matching should include shared values and aims, and clear perception of the benefits to all parties.

d) Distributed leadership

Most of the practices which have called for system leaders have also resulted in greater distribution of leadership within the schools. Principals need to have time to work on their system leader roles and thus need to delegate some of the school management and other tasks more.

In Flanders, some communities of schools added to school leaders' workload and there are calls for middle management to be further developed to take on some of these tasks. In Finland, where the principals are working at the municipality, leadership within larger schools has been redistributed with other staff members. This releases the principal from other responsibilities and develops increased leadership experience and capacity within the schools. In England, the leaders developed strong leadership teams that were able to take on the school roles necessary when the principals were away.

e) Improving school outcomes

Many of the processes seen in the countries visited were intended to improve the education and outcomes for students. In fact, this was one of the criteria for selection of the case studies. Such success is hard to measure, but it seemed that most of the examples seen were on the way to achieving it to some degree. Measuring the impact of school leadership on student outcomes is conceptually and methodologically challenging (see Pont, Nusche and Moorman, 2008), but in broad terms we find:

- Improving and rationalising supply of courses or joining forces to provide a broader curriculum and better education for students can improve school outcomes for some.

- Greater integration of services is a way of reaching students and their families better.

- System leadership can lead to better and more consistent pupil orientation and support.

In England, there is significant evidence to show that where a successful school has partnered a school in difficulties there has been actual improvement in grades of students in both schools within a relatively short (18 month) period of time (Chapter 5).

f) Sustainability

All these examples of approaches to reach systemic improvement are also contributing to sustainability of leadership and of schools. This is happening through developing capacity within and between schools, through the creation of co-operation networks, and through development of institutions that contribute to spread leadership across schools. In Finland the commitment to co-operation has become so institutionalised that it is now part of the organisational culture of schools. Sustainability depends on building capacity within individual schools. This can also help to strengthen leadership succession over the long run.

9.5 The challenges to practice

If the concept of system leadership is to be widely implemented, there are considerable challenges to be overcome. We begin with sustainability, as this is inevitably the most critical.

a) Sustainability

Sustainability is not only a benefit of system leadership, it is also a challenge. Most of the conclusions of the case studies highlight the need to support these innovations if they are to be sustainable. In Belgium, to achieve the communities of schools, the OECD team highlighted the need to develop a new collective and distinctive vision through training and development of leaders. In Austria, the question was raised as to whether the Austrian Leadership Academy will continue to operate, and whether its training will have effects long lasting enough to attain systemic change. In Victoria, Australia, this is also a challenge: system-wide improvement can only be reached when a large proportion of principals are reached by the programmes. In England although there have been a number of short term successes in improving student learning as a result of system leadership, it is still not clear whether they are sustainable into the medium and long term. In Finland as well, while the systemic reform had produced some positive results and is improving leadership capacity and rationalising practices, unless support is maintained the long term impact is uncertain.

When looking across these instances of system leadership from the perspective of sustainability five conditions necessary for effective sustainability stand out:

- *Internal capacity* within the school to sustain high levels of student learning.

- *Between-school capability*, the "glue" that is necessary for schools to work together effectively.

- *Mediating organisations* that work flexibly with schools to help build internal capacity and the competences necessary for effective collaboration.

- *Critical mass* so that system leadership becomes a movement rather than the practice of a small number of elite leaders.

- *Cultural consensus* across the system that gives school leaders the space, legitimacy and encouragement to engage in collaborative activities.

It is clear that these conditions are not all in place in any of the case studies, but they are all seen in some. It is also apparent that those cases that contain more of these conditions are the more successful in implementing system leadership. These conditions for sustainability therefore act as a useful checklist for the strategic implementation and institutionalisation of system leadership in national and local systems.

b) School leadership co-operation in an environment of choice and competition

Co-operation among school leaders working in school systems which have been based on competition and school choice may not be easy. Day *et al.* call it a dilemma of democracy in Flanders, where the education system is strongly committed to competition as a means to increase effectiveness and school quality (chapter 6). At the same time the communities of schools are aiming to make schools work together, so the nature of the collaboration-competition balance seems unclear.

In England, Hopkins notes that system leaders are appearing in contrast to the "competitive ethic of headship so prevalent in the nineties". This is at the heart of system leadership, as system leaders are the ones willing to work for the success of other schools as well as their own. This role is also emerging in other education systems across OECD. However, although system leadership in England is now a recognisable movement, it is not yet a mainstream practice. Although it is strongly advocated by the national government it is still not widely accepted by local politicians, local education officers or governors of schools – who worry that collaboration may lead to a dilution of excellent practice in their leading schools.

So system leadership is a challenge for policy makers, who may have to reflect on how system leaders can work beyond their schools to get systems improvement in an environment of competition and choice. It may be a matter of finding spaces for co-operation and sharing of resources where all benefit and competition is not hampered. Eventually, there would be positive spill over, and co-operation can widen its scope as the relationships strengthen and benefits are perceived by all involved. The challenge for policymakers is thus to develop sound and consistent policy with an appropriate, and probably changing, balance between choice/school competition and collaboration.

There may be a need for developing school leaders that see themselves not as an individual school leader but as a system leader. In England, since 2006 National Leaders of Education have been developing as those "outstanding leaders who are willing to involve themselves in system leadership outside their own school, taking lead responsibility for one or more schools in very challenging circumstances" (Matthews, 2008). In Finland, Hargreaves *et al.* (Chapter 4) recommend the need to employ current principals now near retirement by extending their services to help others in the system.

c) Recognising and supporting system leaders

While taking on this broader role may be beneficial for the education system as a whole, it may not be easy for school leaders with their busy schedules to take on the additional role. The national background reports prepared for this study show that in some countries, individual school leaders are already working long hours; an additional role could be too much. While distributed leadership can support this role, in times of challenges or difficulties, the focus on the individual school will always prevail. In addition, some ask about the accountability of system leaders: who are they accountable to and how? What are the measures of their practice?

While distributed leadership should accompany system leadership, this has not been fully acknowledged in policy and in practice across countries. The practice shows that those participating in leadership teams are not well recognised, nor do they receive incentives commensurate with the tasks they are taking on. Pont, Nusche and Moorman (2008) underline the need to effectively distribute leadership across teams, based on contextual needs and models. But for this to happen, policy makers need to recognise and support this practice.

d) Identifying and recruiting system leaders

It is clear from the case studies that there is currently a lack of clarity about how system leaders can best be identified and the key skills that should be required. There is also a need to differentiate potential candidates in terms of prior experience and current capacity. It may be helpful to think of key target groups along the following lines:

- *Existing:* Those who are currently undertaking system leader roles or have successfully done so in the past.

- *Designate:* Those who have recently taken on, plan to take on or are deemed capable of taking on system leader roles.

- *Aspiring:* Those who have the potential to take on such roles in the future.

Clearly each group would need to be recruited separately but there is some similarity in the way these leaders can be incentivised to take on the role. While appeals to altruism may prove a successful means of attracting high quality leaders, such goodwill cannot be relied upon and it can be exhausted.

More formalised incentives can contribute to encouraging and effectively recruiting these system leaders. These include professional acclaim and recognition of the role they are taking, financial reward, and highlighting the positive challenge and enrichment of a change in the pattern of work.

e) Professional development of system leaders

Generating a pool of high quality system leaders requires appropriate professional development. System leaders need to focus on the promotion of student learning, the schools' contexts and capacity building, problem-based learning, and a repertoire of practices rather than a single style.

Across the case study countries, approaches to developing system leaders could be categorised:

- *Formal qualifications:* In England and Victoria, this approach was seen to have benefits of recognition, and a high level of quality assurance. There may be concerns that a qualification may not meet needs, as it may be too detached from the context and may put off existing and aspirant heads who have a heavy workload.

- *Tailored learning:* These approaches provide an informal range of learning opportunities that can be personalised to individual need, reflect the experience and aspiration of the leader, focus on contexts and around significant problems and combine theory and practice.

- *Through practice:* The Finnish and Belgian approaches have shaped system leaders by promoting their practice. However, this might need to be supported with some more formalised training approaches that provide the required skills for successful leadership. Otherwise, they can have a negative impact by reproducing leadership styles that might no longer be suitable.

f) How to move system leadership to scale

In reflecting on the case studies there appear to be three issues that would become increasingly significant were the model of system leadership be moved to a larger scale. These are:

- *Brokerage:* There needs to be a focus on how the crucial partnership between schools should be brokered. This inevitably needs to be based upon a good knowledge of the context, including the true capacity of each school and the specific challenges facing them.

- *Resourcing:* There are a number of potential costs to consider, such as payment to system leaders to undertake more work and pressure, the financial position of collaborating schools, a short term improvement fund to achieve urgent changes. The amount and necessity for these recourses is highly contextual.

- *Support:* There is also a concern about the provision of ongoing personal and professional support. This is a critical factor for success and needs to be designed into effective policy. It can require the specification of responsibilities, provision of professional development to school boards and local education officers to better support system leaders, and identification and dissemination of best practice.

9.6 Food for thought

School leadership co-operation and collaboration have different traditions and developments across countries. There seem to be clear objectives: capacity building across the system, rationalisation and cost savings, improvements in leadership practice due to a more efficient distribution of tasks, and more coherent supply of educational services for those in the community. This chapter has reviewed the different country approaches to developing leadership for systemic improvement. Through leadership co-operation and collaboration as well as development and training programmes, countries are reaching different degrees of systemic improvement.

Developing systemic approaches to school leadership needs public support. Objectives and expected benefits need to be clear, and incentives are needed. When schools and school leaders realise the benefits they can reap from co-operation, principals will make time to engage. One general conclusion that stands out from the chapters by Elmore and Hopkins as well as the five national case studies is the increased emphasis on student outcomes and the greater linkage between leadership and learning. Whether this can be attributed to system leadership is an arguable point, but it is a very welcome trend.

As we have seen, there are clear benefits to these approaches, which are contributing to leadership capacity building, to rationalisation of resources, to improved co-operation, to a greater distribution of leadership within schools and to improving school outcomes.

Yet, there are challenges to be overcome if this approach is to be made sustainable. These have been seen as: the difficulty of marrying co-operation and competition (policy choices need to be made); the need to recognise and support distributed leadership within the school; the need to identify, recruit, develop and reward system leaders; and the need to find the right institutional support for the practice.

In concluding this chapter and the book it may be worth reflecting on an implicit distinction that has pervaded virtually all of the previous chapters. It is this: the distinction between system leaders working in national programmes and those working in locally organised, often *ad hoc,* roles. There is a tension between those system leaders who operate in national programmes that have incentivised activity through organisation, funding and professional development, such as seen in England and Victoria; and those system leaders whose roles are locally developed and contextually responsive, such as in Belgium and Finland. In such activity, professionals not only deploy their experience and skill to lead improvements, they also define the terms on which such activity is undertaken and sustained.

There are of course variations to this bottom up / top down dialectic, as has been seen in the five case studies. If, however, a shared criterion is to develop effective system leadership in a growing number of schools, then the following suggestion for more short term action - *Incentivise rather than legislate* - may prove instructive.

The argument is that this leadership needs to come more from principals themselves and from agencies committed to working with them. It is clear that the more bureaucratic the response the less likely it will be to work. A more lateral approach may be to create mediating organisations, such as the NCSL and SSAT in England and the Leadership Academy in Austria, to promote system leadership and collaborative activity. Another approach is to foster local education authorities and municipalities to develop and spread practice, as the Finnish have done. The intention that must be maintained is that instead of creating a new bureaucracy the brief for these mediating organisations is increasingly focused on facilitating relationships between schools to maximise the potential of purposeful collaboration.

This chapter has shown that there is already significant system leadership activity in the five case study countries. It has demonstrated that system leadership can contribute decisively to a full range of government and local agendas by capacity building; sharing of expertise, facilities and resources; innovation and creativity; leadership and management; and skills support. The collective sharing of skills, expertise and experience will create much richer and more sustainable opportunities for rigorous transformation than can ever be provided by isolated institutions. But attaining this future demands that we give school leaders more possibilities in taking the lead.

Annex 9.A1

Comparative overview of policy reforms, outcomes and challenges

Country	Purpose	How/Reform	Outcomes/results	Hindrance/challenges
Belgium	Enhance student guidance; reduce administrative burden so that focus is on pedagogical leadership; increase use of ICT; rationalisation of resources staff recruitment, curriculum, evaluation) More equity while preserving autonomy	Communities of schools: these can be created through allocating additional staffing to be used through collective decision making of the communities of schools	98% of schools integrated in community of schools Local labour markets for teachers (can be moved from one school to another within the community so less risk for teachers) Different degrees of co-operation have been reached, more successful ones have created additional co-ordination post to share and distribute leadership tasks Increased collective action for staff and other resources. More co-operation in a competitive environment	An additional layer of bureaucracy Many still remain nested within traditional network structures Centrally initiated – contrived collegiality. No additional support for system leadership training, for evaluation or to disseminate examples Lack of middle management to support communities of schools, as they need to take on leadership responsibilities Lack of support by government for these to be developed effectively, not much follow up
Finland	Reorganisation of public services; budget reduction accommodation; development of good quality leadership	Allocation of some school leaders to new district wide responsibilities; 1/3 of time in district, rest in schools Other municipalities are adopting similar arrangements Finland embodies the concept of system leadership as it is distributed across different levels (organic system leadership), not one strong leader	Rationalising resources; integrating services; more transparency; better problem solving through more interaction and collective learning; developing leadership capacity and succession (redistribution at municipal and school level) More interdependence, less competition Greater co-operation on curriculum, professional development.	Develop system of leadership beyond administrative and social roles More coaching and mentoring of retired principals. Concrete results still to be confirmed

Country	Purpose	How/Reform	Outcomes/results	Hindrance/challenges
UK (England)	Increase performance of low performing schools by a) ensuring that well qualified heads share their expertise with other schools through a variety of systemic arrangements, and b) providing schools with tools for improving leadership practice.	Systemic approach to school Leadership: range of possibilities for schools and principals to work with other schools: SSAT promoting school networks; collaboration between federations in which schools agree to work together and build capacity together even up to merging Individuals working as change agents: School Improvement Partners; National Advisory Leaders	Improving results of underperforming schools and broader curriculum and resources Greater distribution of leadership at the schools Better sharing of knowledge and skills, responsibility and problem-solving Cost-savings and economies of scale: sharing of equipment and of personnel, teaching staff and services such as cleaning/catering. Creating a culture of learning and results orientation Less competition, more collaboration and mutual responsibility	Need to balance policy initiatives for school principals with a policy environment constantly changing to provide more time for reform to take effect Can work when it is voluntarily entered into and when there is enough capacity Need to strengthen capacity of school boards and local education authorities Need to develop new forms of accountability and financial support Need to encourage new culture of collaboration in a competitive environment
Austria	To prepare leaders at all education levels to provide effective leadership Responding to Austrian context Develop leadership skills beyond those skills included in induction programmes Premise: leadership quality is the starting point for systemic innovation	Austrian Leadership Academy (2004): 2 year programme combination of principles of learning, structure and curriculum content : 4 two to three day forums to learn through partnerships, coaching teams, regional networks, virtual network Participants are not only school leaders but those involved in leadership and school management in regional and national departments of education Based on theoretical model: Leadership Competence Model emphasising leadership for learning (developed at U. of Innsbruck)	1500 out of 6000 have voluntarily participated and graduated (25%) High level of participant engagement and enthusiasm about content and processes Effective in instilling new leadership orientation and skills in many participants; LEA appears to have positive effects on individual development and improved practice over the long run Launching a range of innovative school improvement projects Creating a set of relationships across different elements of the overall education and governmental system Education system seems to be on its way towards making system-wide change	Sustainability of the LEA is still unclear, (although OECD visit contributed to strengthen support by Ministry) Not clear whether the effects will extend to the sustained leadership capacity needed for wide scale innovation Programme needs to be aligned with other Ministerial reform initiatives and with other teacher and administrator training No permanent structure of LEA While support exists, some express a considerable degree of scepticism ("messianic tenor" of LEA's message) Programme aiming at change culture is not accompanied by parallel effort to change structure of system. School leadership practices need to be rethought, inc. greater principal autonomy in hiring firing, reducing workload Participant follow up and networking is not consistent

Country	Purpose	How/Reform	Outcomes/results	Hindrance/challenges
Victoria, Australia	High quality schools for all Improve leadership quality in highly devolved schools controlling 90% of budget Increase leadership capacity of current school leaders, support development of leadership teams within schools, increase the number of applicants for posts and prepare individuals to take up leadership positions as leadership development is recognised as strategic issue	Leadership Development Strategy (Learning to Lead Effective Schools, 2006) embedded in *Blueprint for Government Schools* – coherent school reform process Framework based on Sergiovanni's model of transformational leadership; clear statement of what is expected of leaders and types of skills required for selection, recruitment, training development and appraisal of leaders 19 different programmes for different stages of leaders careers, including a course on system leadership All courses have a school based component matching participants' performance plans and schools' strategic plan	Emphasis on coaching, mentoring and peer learning, encouraging networking and collegial exchanges, involving "critical friends" Satisfaction of programme participants, improvement in their leadership capacities and more applications for promotions. Positive gains after participation in programmes Evidence of differential of improvement in schools in 3 years (school climate; based on teachers' perceptions). Evidence of improvement in quality of instruction High performing principals' programme provides skills and knowledge needed to meet new roles in school and larger systems	None respond to specific needs of improving equity and of disadvantaged students Capabilities listed for effective school leaders could be seen as too top down within the system and within a school System leaders developed are not being well used, can be that leadership capacity is generated at a faster pace than being absorbed Model needs to ensure that teachers engage with the reform process Changes in leadership behaviour need to be supported with changes in culture to encourage this type of transformational leadership

References

Campbell D., T. Coldicott, K. Kinsella (1994), *Systemic Work with Organisations: A New Model for Managers and Change Agents*, Karnac Books, London.

Elmore, R. (2004), *School Reform from the Inside Out: Policy, Practice, and Performance*, Harvard Educational Press, Cambridge, MA.

Fullan, M. (2003) *The Moral Imperative of School Leadership*, Corwin Press, London.

Fullan, M. (2004) *Systems Thinkers in Action: Moving beyond the Standards Plateau*, Department for Education and Skills Innovation Unit / National College for School Leadership, London/Nottingham.

Fullan, M. (2005), *Leadership and Sustainability: System Thinkers in Action*, Sage, London.

Hargreaves, A. and D. Fink (2006), *Sustainable Leadership*, Jossey-Bass, San Francisco, CA.

Hargreaves, D. (2004), *Personalising Learning: Next Steps in Working Laterally*, Specialist Schools and Academies Trust, London.

Heifetz, R.A. (1994), *Leadership Without Easy Answers*, Harvard University Press, Cambridge, MA.

Hopkins, D (2007) *Every School a Great School*, Open University Press, Buckingham.

Katz, D. and R.L. Kahn (1976), *The Social Psychology of Organizations*, Wiley, New York.

Kofman, F. and P.M. Senge (1993), "Communities of Commitment: The Heart of Learning Organizations", in Chawla, S. and J. Renesch (eds.) *Learning Organizations: Developing Cultures for Tomorrow's Workplace*, Productivity Press, Oregon.

Leithwood, K., K.S. Louis, S. Anderson and K. Wahlstrom (2004), *How Leadership Influences Student Learning* (executive summary), New York: The Wallace Foundation, New York.

Leithwood, K., C. Day, P. Sammons, A. Harris and D. Hopkins, D. (2006), *Seven strong claims about successful school leadership*, National College for School Leadership, Nottingham.

Matthews, P. (2008), *Attributes of the first National Leaders of Education in England: What do they bring to the role?*, National College for School Leadership, Nottingham.

Pont, B., D. Nusche and H. Moorman (2008), *Improving School Leadership, Volume 1: Policy and Practice*, OECD, Paris.

Senge, P. (1990) *The Fifth Discipline*, Doubleday, New York.

About the editors

Beatriz Pont completed an M.Sc. in International Affairs at Columbia University, was a research fellow at the Institute of Social Science in Tokyo University, and has B.A in political science from Pitzer College, Claremont, California. A Policy Analyst in the Education and Training Policy Division of OECD's Directorate for Education, Beatriz was Project Leader for the *Improving School Leadership* activity. With the OECD since 1999, she has worked on issues including equity in education, adult learning and adult skills, and ICT in education. Previously Beatriz was a researcher on education, training and active labour market policies at the Economic and Social Council of the Government of Spain and also worked for Andersen Consulting in Barcelona. She is currently working as Project Co-ordinator on an OECD-wide initiative on the Political Economy of Reform. *(beatriz.pont@oecd.org)*

Deborah Nusche is a Policy Analyst in the Education and Training Policy Division of the OECD Directorate for Education. She has an M.Sc. in International Affairs/Development Studies from the *Institut d'Études Politiques de Paris (Sciences Po)* and previous work experience with UNESCO and the World Bank. With the OECD since 2007, she has worked on issues of school leadership and learning outcomes assessment. Deborah is currently working on the OECD Thematic Review of Migrant Education. *(deborah.nusche@oecd.org)*

Professor David Hopkins is the inaugural iNet HSBC Chair in International Leadership, where he supports the work of iNet, the International Arm of the Specialist Schools and Academies Trust and the Leadership Centre at the Institute of Education, University of London. Between 2002 and 2005 he served three Secretaries of State as the Chief Adviser on School Standards at the Department for Education and Skills. Previously, he was Chair of the Leicester City Partnership Board and Dean of the Faculty of Education at the University of Nottingham.

OECD PUBLICATIONS, 2, rue André-Pascal, 75775 PARIS CEDEX 16
PRINTED IN FRANCE
(91 2008 03 1 P) ISBN 978-92-64-03308-5 – No. 56159 2008